FLIP the Script

Breaking Down Barriers, Building Relationships, and Engaging Secondary Students

Rebecca A. Knighton
& Jessica R. May

Foreword by Gaelin Elmore

Solution Tree | Press
a division of Solution Tree

555 North Morton Street
Bloomington, IN 47404
800.733.6786 (toll free) / 812.336.7700
FAX: 812.336.7790

email: info@SolutionTree.com
SolutionTree.com

Visit **go.SolutionTree.com/teacherefficacy** to download the free reproducibles in this book.

Printed in the United States of America

FSC www.fsc.org MIX Paper | Supporting responsible forestry FSC® C008955

Library of Congress Control Number: 2024057609

ISBN: 979-8-89374-011-0

Solution Tree
Jeffrey C. Jones, CEO
Edmund M. Ackerman, President

Solution Tree Press
President and Publisher: Douglas M. Rife
Associate Publishers: Todd Brakke and Kendra Slayton
Editorial Director: Laurel Hecker
Art Director: Rian Anderson
Copy Chief: Jessi Finn
Production Editor: Paige Duke
Copy Editor: Jessica Starr
Proofreader: Charlotte Jones
Text and Cover Designer: Julie Csizmadia
Acquisitions Editors: Carol Collins and Hilary Goff
Content Development Specialist: Amy Rubenstein
Associate Editors: Sarah Ludwig and Elijah Oates
Editorial Assistant: Madison Chartier

Acknowledgments

We would like to acknowledge our current and former students for all you've taught us and for inspiring us daily.

We would also like to acknowledge all the teachers out there who are doing the hard work of meeting your students where they are, providing a safe and inspiring environment, and helping your students see the possibility of a brighter future.

We want to acknowledge Rebecca's PhD supervisors, Bonnie Lee and Susan McDaniel, as well as committee members, Dawn McBride and Sharon Yanicki. Thanks also to the research study participants for supporting and contributing to the research that led to the foundational principles of this book.

We want to acknowledge Jessica's school colleagues at Bill Reed Middle School and the former Conrad Ball Middle School who helped her hone her student connections and teaching craft, predominantly Kaitlin Newlin, Tiffany Jones, and Nancee Deason—Jessica's favorite teacher turned colleague as well as her first storytelling educator.

We want to thank our families. Rebecca would like to thank her husband, Daniel; son, Zach; mother, Paula; sister, Jennifer; sister-in-law, Allyn; and brother-in-law,

Eric. Jessica would like to thank her husband Doug; sons, Jonas, Silas, Elias, and Mathias; mother, Rosemary; sister, Nancy; and second parents, Tammy and Alan. We could not have done this without your support.

We want to thank our friends and colleagues. Rebecca would like to thank Cate Phipps Orive, Amy von Heyking, Lance Grigg, Kevin Wood, Mitzi Garnett, Robyn Shank, Sandy Stoltzfus, Kathryn Harris Werner, Amanda Fewell, Evan Daldegan, Veronica Starcher, Arlisha Lawson-Watford, and Meghan Statton for taking the time to give feedback and insight on the activities and ideas in this book, and to Lynne DeSousa for her mentoring. Thanks to Kristen Brown for the time and support, Adam Collins and Jason Harlacher for their guidance on how to enter the publishing process, Vicki Wehmeyer (in loving memory) for her support and insight, and Michelle Malvey for sharing her condo when Rebecca was in dire need of an inspiring place to think and write. Jessica would like to thank Colorado Commissioner of Education Susana Cordova, Thompson School District Superintendent Marc Schaffer, and Assistant Superintendent–Human Resources Bill Siebers for their unwavering support during her time as the 2024 Colorado Teacher of the Year. Thanks also to Sarah Brown Wessling from the Council of Chief State School Officers and her fellow 2024 State Teachers of the Year cohort: You all are the radiance she needed to rekindle her love for teaching. We hope this book will have the same effect on other educators as well.

Solution Tree Press would like to thank the following reviewers:

Jessica Bassler
English Language Arts Teacher
Francis Howell High School
St. Charles, Missouri

Nathalie Fournier
French Immersion Teacher
Prairie South School Division
Moose Jaw, Saskatchewan, Canada

Erin Kruckenberg
Fifth-Grade Teacher
Jefferson Elementary School
Harvard, Illinois

Christie Shealy
Director of Testing and Accountability
Anderson School District One
Williamston, South Carolina

Rea Smith
Elementary Math & Science Curriculum Specialist
Fairview Elementary
Rogers, Arkansas

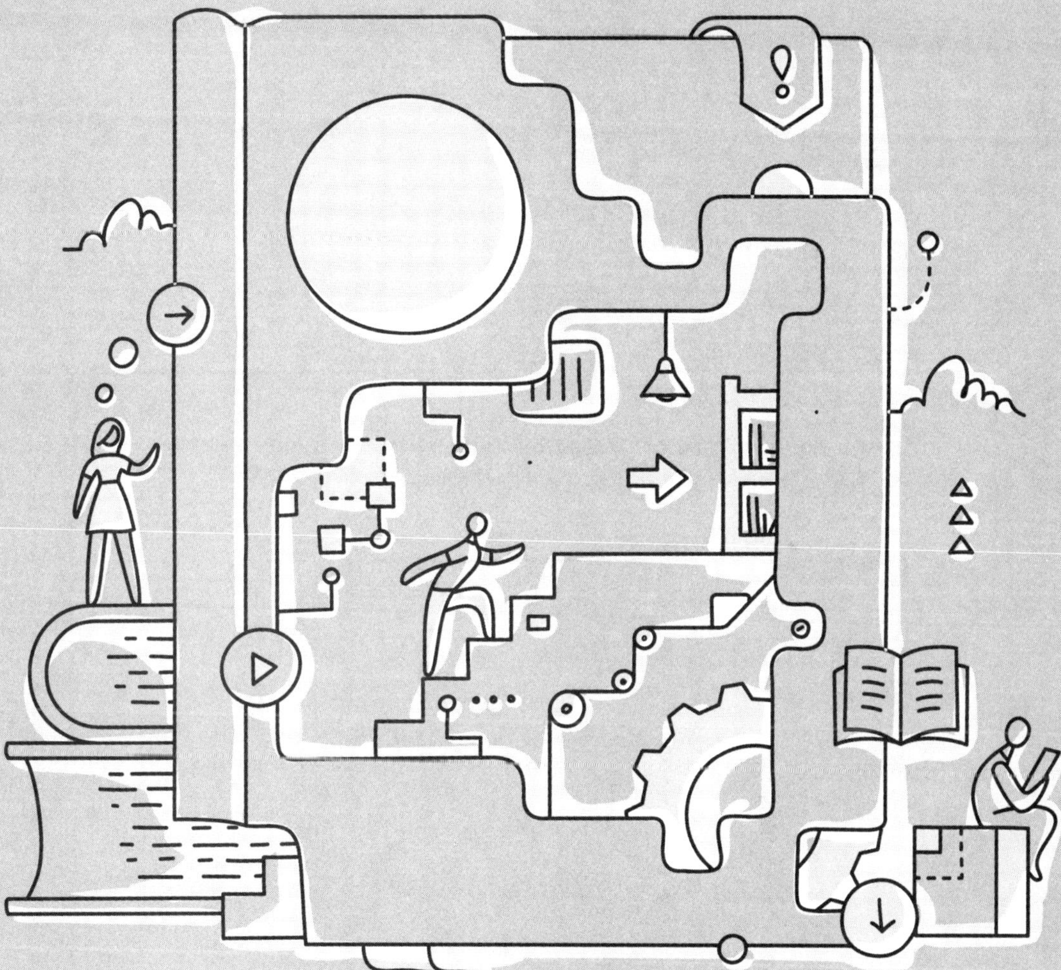

Visit **go.SolutionTree.com/teacherefficacy** to download the free reproducibles in this book.

Table of Contents

Reproducibles are in italics.

About the Authors

Rebecca Knighton, PhD, is a lifelong learner with a passion for understanding humanity's common needs, the barriers we face, and what motivates us. As a senior consultant with the Colorado Department of Education (CDE), Knighton helps district and school leaders transform their districts and schools by increasing their capacity for both humanistic leadership and navigating complex systemwide change efforts, including providing effective professional development, improving culture and climate, and transforming the way staff and students are understood and supported. She began her journey in education as a middle school behavioral interventionist (for general education students), gifted and talented specialist, and leading member of her school's multitiered system of supports and individual student problem-solving teams. Knighton also developed and taught a social-emotional intervention class for sixth graders who struggled with behavior and low school engagement, changing the educational trajectories of the students who participated.

As an adviser and participant in several development teams at the CDE, Knighton served as an adviser during the creation of a new dropout prevention framework and as a key member in developing a guide for systemic improvement in social-emotional wellness and mental health. She has led professional development efforts at the school, district, and state levels and presented at state, national, and international conferences. Knighton seeks to guide staff members to a deeper understanding of themselves and those they lead so their work can be more impactful, building their capacity to help struggling youth change the trajectory of their lives.

Knighton holds a bachelor's degree in biochemistry from Boise State University in Boise, Idaho; a master's degree in teaching literacy across content areas to underserved populations from the University of Southern California in Los Angeles, California; and a doctorate in population studies in health from the University of Lethbridge in Alberta, Canada. Her dissertation focused on teachers who are highly skilled at connecting with and engaging disengaged youth. When she isn't thinking about and creating new ways to guide inspiration and transformation in those she supports, she loves spending time in nature with her husband and their Corgi, Tifa. She also enjoys traveling, especially to Europe to visit her son, or to the Pacific Northwest, where she can experience the power of the ocean and the beauty of the forest at the same time.

To learn more about Rebecca's work, follow her on LinkedIn at www.linkedin.com/in/rebecca-knightonphd.

Jessica May, M. Ed., uses her role as a classroom teacher to foster supportive relationships with even the most difficult students—including those from generational poverty and the at-risk population as well as affluent students. She is well-versed in the basic human tendencies of secondary students along with brain research, which she draws from to uniquely connect with each of her students. May designs strategies to bond deeply with students navigating diverse issues in all areas of life—not just those that arise at school.

May has taught English, mathematics, science, Family and Consumer Sciences, and social studies in northern Colorado's Thompson School District, in both middle and high school, since 1997. She is passionate about explaining how to build the positive relationships with students that the field of education promotes but doesn't always deliver.

Having won Colorado Teacher of the Year in 2024, as well as District-Level Teacher of the Year three times in seven years, May uses the feedback from her students' end-of-year surveys, end-of-semester surveys, and peace circles to fine-tune her craft of becoming a better person and teacher. May also coaches other teachers on classroom management, social-emotional learning lessons, and her biggest passion: reading in the real world through the lens of every content area.

May earned a bachelor's degree in social sciences from the University of Colorado in Boulder, and a master's degree in education from Colorado State University in Fort Collins. She lives in Loveland, Colorado, with her husband of twenty-four years, Doug; their four sons; and two pampered housecats, Mozzie and Scarlett. In her spare time, May enjoys reading youth and adult fiction, watching her beloved Denver Broncos, playing the acoustic guitar, and clobbering her sons—Jonas, Silas, Elias, and Mathias—in UNO™, gin rummy, and backgammon.

To learn more about Jessica's work, follow her on Instagram at jessicamay2024coteacherofyear and LinkedIn at www.linkedin.com/in/jessica-may-58b170301.

To book Rebecca A. Knighton or Jessica R. May for professional development, contact pd@SolutionTree.com.

Contributing Teachers

Lauren Granberg is a teacher in Lethbridge, Alberta, Canada. She has been working in Southern Alberta for School Division 51 since 2014. She is a passionate educator, wife, and mother to three little people. Her background is primarily with middle school students in grades 6–8, with a focus on humanities and fine arts. Granberg prides herself on building strong connections with students through comfort, community, and communication. Granberg believes that a diverse and engaging classroom runs on accountability, flexibility, authenticity, and a lot of strong coffee.

Granberg received bachelor's degrees in both the arts and education from the University of Lethbridge in 2013.

Joel Bryant is a teacher at Winston Churchill High School in Lethbridge, Alberta, Canada, where he teaches social studies and geography classes for grades 9–12. He began his teaching journey as a substitute in 2013 with the Lethbridge School Division, where he taught kindergarten through grade 12 at a variety of schools in the city. Being exposed to this diverse range of student experiences prepared him for his current teaching assignment, working with many students experiencing socioeconomic challenges and a significant number of English learners. He focuses on building positive relationships and leading with empathy to help nurture learning in his classroom.

Bryant is an active member of the Alberta Teachers' Association (ATA) and serves as head representative for his school. Always pushing for better conditions for both students and colleagues, he has served on the division Teacher Welfare Committee and Working Conditions Committee. He is a member of the ATA Social Studies Council and has attended professional development conferences in Denver, San Francisco, Edmonton, Calgary, Banff, and others. Bryant is a strong advocate for digital literacy and has presented to his colleagues at the South Western Alberta Teachers' Convention on the dangers of misinformation in the modern technological landscape.

Bryant received his bachelor's degrees of arts and education, graduating with great distinction from the University of Lethbridge in 2013.

Cody Hall is an experienced and dedicated educator with a diverse career. His journey in education began as a physical education specialist, where he focused not only on developing students' physical abilities but also on fostering character development and confidence. Hall has long believed that physical education is about more than just fitness—it's about teaching life skills like perseverance, teamwork, and self-discipline, which are essential during the often-turbulent teenage years.

Hall has worked in middle school throughout his career, guiding students through physical challenges while helping them build resilience, self-esteem, and a positive mindset. His approach is to create a supportive environment where students feel empowered to reach their goals and develop a sense of accomplishment, both physically and emotionally. Many of his students learn to value effort over outcome, which helps them grow into more confident and capable individuals.

After working in the world of physical education, Hall transitioned into teaching other subjects, branching out into shop and language arts. This shift allowed him to bring his experience in hands-on learning and personal development into new areas of the classroom. His holistic approach remains consistent: Whether students are working with tools or words, he aims to inspire them to recognize their own potential and strengths. Throughout his career, Hall has been committed to cultivating a classroom atmosphere that prioritizes respect, collaboration, and growth. He believes that every student has the potential for greatness, and he strives to provide them with the skills, support, and opportunities to realize that potential.

Hall received his bachelor's degree in education from the University of Lethbridge while studying kinesiology and Indigenous studies.

Angela Tavernini has been teaching high school mathematics since 2012. A self-proclaimed "math nerd," she is equally passionate about teaching academic mathematics skills as she is about getting students at risk to show up and enjoy her class. Her goal is to make mathematics accessible and enjoyable for all students. She wants students to know that mathematics doesn't need to be a scary subject. It's amazing how many more students consider themselves "mathematics people" when they are encouraged to believe it. Tavernini is also deeply passionate about work-life balance and showing up as her best self in the classroom. She spends her time outside the classroom with her husband, her kids, and their two dogs.

Tavernini has sat on her school division's Mathematics Steering Committee. The committee worked toward providing a cohesive approach to quality mathematics instruction across all grade levels. She is also currently a member of the Alberta Teachers' Association Mathematics Council.

In 2021, Tavernini completed her 200-hour yoga teacher training. Although the intention was to expand her learning and offer a different sort of challenge, it ended up influencing and strengthening her philosophy within the mathematics classroom.

Tavernini received her bachelor of science degree in mathematics and bachelor of education degree from the University of Lethbridge. She is also currently working toward her master of mathematics for teachers degree through the University of Waterloo.

Foreword

The infamous quote "We ain't come to play school" (Jones, 2012) comes from a former Ohio State University quarterback. I was a scholarship athlete on the football team at the University of Minnesota when this tweet went viral. I remember reading it and thinking that, even though most college football players shared this sentiment, he'd made the mistake of saying it out loud. Essentially, he was saying his main priority and purpose for being at school was football, and everything else (especially school) was a distraction from the main priority and purpose.

Put another way, the message is: "I didn't become a successful athlete to learn. I just need to perform well."

Many years removed, I understand how misguided and harmful that widely held belief was (and still is if you look at the landscape of college athletics). However, I've learned that this ideology has infiltrated many parts of our culture, professions, and communities. As I consult and speak with organizations and professionals on the importance of belonging, I've learned that many people operate with the script that building relationships is a distraction to their priority and purpose. It might look something like this.

Script A:

I didn't become a doctor to build relationships. I just need to treat patients well.

I didn't become a small-business owner to build relationships. I just need to serve customers well.

I didn't become a politician to build relationships. I just need to represent constituents well.

I didn't become a coach to build relationships. I just need to coach players well.

I didn't become a social worker to build relationships. I just need to protect clients well.

I didn't become a teacher to build relationships. I just need to teach students well.

Maybe you have said, felt, or believed this script before. Maybe you know someone who says, feels, or believes this. Maybe you still say, feel, or believe this as you read my words. And if that is true, that's OK. I'm not trying to shame anyone. There are many people who unknowingly operate with the mindset that the human element of their work is a barrier to and distraction from the actual work. But here's the truth: No matter what role, profession, or field you find yourself in, the human element of that work *is* the work. Here's what it looks like to operate from that script.

Script B:

Doctor: Because I need to treat patients well, I need to build relationships.

Business owner: Because I need to serve clients well, I need to build relationships.

Politician: Because I need to represent constituents well, I need to build relationships.

Coach: Because I need to coach players well, I need to build relationships.

Social worker: Because I need to protect clients well, I need to build relationships.

Teacher: *Because I need to teach students well, I need to build relationships.*

The subtle, discrete, and harmful script that people are a distraction and not the purpose impacts lives greatly, especially in education. It's a script that desperately needs to be flipped. I know this to be true because of my professional experiences, but I most deeply know this to be true because of my personal experiences.

I come from a long line of people full of potential but overwhelmed with problems. If you were to look at my family's history, you'd see my ancestry didn't set me up to break the status quo. If anything, I was on a fast-track to being consumed by the same problems that consumed my parents, siblings, aunts, uncles, and everyone else in the family. That was, until educators flipped my script. They were able to do this because they had flipped the script for themselves; according to the script they'd inherited in education, they had no business investing in my life. Luckily for me, they were different. Rebecca Knighton and Jessica May refer to teachers like these as *positive deviant teachers*, meaning they have solved a challenge that their peers struggle with. These teachers see the world through a different lens and have flipped the script toward their job.

In my childhood, I had ample exposure to educational systems in just about every context you could imagine. I grew up with my biological family and in foster care. I was raised in an urban environment, lived in rural communities, and relocated to a suburban neighborhood. I attended six K–12 schools (both private and public) across three states while living in more than twenty different homes. I was a problematic child because I ran away three times by the age of twelve, and I was living with (misdiagnosed) ADHD and bipolar disorder. I was also a frequently truant student due to battling homelessness three times by age sixteen. My problems were undeniable and ready to overwhelm me, except I kept stumbling into positive deviant teachers' classrooms; these educators changed my life forever. Despite the differences in my age, the community I was in, or the problems I was facing, all of these positive deviant teachers shared something in common: they had the audacious idea that I was *their* business. They acted like navigating my challenging behavior and trauma responses wasn't a barrier to doing their job—it *was* their job.

I reflect, think, and speak of what those teachers did for me on a weekly, if not daily, basis. I went on to break the family cycle and become a college athlete, NFL player, dad, husband, and advocate—not because of a mythological force that destined me for greatness but because I received the support that those who came before me did not get. Positive deviant teachers like the ones in this book are not common, but they can and should be.

This book is created with the purpose of making the positive deviant teacher more common. *Flip the Script* is a timely and practical resource that will absolutely make you a better teacher and, more importantly, a better person. It's a resource I have referenced, referred to others, and quoted many times already in the short time I've had it in my possession. Utilizing relevant research, relatable examples and stories, and self-guided questions at the end of each chapter, the authors walk with you as you intentionally wrestle with what it means to flip the script for your students and, most importantly, for yourself. I am excited that you've decided to embark on this journey!

Gaelin Elmore,
Keynote Speaker and Belonging Champion,
Minneapolis, Minnesota

Introduction

This book was written for teachers by teachers. We hope to help our fellow secondary teachers learn how to build the types of relationships that not only increase their own job satisfaction and well-being *but also* increase student engagement and change students' lives.

We know that positive teacher-student relationships decrease behavior challenges and increase engagement (Roorda et al., 2017), but *how* do we develop relationships with students who push us away and whose behaviors push our buttons? When students disrupt our classes and refuse to engage, it evokes feelings we have to sort through.

- We feel frustrated that they are preventing other students in the class from learning.
- We feel disrespected when they don't appear to value us or the content we care about.
- We feel angry at them for forcing us into conflict and power struggles.

- We feel fearful that we won't have time to get to all our content before testing, that our other students' scores will be negatively affected, and that, as a result, our job security or the respect our administrators have for us will be threatened.

In addition to these challenging emotions, when these students walk into our schools and classrooms, we sometimes see them on a trajectory toward future dropout, and we feel powerless to stop that train. We see these students, and we worry about their futures and how they will be able to make it in the world.

Positive relationships with students improve our sense of well-being and job satisfaction (Aloe, Amo, & Shanahan, 2014), but they can also significantly impact our students' life paths. This is a book about how to connect with and engage secondary students, especially the hard-to-reach students. This requires that we understand human motivation, adolescent development and needs, the role of hope and self-efficacy in student engagement, and how to break down the barriers that prevent connection and engagement. It requires that we explore our own beliefs and triggers and what it means to be an authentic teacher. Research shows that positive teacher-student relationships are even more important for students' academic success and well-being in secondary school, but they are also less common (Roorda et al., 2017). This might be because, as secondary teachers, we sometimes assume adolescents don't want or need a relationship with us (Roorda et al., 2017). It might be because it seems like more secondary teachers focus on teaching content rather than guiding the human development of young people. It might be because adolescents can be harder to connect with.

Adolescents are going through many changes physically, hormonally, relationally, and socially. They are discovering who they are and forming their identities. An adolescent's hormonal fluctuations cause them to experience intense emotions and mood swings, and their prefrontal cortex (the part of the brain that thinks more rationally and helps connect how current choices impact the future) hasn't caught up (Hutchison, 2019). This leads them to make questionable choices. Adolescents are also unduly preoccupied with peer acceptance, which leaves them full of self-doubt and afraid to take social risks (Yeager, Dahl, & Dweck, 2018). These factors can create challenges for teachers seeking to build relationships with and engage adolescents.

Although most adolescent students feel some level of disconnection and disengagement at school, some struggle more than others. The students who struggle the most with disconnection, disengagement, and low self-efficacy are more likely to eventually drop out of school (Anderson et al., 2019; Balfanz, Herzog, & Mac Iver, 2007; Quin, 2017).

Many of these students have a history of *adverse early life experiences* (AELEs), some of which are also called adverse childhood experiences (ACEs), which are difficult or traumatic experiences such as bullying, abuse, neglect, poverty, or exposure to violence (Hambrick et al., 2019; Koplan & Chard, 2015). AELEs set students up to struggle in school by altering their neural pathways and negatively affecting their beliefs about their own abilities. For example, these students tend to struggle with impulsivity, decreased emotional regulation, and difficulty thinking through sequential actions that will help them accomplish goals (Hambrick et al., 2019; Hashimoto et al., 2015). Think about the skills students need to succeed in school. They need to regulate their emotions and their actions because they can't just talk whenever they want to or punch someone when they are angry. They also must organize their time and think through how to complete tasks effectively. Experiencing high levels of adversity in childhood impacts how students' brains develop, leaving them less skilled at these fundamental aspects of doing school well, which can lead to greater difficulty succeeding. These repeated failures, coupled with living in environments where they and their family members internalize the message that they have no power in the world, can lead to low self-efficacy (believing they can't succeed), an external locus of control (believing they have no control over what happens in their lives), and low hope for the future (Anderson et al., 2019; Snyder, 2002). If students don't believe they can succeed, then of course they are going to avoid working in our classes. All of this creates a perfect storm of behavior struggles, low engagement, and difficult teacher-student relationships. As teachers, however, we have the potential to help students flip that script and realize that they can succeed in school and that they do have a future greater than what they imagined.

We know students will engage in classes when they have positive relationships with us, but it isn't as easy as it sounds. We've heard Theodore Roosevelt's quote "Nobody cares how much you know until they know how much you care" (BrainyQuote, n.d.) more times than we can count, but we come back to the question of how. *How* do we build relationships with students who don't seem to want one, or even more challenging, with students who push our buttons? *How* do we build relationships with students when we worry that their behaviors may threaten our job security by lowering other students' test scores or changing how our administrators view us? It starts with understanding that, oftentimes, these students have faced more adversity than anyone ever should and that those experiences have predisposed them to struggle in school. It also helps to know that positive relationships with teachers have been shown to counter the negative impacts of those AELEs so students can succeed in school and later in life (Kelley & Lee, 2018; Noble-Carr, Barker, McArthur, & Woodman, 2014).

Lessons From Positive Deviant Teachers

Although student dropout rates have improved worldwide since the early 2000s, 14 percent of adolescents worldwide are still not graduating (Organisation for Economic Co-operation and Development, n.d.). Additionally, teacher burnout and attrition rates have increased since the pandemic, especially for schools serving underserved students (Education Resource Strategies, 2024), and around 30 percent of people earning teaching degrees leave the profession within five years (Ingersoll, Merrill, Stuckey, & Collins, 2018). Many teachers who quit cite high stress from lack of student engagement and teacher-student conflict as two of the primary reasons (Aloe et al., 2014; Chang, 2013). The good news is that, in nearly every school, the problem of how to engage and build relationships with chronically disengaged adolescents has already been solved. There is that one teacher (or maybe several teachers) who has mastered this. They build relationships with the students who push other adults away. They see engagement and achievement in their classes from students who are failing or getting kicked out of other classes. We think to ourselves, "How do they do it? And how can the rest of us replicate their success?" These teachers are the *positive deviants* in their settings.

Positive deviance is a strengths-based concept—it's the idea that, within communities, there exist members who have already solved a challenge that others struggle with (Pascale, Sternin, & Sternin, 2010). The idea is that the best way to solve a challenge is to understand how members of a community have already solved it and then replicate that. So often we try to solve challenges by bringing in "experts" from outside of a community who then give guidance or lead change efforts. However, outside experts lack a deep understanding of the needs, values, culture, and beliefs that create barriers to solving the community's challenges. Members of the community who have solved the challenge are aware of and understand all those facets, which can lead to greater success in navigating the challenge.

Positive deviance was first developed to address childhood malnutrition in a small village in Vietnam (Pascale et al., 2010). It has since been used to solve a variety of severe challenges ranging from decreasing maternal mortality rates in Pakistan to decreasing high school dropout rates in Argentina and the United States (LeMahieu, Nordstrum, & Gale, 2017). In the field of education, positive deviance has been used as both an innovative research strategy and a quality improvement strategy (LeMahieu et al., 2017).

This concept was the foundation of a research study conducted by one of this book's coauthors, Rebecca Knighton. The other coauthor, Jessica May, and the contributing authors are all positive deviant teachers. To understand how we, as teachers, might better connect with and engage chronically disengaged secondary students, Rebecca studied middle and high school teachers from four schools located in Colorado, United States, and Alberta, Canada, who taught multiple subject areas (language arts, mathematics, social studies, physical education, technology, special education, and library) and who all excelled at connection and engagement. To understand what common factors led to these teachers' successes, Rebecca conducted observations of teachers and interviews with those teachers, their administrators, and a group of adults who had an experience with a positive deviant teacher when they were in middle or high school. One of Rebecca's most important findings was that these teachers were diverse. Their dispositions, classroom management approaches, and teaching styles varied, but one factor that did not vary was they all attributed their successes to treating students like fellow humans and to being authentic (Knighton, 2022). This means if we want to be as successful as positive deviant teachers, we can't just try to replicate what they do. We can't try to be someone we aren't.

We must do the hard work of discovering who we are as teachers and who our students need us to be and then be *that teacher.* We have to discover what discipline approaches work for us and are effective with our students, what relational and connection strategies align with who we are, what processes and structures in our classrooms work best for us and our students, and what teaching styles fit with our personalities. *We need to learn to be ourselves, not try to be like someone else.*

This means if we want to be as successful as positive deviant teachers, we can't just try to replicate what they do. We can't try to be someone we aren't.

While the positive deviant teachers in Knighton's (2022) study did not do or say the same things or even interact with students in the same way, they all shared the following key commonalities that contributed to their success.

- They were less triggered by student behaviors (because of a strong understanding of human development, needs, and motivations).
- They had a strong understanding of human motivation, which enabled them to engage students who did not engage in other classes.
- They had an ability to see and understand their students, anticipate student needs, accept students without judgment, and be real with students, which created environments of safety (a key element that contributes to student engagement).

- They were able to connect their content to real life because they believed their role included both fostering students' academic growth and guiding students' human development as they moved toward adulthood.
- They believed all students could succeed and showed students that they believed in them, especially when students didn't believe in themselves.

These key commonalities were described by teachers, administrators, and adults who had a positive deviant teacher as essential to teachers' success connecting with and engaging students (Knighton, 2022).

So often, educators look for the perfect evidence-based program or external "experts" to solve our challenges, but we propose that without authenticity, positive relationships, the ability to see and understand our students, a focus on removing student barriers, and an understanding of how to inspire motivation within our students, those approaches will be less effective. We propose that all teachers have the answers within themselves about how to develop relationships with and engage students within their school communities. We hope to help you find those answers within yourself through the content, examples, strategies, and exercises we present in this book.

Start With Flipping the Script

To develop the types of relationships with students that increase engagement and even change the courses of their lives, we have to flip the script—our own and theirs. A *life script* is a set of mental expectations and perceptions about ourselves and how our lives will go that is formed in childhood based on our experiences and relationships (Erskine, 2018; Gujral & Kaur, 2018). Psychotherapist Terry M. Levy (2021) describes the formation of our life scripts this way: "Our scripts are written without us even being aware of it. These experiences develop into core beliefs; the mindsets, attitudes and expectations that define who we are, how we relate to others and what roles we play." Flipping the script means shifting the life scripts that determine how we define ourselves and our place in the world. It involves shifting mindsets, but it's also more than that.

Just like us, our students have developed life scripts that influence how they see themselves, the world, teachers, school, and their peers, and those scripts impact how they interpret what happens to them and how they react to it. These life scripts might lead students to believe that they will never be successful in school, that they need to fight a fellow student who disrespects them to protect themselves, or that they can't be a doctor due to their race because they believe the negative stereotypes they see in the media. When we can help students flip the scripts that limit them, it increases their engagement in our classes and has the potential to change the trajectories of their lives in profound ways. To do that, oftentimes we must dig into and shift our own scripts that determine how we view our roles as educators, see students, navigate student relationships, and interpret why our students behave the way they do. Some of our scripts may unintentionally create barriers to building the types of relationships with students that not only increase engagement but also change their lives.

About This Book

This book is designed to help you identify and flip your own scripts and equip you to better connect with students, increase engagement, and support students. It will help you learn how to guide students to believe in themselves and flip the scripts that limit their academic identity and the futures they can envision for themselves.

Positive deviant teachers are highly skilled at building teacher-student relationships, engaging students, and guiding students to flip the scripts that limit them. Positive deviant teachers also feel a sense of job satisfaction and well-being in their roles. This book provides an opportunity for educators to develop the key commonalities shared by positive deviant teachers. We offer you an opportunity to learn about the topics and read real-life examples of how five positive deviant teachers address common teacher-student situations. We also provide opportunities for you to interact with the concepts you're learning by guiding you through self-reflection and annotating sample scenarios. In this way, you'll practice developing some of the skills you may not have learned in your teacher preparation programs, such as how to see and understand students' needs or how to navigate conflict when students push your buttons.

While this book is designed to benefit you as an individual teacher, sometimes the scripts we need to flip are deeply ingrained in our school culture, and the only way to shift them is to engage in this work together. You may use the guiding questions at the end of each chapter as a book study with your colleagues. Additionally, we know that administrators' policies, procedures, and philosophies of leading and teaching influence the culture and climate of the school and impact teachers' ability to engage in the concepts we share in this book. We hope the book study questions will facilitate deeper discussion about the implications of this content and the policies and culture within your school. As you create a plan for facilitating this book study, you may want to invite any positive deviant teachers (those already highly skilled at the content in this book) on your staff to lead it rather than ask them to engage in content they are already experts at; that is, if they wish to do so.

Each chapter includes the following sections.

1. Looking Outward: Themes in Research and Practice
    a. Personal and professional examples about the topic
    b. Reflection questions about the content and how you might personally apply it in your classroom
    c. Jessica's Vignette—a vignette from coauthor Jessica May illustrating a key concept from the chapter
2. Looking Inward: Flipping the Script
    a. Reflections to help you flip your own scripts
    b. Skill building
3. Learning From the Five Teacher Types
    a. Two common student scenarios or situations followed by descriptions of the strategies or approaches five different positive deviant teachers might use in response, such as how to build relationships during the first two weeks of school or how to engage a chronically disengaged student
4. Wrapping Up
5. Book Study Questions

Meet the Five Teacher Types

In each chapter, we highlight common student situations and how five different positive deviant teachers would navigate each situation. Each teacher has chosen a *teacher type* title that represents who they are as educators. Following each scenario, there is space for you to reflect on how you might respond to the scenario yourself. These teacher types are real positive deviant middle and high school teachers sharing their experiences and approaches with you. Feel free to mix and match aspects of the different teacher types or come up with something completely your own based on the content and strategies you learn from this book. While you may not relate to how they describe their appearances or the content areas they teach, we hope that you see something in one or more of these teacher types that resonates with who you are as an authentic teacher and that you will be able to apply in your classroom. In the following section, the five teacher types introduce themselves.

Teacher Type: Caring Connector

For my personal style of teaching, I tried to boil down the two things I consider to be the most central to my approach to life, not just teaching as a profession: (1) caring and (2) connecting. I believe it is crucial to be your genuine self within the classroom, as students will always be able to tell if you are being fake. Besides, if you are trying to model behavior for students, then it is important that they know you are walking the walk, not just preaching "do what I say and not what I do."

Caring

I believe having empathy is the root of being a caring teacher. You need to approach each student without preconceived ideas or biases that could cause you to label them one way or another. If you truly care about their academic success and their overall well-being, you must take the time to understand their needs. Whether you are differentiating an assignment, giving multiple chances to redo their work, or just having meaningful conversations about how you can help them, you have to keep working until you find their key to being a successful student, whatever that may look like for them. For one student, it could be achieving high academic success, and for another it could mean just making it to class that morning. It is crucial to remember that you don't know what each student is bringing with them emotionally into school each day. Sometimes, this requires a lot of patience and can be challenging, as the needs of each student are often very different. As is the case in life in general, showing empathy can often leave you vulnerable, and sometimes students may abuse your willingness to give second chances. However, to me, caring isn't just about giving students what they want; it's about giving them what they need at that time. Sometimes, that means contacting parents or drawing hard deadlines if necessary. If the student knows you care about them as a person and a learner, they will understand that you are doing what is in their best interest (even if they don't realize it right away). Each case is unique, and you have to decide the right course to take depending on the student. This leads into the second part of my personal style.

Connecting

For me, the word connecting *is intimately linked to the idea of caring when considering both a classroom environment and my personal life. Without connection, relationships become superficial and are either easily disposed of or taken for granted. In the classroom, I always start the first few days of each new semester focusing on building these connections. I begin by not just introducing myself but introducing the students to my various hobbies to show them that ~~I am more than an "education ATM;"~~ I am a person with diverse interests outside the classroom and someone who is a lifelong learner with passions for many things. I also spend time getting to know each of my students' interests and hobbies and finding something we have in common. I want my students to know that I care enough to genuinely get to know them, and that I value them as not just a student but as a human being in my classroom.*

I believe that true learning occurs when there is a positive relationship between teacher and student, and this pays huge dividends, not just for improving student learning but for overall classroom atmosphere and my own enjoyment of teaching.

Teacher Type: Gentle Giant

I have a very imposing appearance, especially to middle school students. My large stature and dark beard often give a scary first impression, but I pride myself on being known for my compassion and empathy. Students quickly realize that I am not so scary and am a good example of why you shouldn't judge a book by its cover. I spend a lot of time in class sharing personal experiences of character growth related to each of my lessons, and I think this helps students feel more comfortable in my class.

Gentle

I find it really important when working with middle school students to have a soft side. So many of them are trying so hard to put on a tough face, and it's important that they know it's OK to be vulnerable once in a while. I love showing students that I am willing to listen and empathize with their doubts and fears. In physical education, we see a lot of students struggle with self-confidence, and it's important to be able to make them welcome through conversations and relaxed activities. It's great to play along in class and engage on the same level as the students. Likewise, I like to bring my guitar to class once in a while to show them a different side of myself. Students often joke that I deliver too many TED Talks as this is my approach to discipline—explaining how something was wrong and how it can be changed rather than scolding and reprimanding.

Giant

As a physical education teacher, my job is to know the games and activities that I teach. Every once in a while, I'll need to jump into the action to level the playing field. It's completely unfair, but it helps to engage some of the disengaged students. Showing them that even the "best" students or athletes in the class also experience failure is a fun way to teach perspective and compassion. As a big man whose physical appearance is intimidating to most newcomers to middle school, it is important that I am the one to break the ice with dumb dad jokes and goofiness. Students quickly learn that when the goofiness goes away, the TED Talks are about to start!

Teacher Type: Nurturing Narrator

In my classroom, I often cultivate a community of growth and development through an honest and raw connection with my students. I make sure everyone knows they come in with a clean slate, that their nature with school thus far is not necessarily their destiny.

Nurturing

I create trust in my classroom before I expect students to be able to learn in it. I make sure to always have snacks and my time available for students should they need it. I encourage my students by nourishing their individuality, while fostering a supportive community.

Narrator

I had a really hard time coming up with my personal style, so I asked my former students in an Instagram post (on my teacher's account) how they would describe my teaching style. An overwhelming number of responses described me as "the storyteller." I use a lot of examples in my classroom from my personal life and my own experiences in both my lessons and my expectations. Students know my husband through my words, though they have never met him. I am so thankful for him because I use him as a teaching tool all the time, and sometimes I do have to change the exact story to fit what I need that day. I create a comfortable and safe environment for my students by narrating our story. I set up our day by telling them about my night or a specific memory, something that is relevant to what we're doing or maybe what we've been struggling with as a class. They also feel like they learn a bit more about me each day and then, of course, share a relevant story about themselves. Students find compassion for each other through interest in each other—which I demonstrate through our nurturing conversations each day. Not everyone shares every day, but everyone is given the opportunity.

Teacher Type: Perceptive Pragmatist

I have always considered myself to be an observer. I don't enjoy being the center of attention (yes, I know, ironic for someone who stands at the front of a classroom with all eyes on her).

Perceptive

By taking the time every day to observe my students—their moods and their body language—I think I am better able to perceive what they need, what's going on, who needs to be pushed, and who needs gentle kindness at any given time. I think a lot of power struggles within the classroom don't happen because the teacher has used the "wrong" strategy, or a student is being difficult—I think it simply stems from a mismatch of the teacher's reactionary response with the student's underlying headspace. I always do my best to be in tune with how others are doing so I can take the approach that will meet people where they are at.

Pragmatist

In an ideal world, we would have ideal strategies when interacting with students that would result in ideal student behavior. However, that is not the case. I think how we interact with students varies day to day, even minute to minute, depending on a whole host of real-world factors. I always take the approach of humanizing teenagers. I find it becomes a lot easier to address behavior when I stop worrying about what my "teacher approach" should be and instead just view every interaction as person to person. Students are much more receptive to conversations, even if it's a hard conversation, when they feel they are being treated as an equal deserving of respect and not a subordinate, especially by the time they are in high school. I think the solution to every problem isn't a one-size-fits-all approach; it is what treats the student as a human with a unique history of experiences, helps them learn and grow, and gets the job done.

Teacher Type: Warm Demander

I outwardly love students up while also being equally strict and unrelenting.

Warm

The things that are most important for me to tell students are "I love you" (I also give "mom hugs" when they need one), when they are having a good hair day or how much I love their outfit, and that I'm proud of them for certain specifics I witness them say or do. My students have told me that I'm always happy to see them, that I smile a lot, and I have such a positive attitude. My goal is to make them feel seen and heard. I make sure to always tell them I've missed them when they're gone, so they know I noticed their absence. No matter what they ask me, I always say thank you for asking. I acknowledge their presence every chance I get. It's important to let them know that I read all the work they turn in, and I do this by remembering certain things they had in their assignments. For example, one student wrote a journal entry about not feeling good enough for anyone or herself. Less than a week later, this student happened to come by my room with a friend who had to grab something, so I took that moment to hold her hands in mine, look her in the eyes, and tell her how beautiful and smart she is, and that she makes my day with her bubbly personality. Her eyes started to tear up as she said thank you. I then told her that those who really love her will always think and know that she's enough, and if they don't, they don't really love her, and she should move on. She gave me a hug, thanked me, and walked away taller and lighter.

I make sure that my tone is upbeat, friendly, and calm. I joke with my students and laugh with them as much as possible, including when it's at my expense. I was taught by another teacher that it was better to actually put the bandage on for them instead of making them do it themselves, because it's an easy but profound way to show how much you care for them. My classroom is filled with everything a student could possibly need or want. I'm known for this, and I have students come in asking for things even though I've never had them in class. From a supply of tampons and pads in my closet, to fingernail clippers, to stain removers—I've got it all.

Middle schoolers feel invisible to adults, so I make sure to listen to their "middle school" issues that are huge to them but seem so minor to me. I intentionally make myself step into their minds and shoes to understand their angst. It's my duty and honor to tell them often that, while I can't make anything better, I understand the difficulty they are going through and their feelings. I explain that I am here as living proof that they will get through middle school because I made it through. I give them hope*!*

Demander

While I love them up fiercely, I also hold my students to high expectations. I gently tell them to redo less-than-stellar work because I know they are capable of doing better. I'm always walking around the room, looking over their work as they do it, giving them reminders to guide them in fixing their mistakes before they turn in assignments. If they swear in class, I give them a different word to substitute it with and ask them to use that word instead. Bringing the real world into specific lessons on content—but also including good character traits—are the ways in which I encourage them to rise to the next level of personal attributes. Students have told me they like my honesty and bluntness. As an example, I always tell them they shouldn't be dating in middle school because these years are about figuring out who they are on their own without having to care about another person's needs. I point out the behavior I expect from them when they aren't meeting my expectations and explain what to do next time instead. From the first day of school, I explain that I'll always be transparent with them, so I let them know the consequences for every behavior in class that won't be permitted. I don't write referrals, and I don't send students out into the hall or to the office. Instead, I explain my "three strikes and you're out" policy—any student who strikes out must handwrite thirty or more letters, one for each peer in their class, to acknowledge and then right the wrong that affected each person in the room. I'm intentional about noticing students' positive and negative behaviors in class, followed by quick conversations with them about what it looks like to have good character and how to be a better human. Working with them and alongside them allows me to help them follow through by fixing their mistakes with other peers, with me, or in their home life. To me, everything in class is meant to be a teachable moment, which I grab hold of to help students and to explain how to become their best selves as humans.

As a "demander," I've learned to be vocal, honest, vulnerable, involved, and intentional with my words and actions when interacting with my students. I'm a pit bull, so to speak, who won't let things be subpar. My students know I am there to help guide them and push them to be better . . . each and every day. They trust my efforts even though they may not like them or want to hear them.

A Look Ahead

The book comprises six chapters and four appendixes.

Chapter 1 explores building trust and connection with students in the early weeks of the school year by identifying strategies teachers use to help students feel seen, valued, and accepted.

Chapter 2 discusses the importance of creating a safe environment in the classroom by recognizing and reducing barriers to engagement that students face and by helping them grow, self-reflect, and believe in themselves.

Chapter 3 shows that developing authenticity is essential for teachers to establish trust with students, effectively manage challenging behaviors, and navigate tensions with administrators.

Chapter 4 discusses how to increase student engagement by exploring human motivation and needs as well as students' self-efficacy, hope, and locus of control.

Chapter 5 explores how teachers can navigate conflict with students by understanding their own core beliefs and the underlying factors that lead to their students' challenging behaviors.

Chapter 6 guides teachers to flip the scripts that limit their relationships with students and guide students to flip the scripts that limit their learning and what they think is possible for their lives.

The appendixes include activities to guide students' self-reflection, a middle school and high school scaffolded essay writing packet, tools to help students develop social-emotional competencies, and activities to engage students and build relationships during the first two weeks of school.

This book is for you if you want to increase your well-being and job satisfaction while also learning how to understand, connect with, and engage students in deeper ways. If you are looking for a checklist that will magically increase student engagement, this is not the book for you. In this book, we give you examples of how to build positive relationships, engage students, and navigate teacher-student conflict more effectively, *and* we ask you to engage in deep reflection of yourself and your current practices. This book will transform the way you see your job and relate to your students. Regardless of why we teach, one thing is clear: Having positive relationships with students and increased student engagement benefits students *and* increases your well-being and job satisfaction as an educator. This book will help you do that.

CHAPTER 1

Building Trust and Connection

Sometimes we find ourselves trying to solve our current struggles in education with the latest app, a new curriculum or intervention, or the latest program, but none of those will be effective for struggling students if we don't have a foundation—a positive teacher-student relationship grounded in trust. This is especially true for secondary students, who are highly influenced by social-emotional factors. In elementary school, most students will participate when you place them in a group intervention for reading. If you try to pull a group of eighth- or ninth-grade students together for a reading intervention, however, they will do everything they can to avoid engaging because they don't want to look "stupid" in front of their peers. A trusting relationship with a teacher will set the stage for how safe our adolescent students feel in our classrooms, and that will absolutely determine if they will engage when they feel like they might not succeed. If they feel safe in our classrooms, that will give them the courage to risk failing in front of their peers.

In this chapter, we explore what research and practice show about how to build trust and connection with students—such as prioritizing positive relationships with students, connecting with students early in the year, building trust through self-reflection, and others. Then we practice flipping the script through self-reflection activities. We end the chapter by hearing how the five teacher types respond to two common scenarios related to building trust and connection.

Looking Outward: Themes in Research and Practice

If you've been in education for any period of time, you've heard that teachers need to develop positive relationships with students if we want them to engage in our classes and decrease their chances of dropping out of school (Hambrick et al., 2019; Koplan & Chard, 2015). But how do we do that? We've found that the more we can understand our students—through remembering what it was like to be their age and through understanding adolescent development and shared human needs—the easier it is to build positive relationships.

Prioritize Positive Relationships With Students

When we empathize with our students and imagine what it feels like to be them in our classes, it changes how we interact with them and how they feel about and respond to us. Let's look at some of the key ways teachers can foster a bond with their students.

- **Put yourself in their shoes:** Think about your relationships with your leaders. What qualities motivate you to want to work hard for them? What qualities do you need in your environment and from your leaders to feel safe to try to do something you don't feel confident doing? I (Rebecca) know I am much more productive and have a greater sense of well-being when I work in an environment where I feel connected to my leader and colleagues, feel safe to express my ideas and try something new, and trust my leader. If I am going to engage in something new or try something I may not buy into, I need to trust that my leader has my best interests in mind, values my opinion, is competent, and understands my work. The same is true for adolescent students, especially those on a path toward dropping out with a history of school failure and difficult and painful adult relationships (Culyba et al., 2016; Mason, Hajovsky, McCune, & Turek, 2017; Watson, 2017). Positive relationships with students who are struggling in life and school can change students' lives when teachers use that foundation to challenge them, help them shift their academic identity, learn to believe in themselves, and find hope for the future (Kelley & Lee, 2018; Meltzer, Muir, & Craig, 2016).

- **Foster a sense of belonging:** One of the most powerful things a teacher can provide students with is a sense of belonging. I (Rebecca) attended a conference where motivational speaker Gaelin Elmore (2024) gave the keynote about the importance of belonging. He told his story of experiencing abuse and being in and out of foster care as a child. He was a frequent visitor to the front office, and at sixteen, he was planning to drop out of high school. He said the one thing that changed his life was feeling a sense of belonging from his teachers and coaches. He did not drop out of high school—he graduated with full-ride offers to play football at multiple colleges. He has now dedicated his life to helping teachers and other adults realize the power that belonging has to change the lives of struggling youth.
- **Help students believe in themselves:** In my study of positive deviant teachers, I (Rebecca) interviewed adults who'd had a positive deviant teacher. These were people who had been disengaged students—who had struggled in life and school. They all told me stories about how their positive deviant teachers helped them believe in themselves and see more possibilities for their lives (Knighton, 2022). One of the things that is so important about developing positive relationships with teens is that those relationships can positively change students' lives regardless of gender, race, ethnicity, socioeconomic variables, or special education needs (Cornelius-White, 2007; Liang et al., 2020; Roorda et al., 2017).
- **Provide positive experiences in the classroom:** Many of our highly disengaged students have had repeated experiences of negative feedback from teachers. How can they believe they will ever succeed, and why would they even want to show up or try if all they hear is negative feedback? Imagine having to get up every morning and go to a place where everyone but you seems to be successful at shared tasks and able to relate to each other. You don't fit in with them, and you don't believe you can be successful. All you hear in your head is, "You are a failure. You suck. Whatever you do, don't let them see that you can't do this. Why can't you be like them? What's wrong with you?" Imagine how isolated and hopeless those students feel. It's not hard to understand why they disengage, shut down, or rebel against being forced to be there.
- **Guide students to rewrite their life scripts:** We can help these students rewrite the life scripts that have them believing they don't belong and

> can never succeed. We can create environments where they feel like they do belong, where they feel like we believe in them, and where we help them gain the skills in which they've fallen behind or challenge them if they are advanced. In these environments, our students can begin to feel valued, cared about, and connected. They also begin to engage more because they have hope that they can succeed, and that school does matter for real life. For disengaged students, that can change the course of their adult lives.

Developing positive relationships with students and creating environments in which they are more motivated to engage helps them *and* increases our joy, well-being, and job satisfaction. As teachers, we also want to feel connected to our students (Klassen, Perry, & Frenzel, 2012). We feel good when they succeed, and we feel valued when they engage in the lessons we spent hours developing.

Connect With Students Early in the Year

Establishing an environment that guides students to rewrite the scripts about who they are at school and in life begins by creating connection at the beginning of the school year. It is the first time we meet many of our students, and they are deciding whether they can trust us depending on what we do, what we say, and how we treat them and their peers. If we treat their peers in ways they perceive to be unfair, that decreases their trust in us. If we say one thing and do something else or we don't follow through on what we say we will do, that erodes trust. If they think we don't have their best interests in mind, they will be less likely to do what we ask of them. We also must find a way to connect with our students. It could be common interests (movies, music, hobbies, sports, foods, and so on), similar experiences, or personally knowing their siblings or friends. When students feel connected to us and trust us, they feel safer in our classrooms, but it doesn't stop there. Creating safety also means we need to scaffold our lessons well so they can succeed. Finally, we need to create a culture where students support each other and where no one is judged or shamed for not knowing an answer or not doing a task correctly. It all starts during the first two weeks of school.

JESSICA'S VIGNETTE

Within the first two weeks of school, I always have a very real conversation with my students. It goes something like this:

"I think it's important that you all understand how seriously I take the honor of being your teacher this year. And because of this fierce belief, I want you to know that my students don't fail."

A handful of students smirk at me.

"If you're thinking to yourself that that's not possible, I will always respond by telling you that my classroom may be different from others you've been in, because I always create assignments that purposely set my students up for success. I've been doing this job long enough to know exactly what you, the student, need to do. I have *never* had a student fail my class. So, if you decide to follow all of my specific tasks and strategies, I *promise* . . . I personally *guarantee* you will not fail. Not only will this class become easier, but so will all your other classes."

At this point, no one is smirking at me. I see a lot of stunned faces and the room is silent.

"I'll explain what the handful of doable tasks are when we get to content-related tasks. The main thing I want you to know is that I have your back. Once your name is on my roster, you are my kid forever. I'll love you like a mother and want nothing but the best for you. Depending on what *you* choose to do, this year could be the greatest growth you'll ever have in school, if you do everything I tell you to do and how to do it. Trust me."

I show my students my heart in hopes of connecting with their hearts, and I show them that I believe they are more capable than they think they are. That's where the magic lies.

When the school year starts, many of us feel pressure to launch into content on day one. This pressure might be due to an urgency to cover all content prior to testing in the spring. It might be due to real or perceived pressure from our administrators. It might be because we aren't sure how to design activities that intentionally develop relationships with students. It might be because we believe that we need to set a strict and distant tone from the beginning or students won't respect us the rest of the year. Whatever the reason is, many of us skip taking the time to build relationships with students and create a trusting and safe environment during those first two weeks.

Positive deviant teachers all emphasize the importance of taking those first two weeks of school to connect with their students (Knighton, 2022), which leads to far fewer discipline issues in their classes during the year. If you've been in education for more than one year, you know there are some months that always seem to have higher discipline referral rates, making it much more difficult to teach. In our experience, those months are October and February. Positive deviant teachers don't struggle to teach during these months. The time they take at the beginning of the year to build relationships and establish a safe environment gives them teaching time back during those high-referral months.

Spending the first two weeks of school building relationships doesn't mean we don't teach content, but it does mean engaging in content in ways that also builds connection with students and sets the tone for creating safety and trust. See some examples in appendix D (page 273). For example, one positive deviant teacher asks students to complete a writing project where they let her know more about who they are as people. They are diving into language arts content, but she doesn't grade this first project. She wants students to feel safe to submit their work to her without the fear of failing an assignment. This approach does two things: (1) It helps students begin to trust her and feel safe, and (2) it allows her to get to know her students as humans and evaluate their writing levels. Later in this chapter (page 39), you'll read what five different positive deviant teachers do during those first two weeks of school to connect with their students and create an environment of safety and trust.

Build Trust Through Self-Reflection

As teachers, we are the leaders of our classrooms, and we need our students to trust us if we want them to engage in what we ask them to do. They need to know we have their backs, and what we are asking them to do will benefit them. They need to know that when we ask them to do something, it isn't to try to control them or to serve only our own needs. To do this, we must slow down and reflect on what we are asking students to do and why. Building the types of relationships and classroom structures and norms that lead to higher engagement requires us to examine why we do what we do: What activities do we ask students to do in our classes and why?

Consider the following reflection questions about how you make decisions.

- Do I take time to reflect on how I approach teaching my classes and adjust based on who is in the room and what they need? Or do I do things the way I've always done them?
- Do I make decisions because that is the way I think I have to do it?
- Do I make decisions because I am worried about future test scores?
- Do I make decisions based on what I think my administrator expects to see?
- Why do I design assessments the way I do, and do they tell me what I need to know as I guide student learning and growth?
- Do I believe all students can and want to learn, or do I think some students will never care or try, so why bother trying to connect with and engage them?

Building the types of relationships and classroom structures and norms that lead to higher engagement requires us to examine why we do what we do: What activities do we ask students to do in our classes and why?

There is no judgment in these questions. They are designed to help us gain more awareness of why we do what we do. They help us understand how our preconceived ideas or old patterns impact the types of relationships we are forming with our students and how those relationships may contribute to the level of investment our students have in our classes. Imagine working for a supervisor who doesn't think you are capable of learning and treats you that way. How might that impact how you feel about yourself, your job, and the supervisor? How might that impact the level of effort you put into what they ask you to do?

Students also need to know that we care and that we are putting effort into supporting them. Adolescents need to feel seen and respected as fellow humans with their own thoughts, ideas, and valid feelings (Allen et al., 2013; Hutchison, 2019; Yeager et al., 2018). Sometimes, as adults, we tend to discount students' thoughts, feelings, and ideas because we know their emotions can be intense and that they will outgrow a lot of what they think and feel at this age. But if we want to connect with, engage, and positively impact our students, we need to honor and respect that what they are going through in each moment is very real and valid for them. It is by going through the thoughts, feelings, ideas, and experiences during this phase of life that students evolve into adults.

I (Rebecca) find that teens can have incredible insight and wisdom, especially the students who've had really rough lives. I think it's our job to ask students reflective questions that help them gain deeper self-understanding and wisdom, rather than tell them what to think and how to feel. Have you ever had an experience where someone, maybe a coach or administrator, asked you questions that helped you understand yourself and your situation better so you could figure out how to navigate it? How did that feel compared to experiences you've had where a supervisor just told you what to do? Students often only experience being told what to do rather than being asked questions that help them figure out what to do. Sometimes we don't think adolescents have the capacity to figure things out on their own—that we must tell them what to do—but it just isn't true. They may still need guidance, but the kind of guidance that comes from being asked questions that cause them to think and grow is much more effective than simply telling them what to do. This might sound like, "Help me understand your thinking," or "Can you tell me more about why you answered that way?"

Additionally, students need us to be the kind of leaders we wish we had. They need to know that we are there for them and that we will show up and not flake out. They need to see that we are competent in our content areas so they can trust that what we tell them is true, and they need to see that we are real so they can trust us (Knighton, 2022). Owning when we make mistakes is one of the best ways to gain students' trust. It doesn't make us seem less competent; it makes us seem more human and relatable, and we are modeling that mistakes are OK when we take the opportunity to grow from them. When we don't establish trusting relationships early, students can struggle to learn from us because they fear taking risks and trying when they don't believe they can succeed (Mitchell, Kensler, & Tschannen-Moran, 2018; Tschannen-Moran, 2017; Tschannen-Moran & Hoy, 2000).

Take a moment to read and answer the following self-reflection questions.

WALKING IN OUR STUDENTS' SHOES

Reflecting ON BUILDING TRUST

Think about a leader you trusted, especially if they were a leader who asked you to change or try something new that you were nervous about.

- Why did you trust them?

- What qualities did they have that made you trust them?

- Are you that type of leader for your students? Which of those qualities do you have when leading your students?

- Which of those qualities do you want to develop? How might you do that?

Visit ***go.SolutionTree.com/teacherefficacy*** *for a free reproducible version of this reflection.*

See, Value, Accept, and Believe in Students

Highly important skills that increase the safety, trust, and connection students feel with us are truly seeing, valuing, accepting, and believing in them. As humans, when we don't feel seen, accepted, and valued by the people around us, it is harder to feel safe, especially in settings where we are evaluated. In *How to Know a Person: The Art of Seeing Others Deeply and Being Deeply Seen*, author David Brooks (2023) explains that, as humans, we all need to be seen and acknowledged by others. He writes, "No one can fully appreciate their own beauty and strengths unless those things are mirrored back to them in the mind of another" (Brooks, 2023, p. 11). My (Rebecca's) greatest growth as a person has come from experiences of being seen by someone else as they reflected a truth they saw in me that I did not see myself. We can do this for our students. In my study, the adults who had a positive deviant teacher all emphasized the importance of teachers making them feel seen, valued, accepted, and believed in and how that affected their engagement in class (Knighton, 2022). They told me they tried harder for their positive deviant teachers because they could see how hard the teacher was trying to support them, and they didn't want to let the teacher down. They also tried harder for positive deviant teachers because the teacher believed in them and helped them begin to believe in themselves.

It is more difficult to build relationships and trust with some students than with others. We've all had students who seem like they don't want a relationship with us, who actively push us away, or who seem to enjoy pushing our buttons. These are the students who need us the most.

The way you felt with someone you had frequent conflict with is how some of our students feel in our classes, especially if they have had a long history of failure, conflict, and lack of trust with teachers or adults in general. They come into our classes making assumptions about us and how we will treat them (McGrath & Van Bergen, 2015). They are on the defensive, expecting us to judge them and penalize them for whatever they do. This creates a barrier to relationship building. We can help those students flip the scripts they have about who teachers are and what their relationships with teachers can be. Four of the most effective things we can do to help them flip those scripts are the following: (1) build their trust, (2) show them we really see and believe in them, (3) demonstrate that we value them, and (4) assure them we won't judge them. This can take time, so we must be patient and supportive of each other as we work to break down those walls between the students and us as teachers. Take a moment to read and answer the following self-reflection questions.

Reflecting ON WHAT CONFLICT FEELS LIKE

Is there someone in your life who you frequently have conflict with? Who is that person? What is your relationship with them (spouse, friend, relative, boss, colleague, or other)?

When you are about to spend time with that person, do you go into it open and ready to connect? Or do you go into it feeling guarded and ready to defend yourself?

Imagine you are about to spend time with this person.

- Describe how you feel in your body.

- What thoughts might you be having about how your time with this person will go?

continued →

- What emotions might you be feeling?

- Do you have any assumptions about how they might interact with you? How might these thoughts, feelings, and assumptions impact the type of interactions and the relationship you have with this person?

Visit ***go.SolutionTree.com/teacherefficacy*** *for a free reproducible version of this reflection.*

It is hard to feel seen, accepted, and understood if we feel judged. Not judging others is challenging, and we find ourselves judging even when we don't want to. We judge the choices people make, how they complete tasks, and the perceived effort they put into activities. Think about the students you've had. How many of them didn't manage their time the "right" way or didn't organize their supplies or work the "right" way?

Often, these judgments come from how we were raised and what was modeled for us as what were "right" and "wrong" ways to be in the world. For example, if you were a highly emotional young person and your parents told you that showing emotion was unacceptable, you might grow up to think that showing feelings is a weakness and have little tolerance when others show their emotions. If you grew up in mainstream culture in the United States or Canada, you may have been taught that punctuality was a sign of respect, but in many cultures, the social norm is to arrive late, and it is not a sign of disrespect at all.

We often grow up learning to judge that people who do things differently than us are doing things the wrong way. We learn to judge the parts of ourselves that were "unacceptable" to our families or others in our lives, and then we transfer these judgments onto others. We find ourselves being irritated or angry when others exhibit the behaviors we were raised to believe were not acceptable. The more we can begin to accept all parts of ourselves and be open to the fact that there is not just one right way, the more we can accept our students and truly see them.

As we seek to build relationships with our students, we need to examine the ways in which we consciously or unconsciously judge them. As we become more aware, we can begin to ask ourselves if our judgments are helpful and necessary or if they are creating barriers to student learning. This does not mean we don't hold ourselves and our students to certain standards. It means we don't assume our ways of thinking and doing are the only right ways, and we seek to understand and accept our students more. Judgment creates a barrier to empathy, and we can't truly see our students if we don't have empathy.

In my study, I talked to adults who had been students of positive deviant teachers. They all shared that they didn't feel judged in these teachers' classes. One woman said she felt like she was able to breathe in those teachers' classes when she couldn't in other classes (Knighton, 2022). It's impossible to feel safe to try in an environment where you feel judged. If our students don't feel safe, they are less likely to risk trying an activity they think they might fail at. Think about your own life. Have you ever had a supervisor who misunderstood and judged you? How did that feel? Did you want to spend more time or less time with that person? Did it make you want to try harder for them, or did you want to retreat and shut down or maybe even fight back? I know when I've been in that position, I feel much less confident, and I begin to doubt myself more. This is how our students feel in our classes when we judge them.

Take a moment to read and answer the following self-reflection questions.

Reflecting

ON WHAT JUDGMENT FEELS LIKE

WALKING IN OUR STUDENTS' SHOES

Do you have someone in your life who judges you? Who is that person, and what is their relationship to you?

continued →

How does feeling judged by them impact your relationship with them? Do you trust them? Do you want to spend time with them?

Think of a time when you were judged. Write down what happened. Try to imagine yourself in that moment.

- What did you think?

- What did you feel?

- What did it feel like in your body?

- Did it impact how you felt about yourself?

Visit ***go.SolutionTree.com/teacherefficacy*** *for a free reproducible version of this reflection.*

Learning to see and understand our students without assumptions, biases, and judgments takes practice. We can learn to set our preconceived ideas aside to hear and see what is present in the student. We can pay attention to what does and doesn't work as we interact with students and adjust our approaches accordingly. We can let go of preconceived ideas about who a student is or what they need. We can listen to what they are saying underneath the story they are telling themselves. We can listen for the patterns, the human needs underneath the surface emotion—the connections between their thoughts, feelings, and words. Seeing our students requires us to understand human needs and motivations and also not assume that we know what they are feeling or thinking.

Recognize Barriers to Seeing Students

One of the most important steps in learning to see students is to reflect on what barriers might compromise our ability to listen to them. For example, if I (Rebecca) am feeling disrespected, it will be harder for me to really see who they are because I am feeling personally attacked. Sometimes we have judgments about what students "should" know and be able to do, and also about the "right way" to do something. These also create barriers to seeing and hearing students. We can't see where they really are if we are attached to where they should be.

One of the most common barriers I saw when I worked at both the middle and high school levels was teachers feeling like students *should* always come to class with a pencil. When students forgot a pencil, teachers felt like the student didn't want to learn. But that perspective fails to recognize at least two key factors that explain why adolescents might struggle to remember their pencils. First, the parts of the adolescent brain responsible for thinking ahead are not fully developed (Arain et al., 2013), so, unlike us, secondary students aren't always thinking three steps ahead to make sure they are prepared. This is especially true if a student struggles with executive function skills. The second complicating factor is that adolescents are wired to need peer interaction and connection (Allen et al., 2013; Hutchison, 2019), which can distract them from thinking about what they need for their next class during the passing period. We might think that sixth-grade students forget their pencils intentionally to avoid learning, but in most cases, the pathways in their brains that enable them to think ahead are still developing, and the many peer interactions happening during passing periods may cause them to forget about their pencil until they are sitting in class. By then, it is too late to go and get it. When we make assumptions about why they are forgetting their pencils, it gets in the way of seeing their reality and prevents us from creating effective solutions to resolve this barrier. Jessica is a master at helping students learn to remember their pencils. She assigns two "door guards" each week, and their job is to ask each student who enters the class to show their book to read and their pencil before they can enter. This helps students remember to bring a pencil. It is important to note that if you teach in a community where students can't afford pencils, this strategy won't be effective. In that case, providing pencils in the classroom eliminates the conflict.

Another barrier to seeing students that I've encountered when supporting school districts is adults thinking they know better because they are adults. And while it is true that our brains are fully developed, and we have had more experiences in life, it doesn't mean we understand or know what is best for all students. The only person who can truly know what is best for each individual is themselves. When we were adolescents, we didn't have all the experiences or the brain development to know exactly what our future paths should be, but we did know what classes we seemed to learn best in, whether we were passionate about a subject or not, what we felt confident in, and what called to us. As adults, we can ask good questions to guide students to self-reflect, consider the future, and make decisions about what is best for them, but telling them what is best based on our own filters and ideas isn't always helpful. Adolescents have a developmental need for respect from adults (Yeager et al., 2018).

One of the positive deviant teachers in my study told me about a high school student who was planning to drop out of school and bootleg alcohol up north in Canada because it was hard to get it up there, and he thought he would make a lot of money. Instead of telling this student that his plan was illegal and wasn't going to work out, she asked him questions about the specifics of how it would work to help him come to that conclusion himself. For example, she reminded him that he was underage and asked if he had a plan for someone else to buy the alcohol for him. She asked him to think through what kind of profit he would make if he had to hire people instead of doing it himself. He began to see that his plan might not pan out the way he thought, and he decided to stay in school (Knighton, 2022). If she had simply told him the plan was illegal and wouldn't work out, he may not have changed his mind because he would have felt like she was one more adult who didn't really get it and was telling him what to do. I'm sure we can all remember how much we disliked adults telling us what to do when we were teens. It's also true for us as adults. Think about some experiences you've had with a supervisor. Do you prefer it when they trust that you can find the answer and then facilitate a conversation to guide you to that, or do you prefer it when they tell you what you should do, even if it runs counter to what you know will be effective?

Jessica often says, "To lead humans, you have to know humans." This is a key to successfully connecting with and engaging students. The positive deviant teachers I spoke with understood human needs and motivations very well. As humans, we all have different values, priorities, and ways of coping with and navigating life, but the fundamental human needs of belonging, self-fulfillment, space to be authentic, self-expression, food, shelter, and safety are all the same. We might think we can't possibly understand what it is like to be in middle school these days and navigate the pressures of social media. While it's true that our generation didn't have that exact experience, we can still remember what it was like to be an adolescent and how consumed we were with peer acceptance. We can remember what it was like to feel insecure about who we were, to place high value on peer acceptance, and to fear peer rejection—more than at any other time in our lives. There is a reason most people remember middle school as being one of the most difficult times in life.

The more we can understand and see our students, the more we can connect with and engage them. Sometimes seeing a student looks like understanding what they need (a nap, a snack, help with understanding a concept, permission to complete only part of an assignment, and so on). Other times it might mean calling them out for what they are doing. I (Rebecca) remember a time when I was meeting with a student who always seemed to be in trouble. I was trying to talk to him and help him reflect on his choices. He pointed to one of the posters on my wall and tried to shift the conversation. I smiled at him and said, "I see what you're doing. You are trying to distract me so we don't have to talk about this." He smiled and owned that. And after that small experience, he seemed to trust me more because he knew that I really saw him.

Sometimes it can feel like there is a chasm between us and our students—the intense separation of generations. This has always happened. As we mature and grow older, we forget what it was like to be an adolescent, and we begin treating adolescents the ways adults used to treat us. We forget about how much we needed adults to respect us and how deeply we thought about the world as we began to try to understand it. We forget about the very real dreams we had for our lives. Those memories fade with time. When we remember the challenges we faced in adolescence, we can understand what our students are going through and what motivates them.

Take a moment to read and answer the following self-reflection questions.

WALKING IN OUR STUDENTS' SHOES

Reflecting ON YOUR EXPERIENCE AS AN ADOLESCENT

Remember when you were in middle and high school.

- What did you care about? What motivated you?

- How did you show up in school? What were your fears? What were your hopes? What did you think about? How did you feel?

- How well did you do in school? What affected that?

- What did you think about your teachers?

- What did your teachers think about you? Was their impression accurate?

Visit ***go.SolutionTree.com/teacherefficacy*** *for a free reproducible version of this reflection.*

Looking Inward: Flipping the Script

In this section, you will have the opportunity to engage in two activities, shown in figures 1.1 (page 35) and 1.2 (page 37). These are designed to help you understand yourself better and develop some of the skills discussed in this chapter.

Imagine yourself interacting with a student who is struggling with academic, behavior, or social-emotional skills.
• How do they behave in your class? What is their level of engagement?
• What assumptions and judgments are you making about that student and why they are behaving that way?

Figure 1.1: Examining assumptions about students.

continued →

- What expectations might you have of what they "should" be able to do but aren't?

- What are some other possible reasons why that student may be behaving that way?

- What are some assumptions the student might have about you or about themself that affects how they behave? (For example, you don't like them, they aren't smart enough, you single them out, there is no hope for their future, and so on.)

- What might your relationship look like with this student if you let go of your assumptions or judgments about them?

*Visit **go.SolutionTree.com/teacherefficacy** for a free reproducible version of this reflection.*

This activity may feel uncomfortable. We are asking you to really examine your thoughts, feelings, judgments, and reactions to someone else. We are asking you to be brave and honest, while also being compassionate with yourself. Use the space provided to respond to the reflection prompts.

Step 1: Think about a student you don't understand, someone you struggle to connect with. Try to remember what you think and feel when you interact with this person. Mark all the possible reasons you may struggle to connect with or understand this student.

- ❐ Assumptions you have about them
- ❐ Triggering behaviors
- ❐ Core beliefs you have about how they should act and who they should be
- ❐ Judgments you have about them
- ❐ Past relationships you've had with someone who they remind you of
- ❐ The way they make you feel (for example, they live in poverty and seeing that exist in the world is hard for you)
- ❐ Ideas you have about who they should be rather than who they are
- ❐ Your own personal stress and burnout
- ❐ Thinking you need to "save" them
- ❐ Being lost in thought (about something that happened earlier or that you need to do later)
- ❐ Preoccupation with how others will perceive that you are doing your job
- ❐ Thinking everyone thinks and feels the way you do—overidentifying with the student
- ❐ Racial identity, sexual identity, or political differences
- ❐ Misunderstanding of human development and what's normal for that age
- ❐ Generational norm differences
- ❐ Idealizing the person
- ❐ Other ____________
- ❐ Other ____________
- ❐ Other ____________
- ❐ Other ____________
- ❐ Other ____________
- ❐ Other ____________

Figure 1.2: Examining barriers to seeing students.

continued →

Step 2: Choose one item you marked in step 1 to reflect on. Ask yourself, "Why do I do (or think) this?" and then try to dig a little deeper to understand where that belief or reaction comes from.

For example, if you marked *thinking you need to save them*, ask yourself, "Why do I think I need to save them? Where does that drive come from in me?" Or, if you marked *core beliefs about how they should act and who they should be*, ask yourself, "Why do I think they should be a certain way? Where did that belief come from? Could I be wrong?"

Step 3: Reflecting on the item you chose for step 2, ask yourself, "Is this more important than connecting with and truly seeing this person? Why or why not?"

Step 4: Ask yourself, "What if I let go of this and tried to see this person for who they are? What might happen?"

Step 5: After you understand what might be preventing you from seeing this student, then seek to understand the student. Have curiosity about them. Observe their body language and mood, ask them questions, put yourself in their shoes, remember what it was like to be that age, ask other teachers, or ask parents or caregivers.
Step 6: Consider the following ways to show this student that you see them. • Notice if they need anything. • Notice and comment on their interests (sports teams, TV shows, superheroes, or some other interest you notice them displaying on their clothes or notebook). • Say "hi" to them in the hall. • Tell them a story that shows you can relate, or acknowledge that you haven't ever experienced that, but you can see that they are hurting. • Attend their after-school activities. • Ask about things that happened in their lives.

Visit ***go.SolutionTree.com/teacherefficacy*** *for a free reproducible version of this figure.*

Learning From the Five Teacher Types

This section presents two common scenarios. For each scenario, the five positive deviant teachers you met in the introduction describe how they navigate these scenarios in their practice. The first is how they build relationships during the first two weeks of school, and the second is how to connect with a student who does not trust adults. As you read through these examples, highlight, underline, or circle the parts of each example you relate to.

Scenario: It's the first two weeks of school, and you want to build relationships with your students

The following sections describe how each teacher type approaches this scenario in their classroom.

Teacher Type: Caring Connector

I always start each new semester with a similar approach. I try to focus on getting to know my students and making them feel safe and supported in my room. As a new teacher, I was so stressed out about getting through the curriculum and my students achieving academic success that I wouldn't spend nearly enough time doing this. Nowadays, I realize the benefits of connecting early and often with the students in my room.

I try to always begin my first class by introducing myself, not just as their social studies teacher but by opening up and explaining my interests and how I spend my free time. I do this so they see me as a human being and not just an education ATM! Being vulnerable and willing to share about myself usually helps them open up about themselves as well, with the added bonus of feeling that this classroom is a safe space to take risks in the learning process. I follow up by giving each student a questionnaire, asking them questions about their favorite books, movies, TV shows, hobbies, subjects, and so on. This gives me a basic benchmark of their writing ability and work ethic (some fill it out in great depth, while others put "I don't know" in most fields), and I can use it as a jumping-off point to start a conversation. This type of activity can sometimes be seen as a mundane "make-work" task for the students, and I believe it would be if I just sat at my desk and waited for them to finish. However, from my teaching perspective, the survey is just a way for me to find any type of meaningful connection to their interests. While they are filling it out, I go around the room and personally introduce myself to each student, then I find a shared interest that we have based on the information on the survey. Usually, I can find at least something we have in common, but if not, I will just ask them questions about their responses. Either way, I discover a lot about the students! This is important, as it gives me the information I need to make the course content relevant to them but also shows that I genuinely care about their lives outside the classroom. I will often spend an entire class period doing this to ensure that I get the chance to chat with every single person. While I'm doing this, the students have a lot of down time when they finish the survey, which gives them an opportunity to build connections with each other. The class often starts with students quietly filling out the questionnaire but ends with loud boisterous conversations happening and students moving around the room as they feel more relaxed and comfortable.

In the subsequent classes, I try to focus more on engaging them in the subject area and getting them working in groups. If I focus too heavily on the content right away, it can overwhelm certain students and cause them to disengage. Getting them to work in groups on low-stakes assignments helps them feel more comfortable in the room and experience early success in the course, which can lead to greater engagement and effort down the road. Knowing that they can be successful gives students the confidence to continue to take risks, even if they fail at a task.

Teacher Type: Gentle Giant

The first two weeks of school are typically the get-to-know-you phase of the year. Not just for me with my students but for everyone in the class. I really think it's important in the first few days of the school year to give students the opportunity to share who they are. We play large-group cooperative games that require them to move around and interact with peers. Within the first couple of classes, I put a lot of emphasis on learning the names of all *the students; this usually comes in the form of some game that also requires students to share something about themselves that they think is an identifier. It's neat to do this because it often reveals the commonalities that students have with each other and with me.*

I love being able to share with students who I am and what I've been up to over the summer, talking about my kids and family, introducing them to my passions and interests, and allowing them to see me as a person rather than a robotic teacher. For me, this is a great way to build relationships with students and often is an icebreaker for students to open up and share their personalities within the classroom.

In short, the first step is to open the lines of communication, show students that I am approachable and fun, but I also have expectations and structure. This helps students develop the confidence to explore and experience the class and shows they have fewer reasons to disengage or display challenging attention-seeking behaviors. The second step is to set class expectations and discuss schedules and the scope of the year. I feel like giving students insight into what the school year will look like gives them another spike in confidence. When students know what is ahead of them and what to expect, they tend to relax a little bit.

Teacher Type: Nurturing Narrator

At the beginning of the school year, I find it incredibly important to introduce myself to students through recognizable stories from my life. I put up pictures of people or places and go into a monologue that often opens me up in a vulnerable way. I find when I use parts of my life as a guide to how I came to be in front of them, they're more willing to open up to me in their writing right off the bat. I use time during the week before school to call my homeroom adults to introduce myself and get to know them a little better.

In my slideshow introduction, I tell students the three Cs of our classroom: (1) community, (2) communication, and (3) comfort. I always tell students the curriculum will come when we've established a safe and caring environment for everyone to learn in.

I make a point of learning students' names through continued and consistent use. I also let students know I have opened a line of communication with their adults by referencing them by their first name, "Oh, Mr. Jones it is so nice to see you in person! Jody (mom) told me all about your BMX riding this summer, I cannot wait to read all about it in your writing!" This quick reference point suggests their adult and I have a long-standing friendship.

I also give students a writing assignment in the first week as an introduction, something simple and with loose parameters—a "Rambling Autobiography" or a "Glimpse" assignment—something personal but general. I take in their writing in their whole journal and take the time to read them the same day and then ask students questions about what they've written the very next morning. If a student writes something more vulnerable, I will hold their journal to my chest as I ask them questions—demonstrating my appreciation for trusting me with such raw information.

Teacher Type: Perceptive Pragmatist

I remember frequently hearing "don't smile until Christmas" during the Septembers of my first years teaching as the "key" to successful classroom management. It's advice I never took. It didn't sit well with me and wasn't authentic to who I am as a person. My approach in the first weeks of school is the opposite: smile plenty and use humor. I also only ever act in a way that is authentic and genuine to who I am. For example, if I hate forced social interaction (like icebreaker games), I'm not going to ask my students to participate in them. For students to trust me, they need to experience that what they see is what they get; I'm not going to change personality once we get a few weeks into the school year.

I also frequently take time at the beginning or end of class to just visit—individually or with the class as a whole. Rather than trying to squeeze content in bell to bell, I leave some down time specifically to see students' personalities and let them see mine. For example, a student let me know that he was going to be away for a few days for a hunting trip with his parents. I said, "Oh, cool!" and left it at that since he was on his way to the next class. A few days later, we had some down time, and I brought it up again, "So where do you go hunting? What do you hunt?" Immediately, he lit up and had his phone out showing me pictures and telling me about all sorts of experiences. Connections like these are so *important. Obviously, it's great that this student will now see me as a person who takes interest in him and cares about him rather than just an authority figure. But it's just as important for me. I now also see a student who is likable, interesting, and has skills and talents that I don't have. On days in the future when he might test my patience, I will be seeing him through a personal lens, not as just another student at a desk.*

Teacher Type: Warm Demander

I actually thrive on challenges, especially when it comes to connecting with the tougher students. They are my number one focus right away, day one. After all these years I've discovered that if I can win them *over, then I have better odds of winning over the whole class. This means they're going to be less disruptive and distracting. I can show them that they can be leaders in a different way. I also like knowing that I can change their lives for the better when it comes to their future. This is why I purposely interact positively with them, as well as make sure to memorize their names, even with students I don't have in class. If I've heard they are tough to connect with, I will seek out a way to talk to them when I see them in the hallways to make a positive connection.*

If anyone comes at any living creature with a stick in a forceful way, that living creature will not respond with anything but fear, anger, or flight. To get close to any living creature, humans included, you must approach them with a spirit of love and patience. We know it works with abused animals of all kinds. It's the same with humans of any age. What's truly difficult is how patient teachers need to be with tough students—we must accept that it takes time. I use this approach with most students. Figuratively, I have to circle around them slowly and from far away at first; I have to be patient about getting close to them on a personal level because building trust takes time. In my experience, it will *happen—99 percent of the time. Even with the one student I was never completely able to connect with over the course of my career, I kept trying every day throughout the entire school year.*

When you do break through the barrier—knowing that you've earned a student's trust—there is nothing like it. The feeling is amazing, and bonding with those students will last a lifetime, not just the school year. They will continue to seek you out when life goes right and, more importantly, when life goes wrong; they are extremely grateful for your patience, persistence, and kindness. Just knowing that you have cared enough to take the time and effort to connect with them is priceless. And when that happens, they will be devoted to you forever.

Building RELATIONSHIPS DURING THE FIRST WEEKS OF SCHOOL

WHAT WOULD YOU DO?

What do you normally do during the first two weeks of school?

continued →

How might you change what you do to build relationships with students during the first two weeks of school?

What do you want to keep in mind as you approach building relationships with students?

*Visit **go.SolutionTree.com/teacherefficacy** for a free reproducible version of this reflection.*

Scenario: A student in your class has trouble trusting adults

The following sections describe how each teacher type approaches this scenario in their classroom.

Teacher Type: Caring Connector

This can be a challenging situation, as you are dealing with a student who already has big emotional walls built up around them as a measure of self-preservation. To get a student like this to lower those walls will take a lot of patience, consistency, and empathy from their teachers.

Patience is an absolute necessity when you are dealing with a student who has trust issues. You can't expect them to open up to you in a couple days, no matter how good your intentions are. If they have constantly been treated poorly or been neglected by adults, this will be deeply ingrained for them and will require time and effort to overcome. However, they need to see you put in that effort; if you are always trying to connect with them, they will see that you won't give up on them like some other adults in their life may have.

Consistency is key. Often, students with trust issues have come by those trust issues honestly. Many times, adults in their lives have disappointed them, neglected to follow through, or failed to be someone they can count on. It is important to be consistent as their teacher; if you say you will make time for them, follow through. If you expect certain behaviors in your room, expect those from every student and follow through on consequences. Also, you can't just show consistency with this student; show that you treat all your students that way.

Empathy is extremely important in these situations. Students with trust issues are often used to their interactions with adults being negative and often one-sided. If they are used to being yelled at and told what to do, they will often expect that from their teachers as well. I've found the most success when I just take the time to talk to them. First, I try to give agency to these students by offering them choices in class. Whether it is choosing a different topic for an assignment, choosing who they work with, or being flexible on due dates and offering chances to resubmit their work, this typically increases their engagement and helps them to feel more comfortable and capable in my room. If I ever do have to crack down on them for behaviors, I make sure to follow up with them afterward, sometimes I even apologize to the student if I feel like I was too harsh. This shows that I wasn't angry with them, just the behavior, and that I really do care about them and want them to be successful in my class. By apologizing to them, I show vulnerability. It may be the first time an adult has apologized to them before. This shows them that adults make mistakes too, and as humans, we need to take responsibility for our own behavior.

Teacher Type: Gentle Giant

Building trust with students is essential for creating a positive and productive learning environment. Demonstrating vulnerability, using humor, and sharing anecdotal references can all be effective strategies for establishing rapport and fostering trust.

Personally, I love to share personal experiences where I've faced challenges or made mistakes related to the subject matter or life in general. This shows students that I'm human and helps break down barriers. I find it important to inject humor into lessons and interactions with students. It helps lighten the mood and makes me more relatable. I've got "daily dad jokes" and funny T-shirts that I wear to school. I really enjoy the goofiness and relaxed atmosphere these can create.

Aside from lightening the mood and creating a comfortable space, I take a lot of pride in being real and honest with students. When they feel as though they are heard, understood, and validated, walls start to come down. As such, I'll often begin class discussions by acknowledging common worries or stressors that students may be experiencing, such as upcoming events and challenges. Sharing my own experiences with managing stress and offering strategies for coping helps create a supportive atmosphere where students feel comfortable opening up.

By incorporating vulnerability, humor, and anecdotal references into my teaching approach, I can create a more engaging and trusting relationship with my students. It's important to be genuine and authentic in my interactions, as sincerity is key to building meaningful connections.

Teacher Type: Nurturing Narrator

The first thing to remember is that it's not personal, and it's not a challenge. Having a difficult time trusting adults is often a trauma response, so it's critical to handle these situations with care and respect. You only get one first impression with these really tough and guarded students. Above all else, students want to know you care about them and that you are in their corner. Students who are extra tricky will not authentically complete work for you until they know they can trust you—especially vulnerable works, like being asked to write about their past to a complete stranger (their teacher). It's important to put your ego aside when they don't want to do assignments you've spent hours and hours creating and instead show empathy for their perspective. It's incredibly difficult to be able to work when you're hungry or when you've been up all night listening to your caregivers fight or even party. Quick, small, real check-ins will buy you a lot of grace from these students. At the beginning of the year, I try to find what they care about by asking casual questions. It doesn't take long for even the most challenging students to let you know what they would rather be doing than being in your classroom. That small moment when they let you know that one thing that they like to do becomes incredibly valuable.

I am always in the hallway at the beginning of the day. I greet every student who comes into my room or walks past me. I ask intentional questions as they go by, and I use the things they slowly open up to me about as tools to connect. When students hear you every single day, remember what's important to them. It builds trust, a common interest, and the security that you're listening to them all the time.

Difficult students also crave boundaries and structure. Your classroom needs to be a safe place not only for them but also for everyone else. They want to push you away through inappropriate behavior, and they most likely have been very successful doing this in the past. Tough students know how to make teachers avoid them; their body language is aggressive, their language is shocking, their silence is deafening. They want you to be clear about your expectations and be consistent with them. This doesn't mean you're a drill sergeant; instead, it means that when they cross a line, you will hold them accountable because you care enough about them to want them to be successful in your classroom. Respect their personal boundaries. Sometimes they need time and space to warm up to new adults—this is a reflection of their pain, not of you. Some days you will feel like you've taken a thousand steps forward, only to find they are ice to you the next morning. You have to leave your ego behind for these students—reset every night and offer forgiveness every day.

My board every morning says, "Good morning! I am so glad you're here," and I mean it to each of them. I demonstrate that by celebrating them, avoiding unnecessary power struggles, and resetting the clock every single day. A hard day doesn't erase a welcome and bright greeting from me the next morning. Remember that building connections with tough students may take time and persistence. The key is to create a safe and supportive environment where they feel understood and valued.

Teacher Type: Perceptive Pragmatist

The first thing I do not *do is force my presence on students. If anything, I usually give them space to observe how I go about things—how I interact with the class as a whole and with other students. It's the same strategy I use in my first weeks of school for everyone—they need to know that what they see is what they get, and I am being authentically me. I choose how I first interact with them based on how I observe their personality: Are they more social? Are they more reserved? If a student seems open, I usually limit my conversation with them to topics outside of school, like how their weekend was. If a student is very reserved, I do the opposite and start by only reaching out about what we're doing in class. Without fail, students will start to open up more and may eventually be the one to initiate a "hello" or ask for help.*

At the end of the day, the main things that matters for these students are that I'm able to be authentic, I am not trying to force any connection, and I am just giving it time.

Teacher Type: Warm Demander

My first-two-weeks-of-school boot camp includes activities that require vulnerability from me and my students. I tell them who I am the first day with a slide deck containing my family, my favorites, my dreams, and what I do in my free time. I begin with my love of storytelling, and I talk about my upbringing with my parents fostering 189 kids during my years growing up. I share my life struggles as they come up within the school year when it's applicable. We (because I participate too) role play about how not *to act in class. We dance and lip sync to Aretha Franklin's "Respect." We break down what respect and trust look and sound like, going through the Four Agreements, while being clear about all behavior and work expectations in our room and being transparent about the consequences of students' decision making. And while I'm doing all of this, I explain in detail about me having their backs in all areas of their lives (being their Mama Bear). All these things bring into focus that this classroom is where they are guarded; it's a safe place for students to fall, whether they're having a good or bad day.*

I laugh with my students, I hug them, I cry in front of them, to which I explain that that's what humans need to do to stay healthy inside. We discuss their habits and how they can make better choices for their bodies, minds, and moods. I incorporate all that I can when it comes to growing into a positive person who thinks of others, serves others, and puts their self-care needs first without any guilt. School is the whole package, and that's how I make them feel safe in my room, because I see them as humans first and students second.

I weave the feeling of safety into my classroom through thoughtful videos, explaining how no-technology self-care is incredibly important, and I create lessons that enforce all the activities we did in the first two weeks of school. It's never a one-and-done lesson in my class; we build life conversations on top of each one as an extension, which I make sure each student applies to their lives. If it was a one-time lesson, then I've wasted my time and theirs, and it won't stick. My amazing teacher mentors always taught me that I must continually pull from past teachings into current lessons; otherwise, students don't see those actions and character traits as being important to their own lives.

You can read more about my specific boot camp activities in appendix D (page 273).

Given what you've learned in this chapter, respond to the following reflection questions.

WHAT WOULD YOU DO?

Building TRUST WITH STUDENTS

Imagine you have a student in your class who you have heard has trouble trusting adults.

- What would you do?

- What internal challenges might you run into as you try to build a relationship with this student?

- How might you overcome those challenges?

Visit ***go.SolutionTree.com/teacherefficacy*** *for a free reproducible version of this reflection.*

Wrapping Up

As teachers, we can help our students change how they see themselves and what they believe is possible for their lives. To do so, we must build positive relationships based on trust and connection and create learning environments free of judgment, where students feel safe to try and to grow. Our students need to know we believe in them, especially when they don't believe in themselves. To develop these types of relationships, we must learn how to truly see our students. We need to understand what they need, who they are, and how they learn.

Chapter 1 Book Study Questions

As a staff, explore the concepts presented in this chapter and reflect on how they are evidenced in or might impact your school culture. As you read each of the following questions, think about how you would respond based on your individual role. If you are an administrator, think about these questions as you reflect on how you support your staff. If you are a teacher or support staff member, think about these questions as you reflect on how you support students.

1. In your building, do you feel that trusting relationships are valued (for staff, colleagues, and students)? Elaborate on why or why not.

2. What do you do to ensure your staff, students, and colleagues feel supported and that their voices matter?

3. Do you believe all students can learn and want to learn? Do you think some students either don't care or are not capable of learning? How do these beliefs impact the lessons you design and how you interact with students?

4. Have you ever had an experience where someone, maybe a coach or leader, asked you questions that helped you understand yourself and your situation better so you could figure out how to navigate it? How did that feel compared to an experience where a supervisor told you what to do?

5. Think about a time at work where you felt seen. What did your colleagues or administrators do that made you feel that way? What do you do that makes your colleagues and administrators feel seen? What do you do to ensure your students feel seen?

6. What are your school's traditions or activities that foster feelings of connection among staff and with students? If you don't yet have any, what traditions would you like to start?

7. Based on this chapter, is there anything you may want to try to improve trust and connection in your building?

CHAPTER 2

Creating Safety

In addition to developing relationships in which we see, value, accept, and believe in our students, we also need to intentionally create environments where students feel safe to try and where we encourage both academic and personal growth. Creating safe learning environments for adolescents can be more challenging than for younger students because of how preoccupied they are with peer acceptance. It can be even more challenging when we are working with students who have experienced a lot of adversity in their lives, which decreases their feelings of safety.

In this chapter, we explore what research and practice show about how to create safety—such as creating environments where students feel safe to try, recognizing barriers to student engagement, and helping students believe in themselves. Then we practice flipping the script through self-reflection activities. We end the chapter by hearing how the five teacher types respond to two common scenarios related to creating safety.

Looking Outward: Themes in Research and Practice

Adolescence is a time in life when people are discovering who they are and forming their identities (Watson, 2017). Students need to feel safe to express themselves (Pianta & Allen, 2008; Watson, 2017), and to feel safe, they need environments where they are understood and respected.

Create Environments Where Students Feel Safe to Try

Feeling safe at school is especially challenging for students with a history of struggling in school (academically, behaviorally, emotionally, or socially) because they have internalized that experience, and it clouds the way they see themselves. It is how they define themselves: "I'm the kid who was always in trouble, "I can't do mathematics," or "I can't write an essay."

When I (Rebecca) worked in a middle school, my primary job was to work with the students who were frequent visitors to the front office. I had conversations with them, hoping to understand how to help them be more successful in school. I frequently asked the question, "can you tell me about a time when you were successful in school?" So many of the students I spoke to responded, "Never. I've always just been in trouble." These students had adopted the identity of "the kid who is always in trouble."

We need to help students change that narrative if we want them to try in our classes. Asking struggling students to change the level of effort they put into our classes or their behavior in school is asking them to change their identities. This is a much bigger ask than just engaging in a lesson or learning how to be less disruptive. We have the opportunity to help students rewrite the scripts they've created for themselves and their lives. We can guide them to succeed when they don't think they can. This means they must feel safe enough to risk changing who they think they are. When students trust us and feel accepted and safe, it increases the chances that they will take that risk.

Recognize Barriers to Student Engagement

Supporting students to feel safe to try means we must pause and seek to understand the barriers our students are encountering. When we don't do this, it leads to our frustration and their disengagement. I saw an example of this where teachers required students to fill out an agenda book with their homework and tasks due. This made sense because they were trying to help students develop the increased organizational skills needed to succeed in school. However, teachers were frustrated when some students didn't bring the agenda book to class or didn't use it. It would have been easy to assume the students who wouldn't bring or use their agenda book either didn't care about their classes or didn't want to be organized, but I found that wasn't true. In my conversations with students, I learned filling out an agenda wasn't a useful organizational method for some students. Even if they wrote down the information, it didn't help them remember anything, so they felt it was wasted effort. Some students didn't bring their agendas to class because they lost them, could not afford new ones, and didn't want to tell anyone because they felt bad about their socioeconomic situation. Still other students struggled with executive functioning, lacking the organizational skills to bring their agendas let alone fill them out. Teachers judged these students as being defiant, not caring about homework, or not wanting to be organized. In reality, though, the student lacked resources, or the teacher's organizational method did not work for them.

One of the ways we can create environments where students feel safe to try is to understand the barriers to engagement they are battling and think outside the box about how to help them overcome those hurdles. Positive deviant teachers seek to understand why students aren't engaging and find solutions to the barriers they uncover (Knighton, 2022). They think about the purpose of what they are asking students to do and then seek to find innovative ways to meet that objective. For example, a high school physical education teacher I interviewed shared how he worked to change the dress code for his class so that students whose religion required they wear certain items would be able to honor that while also participating in class (Knighton, 2022). A social studies teacher I spoke with allowed multilingual learners to use their cell phones to take photos of the class objectives and notes he had posted in class so they could translate them later while they were studying (Knighton, 2022).

In the example of the agenda book, positive deviant teachers might have taken time to think about the larger purpose behind using an agenda book, sought to understand the barriers that prevent some students from using it, and then identified alternative ways to meet the larger objective. The agenda book's purpose is to help students keep track of assignments and due dates. What other methods could students use to accomplish this purpose? I (Rebecca) found a lot of success in helping students reflect on how their brains worked and brainstorming ideas about what organizational method would work for them. My students came up with ideas like entering assignments and due dates into the calendar on their phones, texting themselves, or setting up reminders. They also thought of writing due dates and assignments on sticky notes in their notebooks or lockers. Teachers came up with ideas such as providing photocopied pages from the agenda book to students who lost theirs. Utilizing these types of approaches would decrease teachers' frustration, improve student relationships, and increase student organization so they could be more engaged.

To create safety in our classrooms, we need to understand some of the factors that create barriers for our students. Empathy allows us to shift into seeking creative solutions rather than feeling frustrated and making assumptions about their behavior. Two primary factors we encounter in secondary schools that provide insight and empathy are social determinants of health and adolescent development.

Social Determinants of Health

It is helpful to understand how students' home and neighborhood environments impact their social, emotional, and mental development, which, in turn, impact their motivation to engage in class.

In the field of sociology, there is a concept called *social determinants of health*. It is the study of how experiences with social and environmental influences—such as family; racial or economic inequities; social norms; neighborhood resources; and local, national, and institutional policies—impact a person's biological, social, psychological, and emotional development (Braveman, Egerter, & Williams, 2011; Wadsworth & Butterworth, 2011). These experiences can either set a student on a trajectory toward success in school and life or increase the struggles and adversity they face (Davidson, 2015). One factor that significantly increases the challenges students will face is their exposure to AELEs. As detailed in the book's introduction (page 1), ACEs, a specific subset of AELEs, have been studied extensively. In 2014, researchers studied 95,677 children and found several correlations between students' ACEs exposure and school success. They found that students with two or more ACEs were 2.67 times more likely to repeat a grade, 45.2 percent of these students were diagnosed with attention-deficit/hyperactivity disorder (ADHD), 61.4 percent exhibited behavior struggles, and 55.4 percent bullied other students (Bethell, Newacheck, Hawes, & Halfon, 2014).

When students have experienced AELEs (abuse, neglect, poverty, inequality, bullying, parental substance abuse or incarceration, racism, and others), it impacts their brain development (Koplan & Chard, 2015). The prefrontal cortex, anterior cingulate cortex, and the subcortical-cortical dopamine pathways are affected, resulting in decreased coping skills, sense of safety, self-regulation, flexible thinking, goal setting, and ability to engage in concrete thinking and sequential planning (Hashimoto et al., 2015; Herzog & Schmahl, 2018). These changes can also impact a student's belief that they can control outcomes in their life and decrease their personal agency and the belief that they can succeed (Dixson, Worrell, & Mello, 2017). All of this affects student engagement because these students struggle with the basic skills and beliefs that lead to success in school: sitting still, paying attention to and following a sequence of instructions, planning for and attaining goals, figuring out how to solve a problem when they encounter a barrier, regulating negative emotions, and believing that they can succeed and that their efforts will impact their lives. When we see students who seem like they *won't* try, it can help to know that maybe it isn't that they don't care, it is that they need support in gaining these basic school and life skills and beliefs.

Often, the student behaviors associated with exposure to AELEs can create frustration for us as teachers and negatively impact our relationships (McGrath & Van Bergen, 2015), further decreasing the connection these students feel to school or the effort they put into it and increasing the likelihood that they will eventually drop out (Hutchison, 2019). It can feel overwhelming and heartbreaking to think about what our students have gone through. At the same time, it can be frustrating trying to connect with and teach students who exhibit the behaviors and beliefs associated with exposure to AELEs. The good news is research shows that *even one* positive, supportive relationship with a teacher can significantly improve the neural pathways that were disrupted by exposure to AELEs (Hambrick et al., 2019) and improve students' social, emotional, and cognitive success in school and life (Balfanz et al., 2007; Kelley & Lee, 2018). By developing positive relationships with our students, we can both help mitigate the harm they've experienced and decrease the frustration we feel when they don't engage and when they disrupt our classes. Teachers are in a unique position to help students both learn the skills they need to succeed in school and help students shift their self-concept and sense of possibility for their lives (Hutchison, 2019). Positive deviant teachers are highly skilled at this (Knighton, 2022). Chapter 6 (page 199) goes into more detail about how to facilitate that shift for students. In addition to understanding the barriers to safety and engagement that accompany exposure to AELEs, secondary teachers also have to navigate the challenges presented by adolescent development.

Adolescent Development

One of the challenges of teaching in secondary schools is that we need to find ways to connect with our students while teaching our content *and to* navigate the complexity presented by adolescence. Consider the following developmental shifts students face during adolescence.

- **Intense emotions:** During adolescence, the emotional intensity caused by hormonal changes outpaces the brain's ability to regulate emotions (Hutchison, 2019). This is what contributes to students' intense emotions and decreased ability to regulate them. Additionally, during adolescence, students are biologically wired to form cliques (Hutchison, 2019). Hormonal changes and brain development lead students to see others in the world as either for them, as part of their "in" group, or against them as an outsider; they become acutely aware of who accepts and rejects them (Hutchison, 2019).
- **Distrust of outsiders:** Adolescents are more likely to automatically trust people in their group and distrust those on the outside (Hutchison, 2019; Tschannen-Moran & Hoy, 2000). If students don't think we share their values or have anything in common with them, they can perceive us as being part of the "outside" group. This predisposes them to interpret our actions as untrustworthy. Whereas if we can find and communicate shared values with students, they will be more likely to identify with and trust us.

Hormonal changes and brain development lead students to see others in the world as either for them, as part of their "in" group, or against them as an outsider; they become acutely aware of who accepts and rejects them (Hutchison, 2019).

- **Underdeveloped ability to consider long-term consequences:** A source of great misunderstanding and frustration between adults and adolescents is the fact that adolescents' brains are still developing, and they don't always anticipate the long-term consequences of their actions. This sometimes leads to questionable choices and behaviors. Remember the pencil example from chapter 1 (page 17)? When a student forgets to bring a pencil, often it is because they just aren't thinking ahead to the fact that they need one, but a teacher may interpret the student's gesture to mean they don't value learning. As frustrating as it is that students don't think about the consequences of their choices, each time they make an error in judgment, it presents an opportunity for us to guide their growth and learning as we help them develop new neural connections through reflection and awareness.
- **Need for connection with peers:** Adolescents also begin to have a developmental need for peer connection and autonomy (Allen et al., 2013), making it important for teachers to incorporate those into class. If we don't give students time to connect with their peers, they will disrupt class to meet that need. Starting around eighth grade and lasting throughout high school, adolescents are in a phase of development where they seek to understand the world and how they fit into it (Hutchison, 2019). They have a developmental need to understand how their learning connects to real life and are more likely to disengage when they don't see how the content is relevant. Additionally, part of the process of figuring out who they are and how they fit into the world is to question adults and no longer believe that they know all the answers (Hutchison, 2019). Adolescents also have a developmental need to feel respected by adults (Hutchison, 2019; Yeager et al., 2018). Many of us were raised to believe that young people should always respect adults, even if respect is not reciprocated. The tension between that belief and the adolescent need to feel respected can lead to conflicts with our students. Adolescents are also wired to seek novelty (Siegel, 2013). When I think back to the teachers that engaged me the most, they made things interesting and unexpected.

Biologically, these changes in development are what eventually lead adolescents to leave home and launch into their adult lives (Siegel, 2013). Without these changes, they might be content to stay at home forever. However, these factors do make it more challenging to build relationships with and engage secondary students than elementary students.

Take a moment to read and answer the following self-reflection questions.

WALKING IN OUR STUDENTS' SHOES

Remembering

MIDDLE SCHOOL AND HIGH SCHOOL

Remember back to your years in middle school and high school.

- What mattered most to you?

- What did you think of your teachers?

- What do you think your teachers thought about you? Was their impression accurate?

- Did you feel like the adults in your life understood you?

- Was there an adult in your life that respected you? How was that relationship different from the ones you had with other adults in your life?

- Did you respect all of your teachers?

- Did you feel respected by your teachers? How did that impact your level of engagement in their classes?

Visit ***go.SolutionTree.com/teacherefficacy*** *for a free reproducible version of this reflection.*

Anticipating student needs and barriers is an essential part of creating environments where students feel safe to try.

In addition to that, we need to develop carefully scaffolded lessons that meet students at their level of ability and challenge them to grow and develop skills without being so challenging that they give up. When students come into our classes two or three years behind, we can't jump into grade-level content without filling in the gaps. If a student doesn't know how to multiply, they won't be able to learn algebra. If a student is reading at a fourth-grade level, it will probably be difficult for them to read *The Odyssey*. In schools, there is a big focus on ensuring that students have access to grade-level content; however, if they don't have the foundational knowledge or language skills to understand it, then simply providing the content isn't really giving them access to it. We have to fill in the gaps first. Jessica is a master at scaffolding and regularly sees two years of growth in her classes. She understands that when students can't read well, the best way to improve that is to require students to read every day. She finds books that are interesting to adolescents but written in a lower Lexile so they will be able to read and understand it. She truly meets students where they are and not where they "should" be and then guides them to the next level. I've seen her transform what students believe they are capable of.

Help Students Reflect, Grow, and Believe in Themselves

Positive deviant teachers believe that students would if they could (Knighton, 2022). When students don't or won't engage, they believe it is due to some sort of (internal or external) barrier that is getting in the way of engagement. They then work to understand and mitigate those barriers.

Belief

Some of the biggest internal barriers disengaged students face are the beliefs that they won't succeed, there is no hope for their future, or their life is already scripted and nothing they do will change that. For these students, we need to believe they can succeed until they begin to believe it themselves.

JESSICA'S VIGNETTE

I based my seventh-grade language arts class around *The Book Whisperer* model, by Donalyn Miller (2009), which means my students always walk into class and start silent reading for twenty minutes each day.

At the beginning of the year when my students do this, I watch each of them to determine who is fake reading. One such student was Hope (not her real name). She had an extremely rough beginning to life—a story that would break your heart and make you cry. Yet, on the outside, Hope was the sweetest and happiest girl. She and her younger brother were now with a supportive family, so things were looking up for her.

Hope scored a kindergarten reading level for the beginning-of-year reading assessment as a seventh grader, yet she was "reading" a novel a week in class. When she was ready for her next book, I suggested *The Shack*, which I have also read. When she was done with it and came to get my signature in her reader's notebook, we had the following conversation.

Me: What did you think of the book?

Hope: It was really good.

Me: What part did you like the best?

Hope: All of it. I can't choose just one.

Me: What did you think when God let the main character drown?

Hope: I thought it was sad and didn't understand why He would do that.

Me: (*Pause*) Hope, God didn't let the main character drown.

Hope: (*Silence, her eyes well with tears.*)

Me: You're not in trouble. I'm here to help you. Have you really read any of the novels this year?

Hope: (*Crying*) No, I've never read an entire book.

Me: (*I hug her.*) Doesn't it feel good that you don't have to pretend anymore? Do you feel a sense of relief that it's out in the open now and we can talk about it?

Hope: (*With tears of relief*) Yes.

Me: This is the year your life changes for the better and school gets easier for you. I know exactly what you need to do to get better at reading. And if you do *everything* I tell you to do, I guarantee you'll grow so much in reading, to the point that all your other classes get easier, simply because you can read and understand the material better. Does that sound like something you really want?

Hope: (*Tears subsiding*) Yes.

Me: Here's the plan. First, I'm going to give you easier novels to read, and you shouldn't feel ashamed of that because I read them, too, and I'm four times your age. No book is for babies. Plus, you know that, in this class, there is no teasing about such things. If someone does tease you, you tell me, and I'll take care of it while keeping your name out of it. Second, reading is not a race, so your main goal is to enjoy the story. My best friend is the slowest reader I know, but wow, does she understand what she reads. Third, not only will you read twenty minutes in class, Monday through Thursday and all period on Fridays, but you also need to read twenty minutes each night at home from Sunday night to Thursday night. You'll take Friday and Saturday nights off, if you'd like. If you choose to read all seven nights every week, you'll get even better. But either plan you choose will be beneficial. And fourth, anytime you don't know a word, either keep reading and look for context clues, or come up to me and I'll tell you what it means. There is no shame here today. What you've just shown me is courage, bravery, and vulnerability. I am *so* proud of you, Hope. And this year is going to be the best year of your school career. I promise! Are you willing to commit to these four things?

Hope: Yes.

Me: How are you feeling right now?

Hope: I feel relieved, and I feel better.

Me: Awesome! Girl, I got you. Thank you for trusting me with your truth. No one else needs to know except you and me. Now, let's go find you a book.

My conversation with Hope helped her feel safe enough to try something she felt very insecure about. I gave her permission to just focus on growth and improvement and not feel pressure to be at the same level as the other students. Hope did do everything I told her to do that year. I was so impressed by her focus and dedication. When every student took the end-of-year reading assessment, Hope went from a kindergarten level to a fifth-grade level, in *one* school year! We typically want to see one year's growth in one school year, yet Hope shattered all expectations! We were jumping up and down, hugging, smiling, and crying as we celebrated together in the library after I shared the data with her. It was exhilarating!

Hope continued reading over the summer like I told her to do. The following fall, as an eighth grader, Hope continued to read voraciously and would frequently visit me for book recommendations for what to read next. By the end of her eighth-grade year, Hope scored an eighth-grade reading level. She closed her *eight*-year reading gap in two school years because she felt supported, trusted the process, and was determined to put in the work. I have used her as an example every year since.

I ran into Hope's younger brother at the library six years later. He was doing well and ready to graduate from high school and he told me Hope was in her second year at one of our state universities. My heart was soaring. This is the "bonus check" we teachers receive, and it's better than money! A moment like this usually comes many years after we have had our students, but it's delayed gratification like no other!

When a student's experiences in school chronically reinforce their belief that they're "the kid who has never been successful and has always been in trouble," they come into our classes expecting three things: (1) that we will judge them, (2) that they will not be successful, and (3) that they will have conflicts with us. Students who seem disengaged or refuse to work often exhibit these behaviors because they anticipate how we will feel about them or they want to avoid failing or looking "stupid" in front of their peers. We need to create environments where students feel safe to try and fail academically, socially, and behaviorally.

Growth

In addition to helping students believe in themselves, as Jessica did with Hope in the vignette, the positive deviant teachers I spoke to also focused on growth over achievement. Research shows that when individuals focus only on achievement, they can more easily become discouraged, and their effort decreases when they're faced with more difficult challenges, whereas when they focus on growth, their effort increases with greater challenge (Claro, Paunesku, & Dweck, 2016; Dweck & Leggett, 1988). Additionally, when we focus on growth, students feel safer to try, fail, and learn than when we focus only on achievement.

Our students need a safe space to be imperfect (academically, socially, and behaviorally) and where they can grow. The mistakes we've made in our lives are what helped us grow and become the people we are today. Because adolescents' brains are still developing, they sometimes interact socially or behave in certain ways that aren't helpful to themselves or others. They may say the wrong thing or treat someone poorly or disrupt our classes when they are overwhelmed, sad, lonely, craving connection, or doubting themselves. They are still learning empathy and communication and how to navigate and express emotions, but we expect that they should have adult-level skills in those areas when they just don't yet. When a student says or does something that hurts someone else, disrupts our classrooms, or feels disrespectful to us, it is the perfect time to have a conversation with them—to ask them why they did or said what they did and to explain how their actions impacted others. These conversations shouldn't come from a place of judgment or accusation; they should come from a place of truly seeking to understand where students are coming from and genuinely wanting to help them understand how what they did or said affects others. We can teach them empathy in these moments.

We also put a lot of pressure on ourselves to be perfect and not make mistakes, but when we do make a mistake and admit it to our students, it draws us closer together. It also helps us model how to own our mistakes, grow, and repair any damage we caused. I (Rebecca) will share an example from my experience. In the middle school elective class I used to teach, two students were constantly disrupting the class and not listening to me. One day, I lost my temper and raised my voice at one of them. The next day, I saw her in the hall, and I said, "I want to apologize for how I spoke to you yesterday." She said, "It's OK." I replied, "No it isn't. I am not proud of my behavior." She said, "I'm not proud of my behavior either." She wasn't used to adults apologizing to her and it brought us closer together. When I modeled owning my behavior and repairing the damage I caused her, she reciprocated. That afternoon when class started, she insisted that I wait in the hall until she got everyone quiet for me. I stood in the hall for several minutes. When she came out to get me, she exclaimed, "That was hard!" I said, "Right?!" She gained some empathy for how difficult it is to motivate a group of rowdy students to pay attention. After this experience, she was much better about not disrupting my class, and we brainstormed some ways she might be able to focus better moving forward.

Reflection

Accepting that we may not always say and do the right thing and that our students aren't always going to make the right decision or say the right thing doesn't mean that we stop holding ourselves and our students to certain standards. It means we treat those moments when we or our students make mistakes as learning opportunities. We reflect, we help our students reflect, and we find the lesson or growth opportunity in the experience. Reflecting to grow is a life skill that leads to more successful and fulfilled adult lives, but it isn't a skill that comes naturally to everyone. It is a gift we can give ourselves and our students. At the end of this book, we provide some examples of reflective questions we might ask ourselves and some sentence starters for reflective questions you might ask your students (see appendix A, page 233).

The positive deviant teachers I spoke with were skilled at reflecting and growing themselves and guiding students to reflect (Knighton, 2022). One teacher said he used to hate reflecting when he was younger, but now he thinks it is incredibly valuable for his own life; as a result, he guides his students to reflect on themselves often (Knighton, 2022). Guiding students to reflect can happen through the lessons we design, class discussions we lead, and activities we engage our students in. We might ask students to reflect on how the experiences of characters in the passage we just read relate to their own lives. We might ask students to imagine how someone living during the Civil War might have been feeling if they had relatives in the North, but they lived in the South. Then we could ask them if they've ever had a similar feeling or experience and what that was like. We don't necessarily ask every student to share these reflections with the whole class, but we give them space and time to consider the questions we pose. Students who want to share may do so. We want to help our students develop a deeper understanding of themselves and others as well as the content we teach.

Guiding reflection can also be an important part of one-on-one conversations with students. Think about talking to a student who has been disrupting your class. Asking them questions about why they might be behaving that way and explaining how their behavior is impacting your well-being and ability to teach the other students can be much more effective and powerful at shifting their behavior than simply reprimanding them. This only works if you go into the conversation truly open to understanding where the student is coming from and seeking to help them understand how their behavior is impacting others. It's important to use a calm and supportive tone rather than an angry or punitive one.

When we guide students to reflect and understand themselves better, when we are open to learning about our students, and when we explain where we are coming from as fellow humans, it builds tremendous trust, connection, and safety (Knighton, 2022). Students feel seen and understood, and they also see and understand us better. It creates an environment that encourages growth, which adds a layer of safety for students who don't believe they can be successful. However, guiding our students to reflect and grow may seem intimidating if we aren't sure what to say, and we worry that students won't receive it well. It's tempting to feel that, as adults, we should be the expert and tell students the right way, rather than asking them questions that lead them to think through their choices or explain their thinking to us. To an adolescent student, telling feels condescending and disrespectful; it's less effective than asking them questions that help them reflect and grow.

I worked with an assistant principal who combined the adolescent need for novelty with guiding self-reflection. When students showed up in his office, he asked why they were there. They usually said something like, "I don't know," or "The teacher got me in trouble." Then he drew them a map on his window with a marker showing how their behavior led to one thing, which led to another, which led them to him. He did this in a teaching tone—not a punitive tone. He helped them learn to self-reflect, to see the connections between their choices and behavior and what happened to them. It was much more empowering and effective at encouraging growth and changing behavior than simply punishing them would have been.

Creating learning environments that focus on growth (academically, socially, emotionally, and behaviorally) over achievement actually lead to greater achievement (Dweck & Leggett, 1988). However, this can be challenging. Focusing on growth requires the difficult work of reflecting on ourselves, our interactions, and our mistakes. It requires that we believe our students can grow, academically and as people. It requires that we set aside our judgments and assumptions and seek to see and understand our students and then think outside the box about how to help them overcome the barriers they face in our classes. It requires that we challenge the beliefs we were raised to adopt about school, teacher-student relationships, and human imperfection.

Looking Inward: Flipping the Script

In this section, you will have the opportunity to engage in two activities, shown in figures 2.1 (page 69) and 2.2 (page 71). These activities are designed to help you understand yourself better and develop some of the skills discussed in this chapter.

Think about who you were as an adolescent (in middle and high school). Try to put yourself back in that time in your life and answer these questions. Try to answer all of these questions as fast as you can for the next five minutes. Don't filter or analyze your responses, just write them down.

- What do you remember from middle school?
- What do you remember from high school?
- What did you think about? What did you feel?

- What were your fears and hopes?

- What motivated you?

- What did you care about (music, world events, friends, crushes, family, sports, and so on)?

- Who were your friends? (For example, What were they like? What was your relationship with them like? What did you do together? Did your relationship with them influence what school was like for you?)

- How did you show up in school? Why?

Figure 2.1: Remembering who you were as an adolescent.

continued →

- What did you think about your teachers?

- What did your teachers think about you? Were their impressions accurate?

- What part of your school day was the most important to you?

- Did you have a teacher who inspired you? What about them inspired you?

- Did you have a teacher you did not get along with? What was it about you and that teacher that caused that dynamic for you?

Visit ***go.SolutionTree.com/teacherefficacy*** *for a free reproducible version of this figure.*

To complete this activity, choose from one of the following options and use the prompts for reflection.

Option 1: Think back to a time when you were required to learn something new that you did not feel competent doing or that you did not think you would be capable of doing. Try to think of something that was very difficult, something that made you feel totally out of your element. Some examples might be your first job, being a first-time parent, being a first-year teacher, and so on.

Option 2: Remember a time you were required to learn something new and you failed at it. (This could have been a group activity or an individual new skill you were learning.)

- Describe what it was you had to learn and why you had to learn it.

- What did you think (about yourself, about the activity, about the person requiring you to do it)?

- How did you feel (about yourself, about the activity, about the person requiring you to do it)?

Figure 2.2: Reflecting on the value of growth.

continued →

- Visualize yourself back at that time. What did your body feel like during this experience?

- If you shut down, what did that look like and feel like?

- How did someone in a position of authority over you respond during the experience? Did they reprimand you, support and guide you through it, or respond in some other way?

- How did the manner in which others responded to you influence how you felt about yourself and your willingness to engage in that activity again?

Visit ***go.SolutionTree.com/teacherefficacy*** *for a free reproducible version of this reflection.*

Learning From the Five Teacher Types

This section presents two common scenarios. For each scenario, the five positive deviant teachers you met in the introduction describe how they navigate these scenarios in their practice. The first is how they create safety in their classrooms, and the second is how they encourage their students to reflect and grow. As you read through these examples, highlight, underline, or circle the parts of each example you relate to.

Scenario: You want to create safety in your classroom

The following sections describe how each teacher type approaches this scenario in their classroom.

Teacher Type: Caring Connector

For me, this starts even before the students enter my classroom. My colleagues and I always have our coffee in the hallway outside our classrooms each morning and chat and joke about what is going on in the news. I believe that when students see us enjoying each other's company, and engaging with social studies in our everyday lives, they feel more at ease and ready to engage themselves. As the semester progresses, we even start to see our students joining in on these "teacher conversations." I also make sure to greet each student by name as they enter the classroom. I believe there is power in using names; you are showing the student that not only are you happy to see them but also that they are a unique individual and that they are important.

During lessons, I always ensure that no student is put on the spot. If they are uncomfortable joining in a full class discussion, I never force them to speak. Instead, I engage them in small-group or individual discussions to check their understanding. I will always give students the opportunity to present in front of the group or just to me in a one-on-one setting. This allows them to build confidence in a much lower-stakes environment.

Flexibility plays a huge role in feeling safe in the classroom. If students are late turning in work or perform poorly on a task, I will have a conversation with them and hold them accountable, but I always create a plan to help them succeed. Extending a due date, offering an alternative assessment, or allowing multiple attempts at a task are all ways to help students feel safer taking risks in the classroom and improve overall engagement in learning.

Teacher Type: Gentle Giant

Creating a safe space in my classroom is a priority for me, and I strive to achieve this in several ways. First, I aim to cultivate a welcoming presence. From the moment students step into the classroom, I greet them warmly, make eye contact, and offer a genuine smile or a corny joke. I want them to feel that this is a place where they belong and are valued.

Engaging with equality and interest is also crucial. I make it a point to give each student my full attention, listening actively and showing genuine interest in their thoughts and opinions. I ensure that everyone who wants to contribute gets the opportunity, and I make a conscious effort to include diverse perspectives in our discussions.

Showing compassion and empathy is another cornerstone of creating a safe space. I try to understand the unique challenges and experiences each student brings. When a student is struggling, I approach them with kindness, offering support and understanding rather than judgment. I let them know that their well-being matters to me. Additionally, I believe in the importance of displaying my own vulnerabilities. By sharing my own challenges and mistakes, I demonstrate that it's OK to be imperfect and that we can all learn and grow from our experiences. This openness helps build trust and encourages students to be more open and honest with me and with each other.

Ultimately, creating a safe space is about building a community where everyone feels respected, valued, and heard. It requires consistent effort and a genuine commitment to fostering an inclusive and supportive environment.

Teacher Type: Nurturing Narrator

Students struggle to learn in environments where they don't feel safe, so creating a community of trust is a priority for any educator. Students who have experienced trauma are less likely to trust adults from the get-go, so breaking down the natural barriers that they have is an integral part of your tool kit. The onus is on us, not the student, which is the first thing to remember when trying to establish a positive and authentic relationship.

First, I never ask students to do anything I am unwilling to do myself. I make myself the most vulnerable in the room, especially at the beginning of the year. I make relationships by telling stories, and sometimes I exaggerate or modify details for the story to suit what I need it to accomplish. I teach middle school (grade 8), which just happened to be my least favorite school year during my adolescence. I found no safety or connection when I was young and felt exposed in an already powerless time of my life. I start each year with tales from my personal vault, stories that are raw but cement to students that I know it's not easy to sit where they sit. I tell stories not from my desk and not with slides; I walk around and make contact with students while I speak. I invite students to take one of the dozens of pillows from around my classroom and just listen. This allows them to shut off for a time, and it allows me to become their narrator.

Second, every day I wait for students at my door. I greet them, I remember details about them, and I purposely ask them about their important things. I have the lights off in my classroom as students come in; we call it a cavern, and I fill the space with eleven lamps that only turn off when the sun rises high enough that they're no longer needed.

Third, I do not create a seating plan that is always conducive to behavioral management. I believe students work best when they're comfortable. I create seating plans that sometimes do cause me to be more active but still establish my classroom as a place that students want to be—because they can sit with someone who makes them feel safe.

Fourth, when students journal to me, I intentionally keep their writing on my desk and even go as far as to walk around with their little journals in my arms for the rest of the day. I want students to know that I care about their stories, and I appreciate them.

We often ask children to do things that we, as adults, are not capable of doing. We ask students to regulate their emotions, engage in undesirable activities, interact with unsafe or unknown peers to teach them perseverance, and respect authority. We say this teaches them kindness, tenacity, compassion, and so on; it might, in some cases. These are all important attributes of character, and students should develop them over time. However, adults are not expected to have this same plethora of duties at every moment, and it is important that we, as educators, are mindful of the vast range of skills we're putting on small people. Letting students take one or more of these things off their plates in any way you can for your classroom will help establish trusting and authentic relationships with them.

Teacher Type: Perceptive Pragmatist

I think the biggest way to create safety in the classroom is through connection. I do my best to build rapport with every student in the room. Conflict will arise between students, but when they feel I have their backs, they feel comfortable coming to talk to me; they also know that any intervening I do comes from a place of care and not that I am "picking on" them. I also think building connection within the class prevents a lot of major conflicts to begin with as it's not the vibe of my classroom, and students generally don't want to do anything that would disappoint if that relationship were established.

I also make sure to firmly vocalize when something is happening that is inhibiting a safe feeling for others. For example, I have a couple words that I refer to as my "forbidden words." Luckily, these aren't words that typically come up, but if I hear any of them while students are conversing, I stop and address the issue with the class. I don't single out the student. I say to the whole class, "I just heard a word that we don't use in this class," and we then have a discussion about it if necessary. I don't come from a place of scolding—it's just a conversation about why that word is particularly unwelcome. The reason I bring it up with the class is that there are other students who would have inevitably heard it be said, and I want them to also be in the conversation about why it's not OK. This hopefully prevents others from using the words and lets students feel they have "permission" to call out behavior that makes others feel unsafe. They can use me as an excuse if they would otherwise be uncomfortable doing it on their own.

Relationship building doesn't just create safety for the students; it is also for me. My classroom is my home away from home, and I don't ever want to feel like I'm walking on eggshells or can't be myself. The more comfortable students are, it generally translates to me also being comfortable. Although it's not necessary, it is a bonus when students have your back as much as you have theirs. Very early in my career, a student was having a rough day and had an explosion and stormed out of the room. It wasn't about me, or my educational assistant—he was having a bad day, and we were on the receiving end of it. The rest of the class clearly felt bad about the incident and were extra polite, quiet, and gentle with us for the rest of the afternoon, almost as a way to make up for his behavior. The student and I also talked and repaired any damage after he had calmed down. Without an established relationship, the rest of the class could have easily devolved into chaos, and there would have been no repair with the student.

Teacher Type: Warm Demander

My first-two-weeks-of-school boot camp includes activities that require vulnerability from me and my students. We (because I participate too) role play, lip sync, dance, do demonstrations, discuss what respect and trust look and sound like, and go through the Four Agreements. I tell stories about my upbringing with my parents fostering 189 kids, explain in detail how I have their backs in all areas of their lives (being their Mama Bear), clearly detail all behavior and work expectations in our room, and I am transparent about the consequences of their decision making. All these things bring into focus the idea that this classroom is where they are guarded; it's a safe place to fall, whether they're having a good or bad day.

There are many other ways I weave the feeling of safety into my classroom with lessons that enforce all the things we did in the first two weeks of school. It's not a one-and-done lesson. If it is, then I wasted my time because it won't stick. Teachers must continually pull past teachings into the current lessons; otherwise students don't see those actions and character traits as important.

Use the following prompts to reflect on what you've read from these five positive deviant teachers.

Creating

SAFETY IN THE CLASSROOM

WHAT WOULD YOU DO?

How do you currently create safety for your students in your classroom?

Given what you've learned in this chapter, what might you add or change in your current classroom to create a greater sense of safety for students?

Visit ***go.SolutionTree.com/teacherefficacy*** *for a free reproducible version of this reflection.*

Scenario: You want to encourage your students to reflect and grow

The following sections describe how each teacher type approaches this scenario in their classroom.

Teacher Type: Caring Connector

Giving students opportunities to improve their work or behavior is the cornerstone to growth in the classroom. This is intricately linked to meaningful formative feedback.

Giving written or verbal feedback on the students' work will show them that I care about their success and means much more to them than a number at the top of the page.

However, if I give the feedback but do not provide opportunities to improve the outcome, they won't see any value in reflecting and growing. For this reason, I always give students the opportunity to resubmit any of their projects, tests, or essays. I don't want to put in hours of work on feedback only to have students ignore it, so I often dedicate class time specifically to having them read the feedback and implement changes. I saw a huge improvement in the number of students taking the time to improve their work when they don't always have to do it outside of school hours. I always circulate the room during this time to ensure that students understand the feedback I've provided and answer any questions they have about improving their work.

For formal essays, I always have a formative and summative deadline. Students submit a rough draft for the formative deadline, and I provide written feedback, but no grade. This is important, because if I grade the rough drafts, many students will see it and think good enough! *and proceed to submit the same draft for summative assessment. With no grade, they only see suggestions to improve and take the time to reflect on their work and make changes. I have seen a significant increase in improved writing skills and overall student confidence because of this practice.*

With regard to student behavior, such as absences or missing work, I always have a conversation with the student. I approach this from an empathetic perspective, never starting with accusations or frustration but instead by asking them how they are doing. I want them to know that I'm more concerned about them than the coursework itself. Often there is something going on in their life outside of school that is leading to the behavior, so I can be flexible and extend due dates or offer extra help. Students are usually very grateful for this and take the opportunity to demonstrate growth. Sometimes there isn't anything going on, and it is just not a priority for the student to be at school or complete their work. Having these conversations also allows them to reflect on their behavior. Often, they will apologize and own up to the fact that they haven't been giving their best effort. Then we make a plan for how they can be more successful going forward.

Ultimately, empathy is the guiding factor behind all these practices. If the students know that I care about them, what is going on in their lives, and their academic success, they will be more willing to engage and improve.

Teacher Type: Gentle Giant

When it really comes down to it, I try to lead by example. I'm constantly looking for ways to encourage students to think about learning. Many times, we hear the question, Why do we need to learn this? This is my favorite question to answer. That simple little crack in a student's shield is them letting their guard down for you to explain as an educator why it's worth digging in. Sometimes we don't actually need *to learn the concept, but it's imperative to experience the frustration of failing, joy of finding success, or simple pleasure of completing a task. There is no secret to getting students to reflect on learning and wanting to grow. To me, it's giving them the freedom to take charge and being there to celebrate with them or steer them straight when they've lost control. Asking students what their reason is rather than telling them what mine is seems to be a pretty good way to show them that learning anything can be valuable.*

I talk freely about how accessible knowledge is and how freely we can learn new skills. I tell students how I've tried to learn new things and how finding enjoyment in learning new skills can compound. With learning comes struggle, and this is where reflection comes in. I think this is a pretty natural process. When things work out or when they don't, we are programmed to think about why; I try to share this with students. When we know what works well, we do it again. If things are awful, we know to change the way we do things. I try to make reflection as simple and natural as possible, allowing for communication between peers and groups, introducing and providing prompts for journals, and finally using discussions and debates in class.

Teacher Type: Nurturing Narrator

Having students reflect on their own learning can be challenging as they often want to "check a box" and be done with the assignment or conversation. It takes a really solid relationship with more behaviorally diverse students to push them to self-reflect. The first thing I always do is build in purposeful time. You can't rush a relationship, and your first impression matters to them. Students who struggle in the classroom most often have an antecedent, and figuring out what that is becomes a major factor in being able to ask them to reflect and grow. There are students sitting in your classroom who haven't eaten, haven't slept, and haven't felt love. School is their only safe place, and pushing them to do work when they are in this mindset is not conducive to a healthy relationship. Students who come in and put their heads down, their hoods up, or engage in other evasive tactics get my gentlest approach. I never address them in front of the entire class but instead wait for independent work time to begin. I always go to them and ask them to sit at the blue table, where I often have snacks and my laptop at the ready. I guide all these students in the early days of assignments, often typing for them or even just talking them through ideas. Finishing any assignment is a win for them in a day, so I always celebrate whatever they've accomplished at the end of a class period. Some days I reflect on their eighteen hours at home and have to remind myself that this may be the hardest part of their day, so I am mindful not to rush them to complete work at the beginning.

I often have over thirty students in my class with no educational assistant, so there are very few moments where I sit behind my computer. I am always working with students, which truthfully can be taxing at times. The blue table in my classroom is the most popular place to be by the second week of school. It's the closest to my desk, and the toughest students are often there before even starting the period at their desks. I sometimes have to remind them that it is like the couch on Friends*: It doesn't have a permanent reservation for them, and other kids need my help too. They laugh, take a granola bar, and slowly start to work more independently day by day. Students grow at their own pace, I celebrate small moments, and those turn into big moments without us even noticing most times.*

One thing I do that I want to mention to other educators is that our highfliers can struggle with substitute teachers. One strategy I use to help these students grow is to sit down with them one on one, before a substitute teacher comes in for the first time, and we write their "student profile." These are notes for the substitute to ensure my more complex students will have a good day even with a new person. Here is one example.

> 8C (class and period): Johnny L.—Johnny is very charming, but he often has a hard time regulating his words and his actions—he will try to bait you into a power struggle. He will work, he just needs positive reinforcement—never call him out publicly; he will respond in a really colorful and aggressive way. He is very trustworthy, and if he leaves, do not chase him. Call our Student Assistance Information Center (SAIC) teacher at 33211 and she will follow up after a certain amount of time should he not return. He will come back when he is ready most times. Johnny will not give you his phone. If he is on it, just gently remind him to put it away, and he will. If he does not, please ask him to go to SAIC until he is regulated. During individual work times, please allow him to sit next to Caleb S. They have agreed to help one another be successful while I am away. Remind Johnny of the conversation we had before I left should he become defiant. If he cannot self-regulate, please call one of his trusted adults listed above.

This is an example of a student profile that a student wrote with me last year. In previous years, he often ended up suspended whenever he was faced with a new authority in the classroom. However, last year, because he wrote his profile and we shared it with his parents as a tool for his success, he had a real responsibility to be accountable to his own words. He did access different learning spaces when I was away, but he was not suspended on any of the days I had to be out of the classroom.

Students need trust, patience, flexibility, and forgiveness. We grow together and we reflect together as we start to build relationships in my classroom.

Teacher Type: Perceptive Pragmatist

The first step to having students reflect and grow is making sure they feel safe in the classroom. If they are nervous about others' comments when they share a response or feel like they can't make a mistake, there won't be much growth. Also, I now try to explicitly make comments like, Mistakes are good, as long as you learn from them! or I could never be disappointed if you tried the best you could at the time! For a long time, I assumed that my being warm and friendly was enough for students to know that their academic standing in my class did not correlate with my feelings toward them as people. However, there were a few instances where I ran into former students, and they almost seemed embarrassed or apologetic about their academic performance in my class (even years later). Since then, I have made it a point to talk about what growth and success look like, and it has nothing to do with a mark on a test.

After tests, I give the students a pep talk regarding what they should be thinking about when they see the results. Students are so quick to look at a mark and either be happy or disappointed by the number alone. Instead, I ask them to think back to test day and ask themselves, "Did I give it my all? Is it the best I could do based on that day and everything else I had going on?" If so, there's nothing to be upset about. If not, what could you change? Should you come in for more one-on-one help or spend more time practicing earlier in the chapter? In that case, it's something to learn from and try to work on for next time. I also have a rule in my class that I shouldn't ever hear students asking each other, "What did you get?!" as soon as they get a mark back. Comparing marks does nothing but create unnecessary competition and an unhealthy focus on the mark alone. Instead, students who really want to discuss the test with each other change their focus to ask about approaches to specific questions so they can see how others think and learn from each other.

Teacher Type: Warm Demander

I absolutely love this part of my job. To get students to ponder ideas that focus on the bigger picture of life is truly the greatest lesson we can lead students to adopt in their own lives. I always want everything to come back to how things affect others and themselves. I use videos as my go-to source because most students are visual learners, they need the video to be fairly short, and I love the inspirational music that is usually used for amazing videos that teach a big life lesson in minutes.

My favorite go-to video is the one where Admiral William H. McRaven addresses the University of Texas at Austin Class of 2014. He starts by saying, "If you want to be successful, make your bed" (Nate Wylie Studios, 2014). It shows several fabulous real-life video clips of Navy SEAL trainings with incredible music in the background while the Admiral is giving his speech. Before playing it, I ask my students to draw or write what they think hope is, since that's the main lesson in the video. After the video, I put a slide up with the following questions for table discussions, instructing each tablemate to share their answers.

1. *What part of his speech stuck with you?*
2. *What part made you feel good?*
3. *What do you think about the message of* hope*?*
4. *What life lesson did you learn from his speech*?

I follow up that verbal activity with the following solo written activity, called the Thirteen Word Sentence.

1. *Grab a piece of notebook paper. Now that you've heard your tablemates' thoughts about this speech, I want you to sit quietly to be with your own thoughts.*
2. *Then, in a thirteen-word sentence (thirteen words exactly), write how you will apply this message of hope to your own life.*

I always have a "Do Now" reflection or journal time at the beginning of class each week with questions that get students to think about their own life and how they can apply what they've learned so they purposefully see their own thoughts and growth in themselves. After they complete theirs, I always verbally give my own personal answers to the whole class, modeling vulnerability and my human side. Plus, students love this; it is *relevant to them because they want to understand life. I explain that by journaling and having reflection time, they are becoming less confused about the world and being a human, which lessens their fears of being an adult—a very real fear that secondary students have verbalized each year. This is also a good practice that leads to more feelings of safety in the classroom, so this activity kills two birds with one stone. As a bonus, I learn even more about them and they learn about me, which deepens our relationship.*

By the way, these reflections and journal times aren't always about heavy topics. Sometimes it's about what students did over the weekend and why they did or didn't enjoy it or reflecting on what they would do differently the next time they make a cake in Family and Consumer Sciences class. I mix up the prompts according to what I know is going on in our school or our community. For example, a Texas-based mega convenience store called Buc-ee's opened over the weekend just to the east of our town, and it was a whole hullabaloo! So, their Monday journal time was spent drawing or writing about visiting it over the weekend or reporting what they'd heard about the store. Mix things up and have a great time choosing prompts that mean something to your students.

Given what you've learned, respond to the following reflection questions.

WHAT WOULD YOU DO?

Encouraging STUDENT REFLECTION IN THE CLASSROOM

Do you encourage the students in your class to reflect on themselves? If not, how might you start?

How comfortable are you with guiding students to reflect on themselves when it comes to schoolwork? What about with topics outside of school?

Is there anything from this chapter you would like to apply to help you guide student reflection?

Visit **go.SolutionTree.com/teacherefficacy** *for a free reproducible version of this reflection.*

Wrapping Up

Creating environments and relationships with students that help them feel safe to try are essential for increasing student engagement and are foundational if we want to help students change their educational trajectories. This is especially true for students who have experienced AELEs. Understanding adolescent development and how students' success in school can be affected by AELEs help us understand and accept our students' behavior, their reactions to us, and their choices. When we can help our students begin to believe in themselves, reflect both academically and personally, and grow in ways they did not know they could, it changes their academic identity, engagement in our classes, and their vision and hope for the future.

Chapter 2 Book Study Questions

As a staff, explore the concepts presented in this chapter and reflect on how they are evidenced in or might impact your school culture. As you read each of the following questions, think about how you would respond based on your individual role. If you are an administrator, think about these questions as you reflect on how you support your staff. If you are a teacher or support staff member, think about these questions as you reflect on how you support students.

1. What is one thing you learned about adolescent development that you would like to incorporate into how you lead the students in your classroom?

2. What is one takeaway about the impact of social determinants of health on students that you want to remember when establishing your school culture and climate?

3. Does your school create safety for students to feel safe to try, fail, and grow? Does it provide safety for staff to try, fail, and grow?

4. Do you feel like there is a cultural divide between you and your students or between adults and students in general in the school? How might you bridge that gap to improve relationships and increase a sense of safety?

CHAPTER 3

Developing Authenticity

Think back to a leader you most admire—someone you wanted to follow. This person likely had some degree of authenticity. When someone is authentic, their words and actions are congruent, which makes us feel like we can trust them. When someone puts on a front, people can sense it, and it leads to decreased trust. This is especially true for adolescents with a history of adversity (Knighton, 2022). This chapter highlights the importance of authenticity as we seek to connect with and engage our students.

In this chapter, we explore what research and practice show about how authenticity encourages connection and engagement and improves relationships with students. We also discuss how teachers can find their path to authenticity. Then we practice flipping the script through self-reflection activities. We end the chapter by hearing how the five teacher types respond to two common scenarios related to teaching from a place of authenticity.

Looking Outward: Themes in Research and Practice

We are leaders in our classrooms, and we need our students to trust us if we want them to engage in our content. Discovering and developing connection is an important aspect of building trust with students, but it takes more than that. Authenticity is essential for teachers as leaders in their classrooms.

Being Authentic Encourages Connection and Engagement

The fields of business and management have done extensive research about leadership and the importance of trust. For example, best-selling authors Frances X. Frei and Anne Morriss (2020) wrote an article for the Harvard Business Review in which they describe the "Trust Triangle," the three qualities that motivate people to follow a leader: (1) authenticity (seeing the leader's true self), (2) empathy (feeling cared about), and (3) logic (knowing the leader's reasoning makes sense). These three qualities are also important to consider as we teach and lead our students. The two that surfaced in my study of positive deviant teachers were authenticity and empathy. In this section, we'll examine the first of these qualities: authenticity.

To effectively connect with and engage chronically disengaged students, we must be authentic (Knighton, 2022). *Authenticity* is being real and being true to one's own spirit, values, and character (Authentic, n.d.). Researcher and storyteller Brené Brown (2010) explains authenticity as letting go of who we think we are supposed to be and embracing who we really are. Being authentic means being vulnerable, real, and honest with ourselves. It means taking off the masks we wear. It takes courage and continual self-reflection, but being authentic helps decrease the friction and stress we feel and increases our internal sense of peace. Truly unpacking the layers of ourselves as we become increasingly more authentic can take decades, so this book focuses on how to become more authentic in our roles as educators.

As teachers, our aim is to learn who we are within the context of our roles in schools and then to be that. This isn't something that happens instantly. Many of the positive deviant teachers I (Rebecca) interviewed said it took them three to five years to discover who they were as teachers. We may come in with some sense of who we are, how we relate to students, how we best lead learning, and how we navigate conflict, but it takes frequent reflection on ourselves and how our students respond to us through our lessons, teaching, conversations, and discipline strategies to truly discover how to be effective as an authentic teacher.

I remember an experience during my student teaching in a high school biology class when my supervising teacher wanted me to discipline students the way he did. He wanted me to come down harder on students who disrupted class and kick them out. This is not congruent with who I am. I believe the best way to navigate student behavior is to have a conversation with a student, but because I felt pressure to "kick a kid out," I did it. The student was a boy who often disrupted class, not just for me but also for my supervising teacher. He was used to being kicked out. Even though I told him to leave the room, when I joined him in the hall, I switched back to my authentic self. In a kind voice, I explained that it was really hard for me to teach when he was disrupting class and that I needed him to stop. He was surprised and said, "That's it?" I said, "Yes." We went back into class, and he didn't disrupt my class anymore—not just for the rest of that class period, but for the rest of my time teaching in that class. I can't prove it, but I don't think the interaction would have been as effective if I'd tried to discipline this student the way my supervising teacher expected me to. It would have been inauthentic, and I think the student would have sensed that.

Take a moment to read and answer the following self-reflection questions.

WALKING IN OUR STUDENTS' SHOES

Reflecting ON AUTHENTIC LEADERSHIP

Think about a leader in your life who seemed authentic to you, who didn't try to be someone they weren't, and whose actions aligned with their words.

- How could you tell they were authentic?

- How did you feel when you were with them?

continued →

- On a scale of one to ten, with one being the lowest level of motivation and ten being the highest, how motivated were you to follow them? Explain your scale number.

Now, think about a leader in your life who did not seem authentic.

- In what ways could you tell they were not authentic?

- How did you feel when you were with them?

- On a scale of one to ten, how motivated were you to follow them? Explain your scale number.

*Visit **go.SolutionTree.com/teacherefficacy** for a free reproducible version of this reflection.*

Being authentic as a leader increases the trust others feel for us and their willingness to do what we ask them to do. Students can tell if we are trying to be someone we aren't or if we are putting on a facade, and that decreases their trust in us. When we are authentic, it also gives our students permission to be authentic, which can improve their self-concept and hope for the future (Knighton, 2022). We feel vulnerable to show our authentic selves as teachers, but it greatly improves our student relationships and our effectiveness when we do so.

Being Real Improves Student Relationships

Adolescents tend to think that teachers who are authentic are more effective (De Bruyckere & Kirschner, 2016). Being authentic means three things: (1) that we show up as our true selves with students (which often requires some level of vulnerability), (2) that we show students that we understand real life, and (3) that we manage our classrooms in a way that is both congruent with who we are *and* meets our students' needs. One of the challenges we can run into as we strive to discover and be an authentic teacher is the potential tension when there is conflict between who you are as an educator and administrator expectations and policies.

Showing Vulnerability

One of the most important things we can do to build trust with adolescents is to show them that we are real *and* let them know we understand what they are experiencing (Knighton, 2022). Adolescents need to know that we understand real life and that we've experienced boredom, loss, frustration, failure, disappointment, and heartache like they have. This doesn't mean we should constantly overdivulge aspects of our private lives, but it does mean, when appropriate, we share stories about our experiences that they can relate to, for the purposes of both connecting and teaching. Students also need to trust that we are who we say we are. This is especially true for students with a history of AELEs. Their survival has depended on reading people. In our experience, these students can sense if someone is real or not, and they won't trust people who aren't.

This is especially true for students with a history of AELEs. Their survival has depended on reading people. In our experience, these students can sense if someone is real or not, and they won't trust people who aren't.

Some students who have struggled with difficult lives may tend to assume that teachers have had an easy life and could not possibly understand them, and that decreases their feelings of connection and trust with teachers.

I (Rebecca) experienced this during my student teaching. I worked in a highly impacted middle school with a group of students that the teachers said were the most disruptive they had ever seen. I practiced all the engagement strategies I was learning in my teacher preparation program; some of them worked for most students, but there were still a few students who did not trust me and would not engage. Then, in the middle of the term, I received word that my dad had brain cancer. I came into school carrying the weight of that news. I wasn't outwardly expressing my grief, but I also wasn't putting on a front and attempting to feign joy. Then, the strangest thing happened. The three students who had been unresponsive to my attempts to connect each came up to me that day and connected in one way or another. It was as though they saw pain in me, and that pain made me more trustworthy. I was no longer some middle-class white woman who didn't get it. I was someone who understood deep pain and loss.

I'm not saying we need to go into school and outwardly share all our pain with our students. However, when we try to cover up who we are to appear like we have it all together, that may decrease our ability to connect with them.

We can show students we understand real life simply by naming what they are feeling. If you're teaching something you know teenagers couldn't care less about, you could simply say, "I know this might seem boring and irrelevant to you. I know when I was your age, I would have thought the same thing, but this is why we are doing it, and this is the value it has," and then connect it to something that does matter to them. One of the teachers in my study told his students (the day before "take your child to work" day), that if they weren't going to work with one of their parents the next day they shouldn't come to school because they would be bored since so many other people would be gone. The students were surprised by his candor. From that experience, they felt like he would tell them the truth, which led to increased trust (Knighton, 2022).

JESSICA'S VIGNETTE

Telling stories is my natural teaching method. I've discovered that my superpower lies in my vulnerability, which, for me, falls under storytelling.

Most people believe and feel that vulnerability is a weakness, but it's actually "an astonishing form of human strength" (Kim & Hill, 2018, p. 8). When I embrace my vulnerability through a personal story, I change the power dynamics in my classroom. I open a channel that "gives up my power in order to gain access to a new kind of power" that encompasses everyone in my classroom. Authors Grace Ji-Sun Kim and Graham Hill (2018) write that "power is healing and nurturing when released, when it is used for others' wellbeing and human flourishing" (p. 78).

When I know there's a lot of teasing going on between students, I purposely bring up an experience I had in sixth grade to home in on body image, because every middle schooler has something about their body they wish looked different. Compared to elementary school and high school, middle school is difficult for both girls and boys. Whether girls develop faster or slower than their peers, they are often teased about their chest size. Boys are either super tall or they haven't hit a growth spurt yet. And whether a student has "baby fat" or is extremely thin and boney, they seem to despise their shape.

This is my story: My sixth-grade year was the last year of elementary school before I headed to junior high. I was still a very skinny and underdeveloped twelve-year-old female. I was friends with everyone, and it was very obvious which girls were in the later stages of puberty. Our friend group was made up of both boys and girls, and we all got along well with very little drama. One day, Ethan, one of my male friends, said, "Jessica, did you know the walls are jealous of you?" I was very taken aback because I thought, "Something is jealous of me? Wow! I can't wait to hear this compliment." I answered back, excited, "Why?" In front of all our friends sitting at our table, Ethan said, "Because you're flatter than they are!" He laughed with full gusto, and all I wanted to do was run to the bathroom to cry and hide how flushed my face and neck were. I was devastated. How could my friend be so cruel? Didn't he know

I couldn't control the size of my chest? And did he think I didn't already know how flat my chest was?

I explain to my students that no one has to tell another person how they look because they already know since they see themselves in the mirror, in the shower, and while getting dressed. I always have some students snicker at this. I remind them that no one can change how they grow and how their genetics are influenced by their parents. I also explain that there's no good reason to say those things out loud, and if they do, it's not cool because it's just mean.

After telling this story to my classes each year, I finally realized why Ethan said what he said. I end with this aha moment: He was trying to get other people to focus on me instead of him because he was afraid of being teased for having above-average ears that stuck out from the sides of his head.

The ultimate lesson is twofold. First, people who tease you about your looks are self-conscious about their own looks and bodies; it's about them, not you.

And second, the words we say have the power to hurt or heal, and some stay with us for a lifetime. Until I worked through my body image issues with my therapist, I always felt my body wasn't good enough, from the age of twelve until I was about forty-six. That's thirty-four *years* of feeling inadequate because of a "joke." Those words came not from an enemy, not from a stranger, but from my *friend*. The lesson is this: Stop "joking" about the physical characteristics of others because it's never a joke to them.

We can also show our students that we understand how they feel when we get a sense of what they are struggling with and then tell them a relevant story from our own lives. For example, if many students doubt they can succeed in our classes, we can tell them a story about how we once felt we couldn't succeed at something and how we overcame those feelings. This helps students see us as fellow humans, and it models for them one strategy for facing self-doubt. Being real with students isn't about oversharing, it's about sharing enough so they can see that we understand them and what they are going through.

Being real with students isn't about oversharing, it's about sharing enough so they can see that we understand them and what they are going through.

Any personal story we share needs to be something students can relate to. One of the purposes of sharing is to create relatability, which helps students feel like we get it and increases their trust in us. The other purpose of sharing is to model how to navigate challenges through giving examples from our own lives or from people we know.

Striving for Authentic and Effective Classroom Management

In addition to being real, another aspect of being authentic is to align our classroom management and discipline strategies with who we are while also meeting our students' needs. Different classroom management styles are effective for different teachers. What does not work is trying to manage our classrooms in a way that feels incongruent with who we are. If I feel strongly that I need to give students some freedom in my class but still try to enforce a very strict classroom management style because I think I *should*, it will feel uncomfortable for me, and it won't work for my students. They'll sense that I don't mean what I say. I have seen very strict classroom management approaches work well, just as I have seen much more laid-back classroom management styles work well. Classroom management styles work when they are aligned with who you are while also meeting the needs of your students, and they don't work when they aren't. The same goes for discipline strategies and teaching and assessment styles. Being authentic and real is vital, but we need to combine that with caring about, teaching, and guiding our students.

We have to set up our lessons and our classrooms in ways that meet their needs in addition to being aligned with who we are. If we are only focused on what we need as teachers and not on what our students need, then authenticity won't lead to connection and engagement. At the same time, if we only focus on what our students need and not what we need, we won't be effective teachers and leaders either. We need to balance what we need and who we are with what our students need and who they are.

Navigating Tension With Administrators

Another factor to consider is how your approaches align with your administrator's expectations. Tension arises when our administrators expect all teachers to use the same classroom management approaches, discipline strategies, and teaching and assessment styles. It can be challenging to use the strategies in this book if the norms and expectations in your building don't allow flexibility in how staff relate to students, navigate student conflict, and customize lessons. Students are more successful when there is some consistency within the building (Houchens et al., 2017), but staff are more motivated when they have autonomy (Pink, 2018). These two elements can be at odds, and teachers must become skilled at navigating the tension between contributing to consistency in the building and retaining personal autonomy and authenticity. Teachers need the space to be their authentic selves in the classroom to stay motivated and engaged. In my study, former students talked about how much more engaged they were when their teachers were motivated and cared about their content (Knighton, 2022). If you are using this book as a book study in your school, spend time as a staff discussing how to balance these seemingly contrary needs. There is a way to bring yourself to your classroom, lessons, and student conflict even when what is authentic to you may not match the common schoolwide norms. It may just require examining the reasons why certain policies or norms are in place and using a little creativity. For example, your school may have a policy that students must line up outside each classroom before entering so that teachers will greet them as they enter the room. This approach might not fit how you authentically connect with students. If you step back and look at the reason the policy exists (to encourage staff to connect with students as they enter the classroom), then maybe you can find a way to connect with each student as they enter your classroom that doesn't require that they line up outside your door. Ideally, your whole staff and administration might engage in conversations about the bigger "why" of policies and expectations and explore how those objectives might be met in ways that also allow more autonomy and authenticity among staff.

Being authentic can sometimes feel uncomfortable if you want to try something new that's not aligned with your school's culture. I (Rebecca) experienced this in my second year of teaching when we added an elective class for students who struggled with externalizing behavior—those students who acted out in class and frequently visited the front office. The class was designed to help those students transition into and be more successful in middle school. As I thought about how to lead this class, I considered who the students would be and what they would need. Combining what I knew about adolescent development and behavior and the results from a behavior screener we used to identify these students, I knew many of them felt they weren't accepted and didn't belong in school. They needed to develop self-awareness, self-regulation, self-reflection, and organizational skills. They needed to feel safe and accepted. I also knew these were not the students who were easily controlled by adults.

I knew that what these students needed and what my principal would expect to see if he walked into my classroom were at odds. He would expect students to be seated quietly doing whatever I told them to promptly and without resistance.

But my students needed the space to speak up, push the boundaries, sit in unconventional ways, challenge what I asked them to do, move around the room, draw pictures instead of looking at me when I spoke, and a lot of other seemingly imperfect classroom behaviors. If my administrator had walked in, he would have seen these behaviors and questioned my ability, but he would have missed the deeper real-life learning that was going on. Students were learning to articulate that they can pay attention better in class if they are allowed to draw in their notebooks while they listen. Students were reflecting at the end of each class on what self-regulation and communication skills they did well that day and which ones they needed to improve on. Students were feeling like they belonged in school for the first time. And students were articulating how they were feeling that day and asking for the supports they needed to participate. Students in my elective class went from receiving anywhere between four and thirty-six discipline referrals in fifth grade to fewer than three in sixth grade. In seventh and eighth grade, their referrals continued to decrease. These students needed a different learning environment than what you'd typically think an ideal classroom should look like, and that is what I gave them.

Navigating the tension between administrators' expectations and students' needs can take its toll. Though my efforts were successful, I wasn't sure they would be at the time. I was a second-year teacher, and this was the first time we'd offered this elective. What if I was wrong about my approach? I was torn between what I knew the students needed and what kind of judgment or negative consequences my administrators might impose on me if they walked into my very nontraditional classroom setup. That tension between the pressure of what I thought I should do and what I knew students needed created great stress for me, made me feel inadequate, and sent me home in tears two or three times a week. I know I'm not alone in that experience. I think many of us live with the tension of how we think we *should* do things based on how other teachers do things or what we understand the district or principal mandates to be (whether those are real or imagined) and what we think would meet our students' needs best in a way that feels authentic to us. That can create stress, harm our well-being, and make us less effective. While we're not encouraging teachers to ignore district or administrator mandates, we are advocating that they clarify what those mandates are (and have conversations about the bigger purposes of those mandates) and seek creative solutions that enable them to retain their authenticity and autonomy in meeting students' needs while also meeting the bigger why of the mandate.

In addition to this anecdotal evidence, research supports the idea that teachers who are authentic, while also being caring and respectful, have better relationships with their students, and their students are more engaged and have higher achievement (Allen et al., 2013; Knighton, 2022; Oberle, Gist, Cooray, & Pinto, 2020). So why don't we emphasize the importance of authenticity and give teachers permission to be themselves? Maybe it's because we don't know how or maybe it's because of the pressure to create uniformity and standardization. Whatever the reason, we can successfully navigate this tension. We can ensure that teachers provide high quality instruction and effectively guide student learning while also giving teachers the flexibility to be themselves and meet their students where they are at. Encouraging educators to be authentic isn't just important for student success; it also has the potential to improve teacher effectiveness, job satisfaction, and well-being, which can decrease attrition rates by improving student-teacher relationships and increasing student engagement (Chang, 2013; Harmsen, Helms-Lorenz, Maulana, & van Veen, 2018).

Finding Your Path to Authenticity

Where are you on your journey to authenticity and facilitating student learning? Maybe you're a new teacher who is just figuring out how to facilitate student learning or a veteran teacher who has mastered it. Maybe you know who you are but you're still experiencing barriers to being authentic with your students. Maybe you're still sorting out who you are and learning what values resonate with your deepest self. Or maybe you're somewhere in the middle. Now that we've discussed *why* authenticity is important, we turn our attention to *how* to become more authentic as a teacher. How you engage with the content in this section will depend on where you are on the journey toward authenticity.

When we are our true selves, we are more able to be present and open in the moment. This enables us to be more aware of how our students respond to us and what their needs are.

When we become teachers, we have a lot to figure out: how to organize our classroom, discipline our students, effectively engage students in content, interact with students, and more. To be effective and authentic teachers, we need to understand and balance two things: (1) what is effective with our students, and (2) how we lead our classrooms in a way that aligns with our authentic selves as opposed to how we think we *should* do it or how someone else does it.

It is challenging to be an authentic teacher. Not only do we need to know ourselves well and feel safe enough to be real and present, but we also have to know our content well enough to be able to guide our students through it when real-life detours occur within our classrooms. When we are our true selves, we are more able to be present and open in the moment. This enables us to be more aware of how our students respond to us and what their needs are.

When we are present and open, it also encourages our students to be more open to learning (Wood, 2020). We don't usually learn how to be authentic teachers in our teacher preparation programs. It is important to learn the basics (lesson planning, pedagogy, classroom management, and so on) and learn a template of how to do our work, but it shouldn't stop there. We also need to discover who we are as teachers and how to accomplish tasks in ways that are true to ourselves because that knowledge increases our students' ability to trust us (Tschannen-Moran & Hoy, 2000) and impacts their engagement in our classes (Romero, 2015). There is a temptation to think we should teach or manage conflict in a certain way based on how other teachers do it or based on our teacher preparation program training, but we are more effective, and students trust us more, when we are ourselves (Knighton, 2022).

Being an authentic and effective teacher means knowing yourself and creating classroom policies, procedures, and norms that align with who you are. But most of us don't automatically know who we are as authentic teachers and leaders. We don't know how we best connect with others, how we best manage conflict, and what kind of leader we are. We don't know what leadership style matches our personality and values, who we are as leaders, or how skilled we are at seeing those we lead and understanding what they need. We don't know how to set up our classrooms to match our teaching style and the learning needs of our students or what classroom management style works best for us and our students. We don't know what type of discipline strategies align with our values and personalities while also serving as an effective means of conflict resolution with our students. We don't know how to design our lessons and assessments to align with how we teach best and what our students need. You may not have had much practice trusting yourself or feeling empowered in these aspects of your professional life. That's OK. Wherever you are on the journey toward authenticity, you can start practicing now.

What does this look like in practice? As you learn and grow, pay attention to what approaches feel most congruent with who you are *and* best meet your students' needs. One way I (Rebecca) determine this congruence is to notice how my body feels. If I feel tense, my breathing gets shallower, I feel internal friction, and I feel exhausted afterward, then I know it is not congruent with who I am. Whereas if my body feels at ease, my lungs feel more expansive when I breathe, and I feel an inner stillness or peace while also energized, then I know it is my true, authentic self. Sometimes it is hard to distinguish—if I am doing something new that I might not feel confident in yet, I might have an increased heart rate and feel tension in my belly, but I still have a deeper sense of calm underneath it. Another indicator is how students respond to us. When we are authentic, students seem to connect with us and respond to what we ask them to do more than when we wear a mask or try to be someone we're not (Knighton, 2022). We will see our students respond with their body language, the questions or personal stories they share with us, and their level of engagement.

To discover who we are as authentic teachers, we must reflect on ourselves, our students, what is effective, and what's not. Understanding ourselves at this level will take time. It also takes the willingness to examine what works and what doesn't and then change if needed. If we are continually focused on the past or the future, it will be more difficult to reflect on ourselves and how our students respond than if we are present with our students at that moment. Additionally, if we berate ourselves for our mistakes, we will be less likely to learn, grow, and do something differently the next time. Whereas if we are open and curious in our interactions with students, we will be more able to learn, grow, and change (Wood, 2020). Sometimes, we need to be creative about how to meet our students' needs and those of the curriculum and standards in a way that aligns with who we are and how our brains work; what environment we need to function best; and how we best communicate with, lead, and teach others. This process can take years, but we are hoping this book can help you in that process of discovery and begin to improve your own sense of well-being, your relationships with your students, and your students' successes in your classroom.

Use figure 3.1 to reflect on your interactions with students and what authenticity looks and feels like for you in those moments.

During the interaction, what did I say and do? What did my student say and do?	What did I think and feel?	How did my body feel?	How did the student respond to me?	Was I being authentic during this interaction? If not, what might be some reasons?	What are my takeaways or notes to self?

Figure 3.1: Authenticity reflection journal.

Visit ***go.SolutionTree.com/teacherefficacy*** *for a free reproducible version of this figure.*

Looking Inward: Flipping the Script

In this section, you will have the opportunity to engage in two activities, shown in figures 3.2 (page 102) and 3.3 (page 106). These activities are designed to help you understand yourself better and develop some of the skills discussed in this chapter.

Learning who you are as an authentic teacher can take several years and requires constant reflection on yourself; your students' responses to your practice; and the effectiveness of your teaching methods, activities, and structures. This activity can help you begin to reflect on what works and what doesn't. It will also give you a technique to help you physically distinguish when something you do is or is not congruent with your authentic self.

1. Think back to a lesson you taught or an activity you facilitated that did not work at all—a lesson where you felt uncomfortable and your students did not engage. If you have not experienced this as a teacher yourself, think about a time when one of your teachers did this.
    - What was it about that lesson or activity that made it so unsuccessful?
    - What were you doing as the teacher?
    - What were the students doing? How were they responding?

Figure 3.2: Noticing what it feels like to be authentic.

- What resonated with you the most?

- What did you hear or notice that did not seem to resonate with the students?

- What thoughts were going through your mind about yourself, your teaching, and your students?

- How did your body feel (notice if you were tense or relaxed, if your breathing changed, if your heart rate changed, if you felt anxious, if you were sweating, or if you had other physical responses)?

continued →

2. When we are doing, saying, or creating anything that is congruent with our true selves, it feels different in our bodies than when we are trying to be like someone else. For this activity, we will ask you to engage in several visualizations so you can feel that difference in your body.

    a. Remember a time when you felt totally in your element—doing something you felt competent in, that aligned with your values, and that you enjoyed doing. Imagine being in that moment again.

        - What are you doing?

        - What are you feeling?

        - How does your body feel? (Are your eyes, jaw, and forehead relaxed or tense? Is your neck tight or not? Are your shoulders up and tense or low and relaxed? Is your breathing slow and full or short and quick? How is your heart rate? Are you warm, cold, sweaty, or comfortable?)

b. Remember a time when you were doing something that did not align with your true self. This might be a time someone else was requiring you to do something that did not align with your values or beliefs. It might be a time when you felt peer pressure to pretend to be someone you weren't. Imagine being there.

    - What are you doing?

    - What are you feeling?

    - How does your body feel? (Repeat the body scan from the previous prompt.)

3. How did those two experiences feel different in your body?

This is important to notice and memorize about yourself because this is your barometer to know when you are or aren't doing, saying, or creating something aligned to your true self. As you reflect and grow as a teacher, recognizing what feels congruent with who you are and what doesn't will help you become a more authentic teacher.

Visit ***go.SolutionTree.com/teacherefficacy*** *for a free reproducible version of this figure.*

Students have specific needs during adolescence. This activity will help you think through how to meet those needs while also being true to yourself and your needs. As you answer the following questions, try to be honest with yourself about what you need as a teacher and not what you think you should want or need. Feel free to think outside the box.

Our students' needs:

- To feel connected to their peers
- To experience respect from adults
- To have autonomy
- To have control
- To understand the connection of our content to real life
- To see adults as fellow humans who they have some sort of connection with
- To witness adults being real so they can relate to them and trust them
- To experience acceptance and non-judgment
- To feel safe to learn and grow
- To experience novelty

1. Put a star next to the student needs that you already address well. Circle the needs you want to address better and underline the needs you philosophically disagree with or struggle to accept.

2. What *classroom norms, rules, and procedures* do you currently have in place that ensure these needs are met and fit with your authentic self?

Figure 3.3: Being authentic while also meeting students' needs.

3. Choose two needs that you circled from the previous list. How might you change your current classroom norms, rules, and procedures to ensure those needs are met?

4. Choose two needs that you circled from the previous list. How might you change your current discipline and conflict resolution strategies in a way that ensures those needs are met while maintaining your authenticity?

5. Choose two needs that you circled from the previous list. How might you design your instruction in a way that ensures those needs are met while also upholding content standards and being congruent with your authentic self?

6. Look at the student needs that you underlined and choose two or three to explore.
    a. Why do you disagree with or struggle to accept this student need?

continued →

b. Remember when you were an adolescent. Do you remember experiencing this need? How did it feel when adults dismissed it?

Visit ***go.SolutionTree.com/teacherefficacy*** *for a free reproducible version of this figure.*

Learning From the Five Teacher Types

This section presents two common scenarios. For each scenario, the five positive deviant teachers you met in the introduction describe how they navigate these scenarios in their practice. The first is about being authentic with your students, and the second is about determining your authenticity. As you read through these examples, highlight, underline, or circle the parts you relate to.

Scenario: You want to show up as real and authentic with your students

The following sections describe how each teacher type approaches this scenario in their classroom.

Teacher Type: Caring Connector

When I first started teaching, I was hyper-focused on student academic achievement. Wanting to be perceived as professional by both my students and peers, I attempted to keep strict rules within the classroom and run a tight ship, as it were. I had a bit of a wake-up call one day when a student said to me "Wow, you really need to chill out!" That night, I reflected on my practice and realized I was being the teacher that I thought others wanted me to be rather than the teacher I actually am. From that point on, I focused on being my genuine self in the classroom. I shifted focus from worrying about student performance on standardized assessments to creating meaningful relationships with my students and trying to engage them as lifelong learners.

By taking a genuine interest in their lives, and being vulnerable enough to share about my own, they started to see me as a person they could feel comfortable around. I started to reveal my sense of humor in the classroom, making students groan with all my stupid puns and dad jokes. I stopped the constant stand-and-deliver direct instruction and shifted toward more group work and role-playing activities to increase engagement. I also increased the flexibility in my assessment style, allowing students to demonstrate their understanding in multiple ways and to reattempt any work to show improvement.

The changes I started to see in my classes were amazing. Students let down their guard and opened up about their lives. They took more risks in terms of participating in class discussions and injecting their unique personalities into their project work. A byproduct was that their academic achievement improved as well! Overall, I saw happier, more engaged, less stressed students. By being my true, authentic self in the classroom, I had a lot more fun teaching than I ever had up to that point. My own stress level had reduced, and I truly looked forward to going to work each day.

Teacher Type: Gentle Giant

Authenticity in the classroom is crucial for fostering a meaningful and engaging learning environment. When teachers show their human side by sharing real-life experiences, they create a bridge between knowledge and application. This approach not only makes lessons more relatable but also builds trust and rapport with students. By being authentic, I can demonstrate vulnerability, perseverance, and character. This encourages students to see me as an approachable mentor rather than a distant authority figure. I tell students about my weekends and ask about theirs, share stories of how I learned and failed on first attempts just like they do, and try to relate to their experiences by sharing about my own or others I've seen. This connection helps students feel more comfortable, valued, and motivated to participate actively in class.

In many ways, I am a performer in class, whether demonstrating my own skills and abilities, using humor and jokes to break the ice, or telling stories about my weekend adventures. I embrace this part of teaching and know that it has to be real. Talking the talk is one thing. I've found that walking the walk by demonstrating vulnerability and doing it with genuine authenticity is the key to building long-lasting connections and relationships with students. Sometimes this can mean not knowing the answer or looking silly in front of a class because my attempt at a skill demonstration was a failure, but these moments are equally valuable. Students get to see what I do after I mess up, how I solve problems, or how I discover new ways to attempt things. To me, authenticity is about demonstrating and modeling the things we talk and teach about daily and connecting these lessons to life outside of school.

Teenagers are not stupid; they know when you are pretending to be someone you're not. By modeling authenticity in the classroom, you are helping them be comfortable expressing their own unique identities as well.

Teacher Type: Nurturing Narrator

As students come into the building in the morning, I am always in the hallways with them. I float through the halls each morning greeting every student I see. Being present is a huge part of being authentic. I am not on my phone or behind my desk at the start of their day. I want them to know I am here to touch base and offer a safe place to chat. Some students start their day with no one to talk to, have had a really hard night, are starving, or have many other complicated possibilities at play for them. I meet them where they're at and check in with their needs. The onus is not on the students to make a connection with me; it is my job to make them want to come to me and chat. I also make notes about my students' lives, and I ask them intentional questions that demonstrate my care. I do this for all the students in our hallways, not just the ones in my class.

I start every day in my own class with a story; even in grade 8, they love to hear stories. I call it "coffee talk" each morning because my students know my love of coffee, and it gives them the perception that the coffee talk is for me. We sit and I start with a grievance usually from my previous night, usually to do with my own kids. It's usually something simple, but it opens the conversation for them to share something from their night or make some sort of connection. It also lets them know that I am human. We talk for nearly twenty minutes each morning. We always have a soft start to our day. Students slowly warm up before we start lessons.

Teachers gain students' trust the same way they do with adults—by being real. Students know that if they tell me something in confidence, I will always fall on the sword for them and take the heat. Students don't trust that they can tell adults all things, so having a safe spot to confide in someone who is strong enough to make a change for them is really valuable and powerful. Students who are struggling, be it with behaviors or learning, will not work for someone they do not trust. Establishing a relationship with students comes first—always. As teachers, we are sometimes confused about whose story we're in. We're not in our own story each day—we are not the protagonists. I tell myself more days in a year than I can count (especially after a hard day) that these students' stories are still unwritten, like books with many pages still blank. When they look back at the chapters that I am in, I want them to know I was reading their story in real time—that I cared for and knew them.

Teacher Type: Perceptive Pragmatist

One of my main goals in the classroom is to be human. I don't want my students to see me as a cold, robotic authority figure. However, in the opposite direction, it can come off just as inauthentic to be too personal and share too much about yourself, not to mention that it can be uncomfortable for some teachers. The things that I do to be real and authentic actually require very little of me sharing about myself . . . that part can happen naturally, or not, over the course of the semester. No matter what the dynamics are of the class I am teaching, there are three approaches that I think contribute to showing up as real and authentic and can be demonstrated early: (1) embrace mistakes, (2) have a sense of humor, and (3) don't ask anything of my students I wouldn't want asked of me.

1. ***Embrace mistakes:*** *Too often, I see teachers (particularly student teachers or inexperienced teachers) being insecure about making a mistake during a lesson. I teach mathematics, so I make miscalculations, miss signs, and make those kinds of mistakes all the time. The best way to handle it is just to own that you made a mistake, thank whoever noticed it (if a student pointed it out), and fix it. I often see teachers get flustered and then try to make excuses and explain away the mistake. If you want students to see you as human, and you want students to be OK with making mistakes and learning from them, you need to model it. By overexplaining or not owning it, you show students that you aren't OK with mistakes, which in turn means they will be hesitant to make them in front of you. This is along the same lines as when a student asks a question that I don't know an answer to. I never pretend to know what I'm talking about if I don't. My response is, "Oh that's a good question, let's look it up," or "Hmm, I need some time to think about that and I'll get back to you." In the past, students have expressed that they appreciate this response since they can see right through teachers who don't know and are giving an embellished or made-up answer.*
2. ***Have a sense of humor:*** *I am not suggesting needing to take on the role of a stand-up comedian, or even needing to be funny, but not taking things too seriously goes a long way. The ability to laugh at things that happen in the classroom is a great way to bond with students. When you see what other people find humor in, it tells you a lot about who they are.*
3. ***Don't ask anything of my students I wouldn't want asked of me:*** *We've all been asked to do something outside our comfort zones, like playing an icebreaker game or being called on to answer a question. And yet, so many use those exact activities in their classroom because they feel like that's what they're supposed to do. It feels fake and forced if it's not something you enjoy doing (and if these are things you enjoy, all the power to you). I am very open with my students about why I choose to do, or not do, certain things in my classroom. I do not randomly call on students to answer questions in my classroom, and I tell them I won't and why. Another small example is that, as a student, I didn't like when we moved on to a new chapter before taking the test for the previous one, so I do my best to always completely wrap up a chapter before moving on; I also explain this to the class. It gives students a chance to understand who I was as a student and why I make the decisions I do as a teacher. Maybe it gives them something to identify with.*

I have always said that if you are genuine to who you are, the students will embrace it. I have seen the same students love their warm, fuzzy, nurturing teacher just as much as the old-school, tough-love, sarcastic teacher because each is being who they are. Students can sense a teacher being fake very quickly, and it generally doesn't go well for the teacher.

Teacher Type: Warm Demander

Sharing my life with my students from the get-go has been the most important lesson. I start by letting them know who I am so my students don't have to wonder who they are dealing with, which usually makes them feel anxious and nervous. If I lay it all out there and let them know what kind of person I am, I remove the amount of time students are trying to figure out who they're dealing with (which can take anywhere from a month to the whole year). Instead, their brains are ready for the learning part of my class.

As part of my beginning-of-the-year slide deck, I share things I love: Flair markers, Starbucks bottled mocha, turkey bacon, the Broncos, reading, and giving "mom hugs." Along with that, I explain other favorites, such as giraffes because they have the biggest heart of all land mammals and starfish because of the story of throwing them back into the ocean to survive when they wash up on the shore and why that matters to me. I make it clear that they are my starfish, and I'll always help them with whatever they need to "survive."

The next several slides are full of silly pictures of me and my family with their names and ages on each slide. I describe each family member's characteristics and talents, as well as their jobs because they don't all have college degrees. One of the pictures is of my husband two days after his open-heart quadruple bypass surgery with two of his doctors and me. I explain my husband's condition and his need for a heart transplant. I do this because it shows my human side and lets students know that I have struggles and worries. I'm very honest about the need to look at my Apple Watch or my phone for texts from him because he's homebound. I'm real, but brief, about how my four sons and I are dealing with this experience.

Then I show my students a slide with numerous pictures of me, my sister, my mom, and our foster kids, explaining that my parents fostered children from the time I was three years old until I was twenty-seven. By the time I moved out after college, I'd had 189 foster brothers and sisters. I go into detail about what I learned from my mom as she mothered children who weren't her own, but they were in a sense. She showed me how to be patient, understanding, loving, calm, and direct. She modeled how to show compassion to kids stuck in bad situations—through no fault of their own. She was a manifestation of complete love and kindness, all of which I embrace and try to practice daily, both in the classroom and in my life. My mother had the innate ability to separate behaviors and situations from the actual child. In this way, she could make any scared and confused child feel welcome, safe, and calm. My intentions are to do the same for each of my students every single day.

After answering all their inquisitive questions about fostering, I then turn back to a lighter topic. I show a slide of deeper favorites and explain my whys—from playing guitar, singing, and spending time in Nashville to why I chose to continue teaching. I also share my deep love of reading and getting my students to love reading too. This is when I share a picture of two former eighth-grade girls engrossed in thick novels—two of my students who swore I'd never get them to like reading. And even though I don't teach language arts every year, my passion for getting middle schoolers to read will never go away because it truly is the Golden Ticket for life success.

The next slide shows what my dreams are, which always seems to shock students because I'm an adult. The slide shares my desire to own a red 2000 Corvette with chrome rims and a black convertible top; to own a sod farm with a herd of Great Pyrenees dogs running amok, so we can call our farm Pyr Heaven; and to write a book, which I get to explain is now no longer a dream, but a reality!

From there, I have a slide about my pet peeves: breaking pencils on purpose, cussing (though I do my fair share of that outside of school), leaving trash behind, touching my personal stuff without asking, and of course no-name papers!

On the last of my own slides, I purposely show examples of how tidy and organized my classroom should always look at the end of class. I don't skirt around my expectations, and I explain this characteristic comes from my childhood due to things being stolen from me (not that I ever think my students will steal). I tell my students that if they need something, all they need to do is ask me. I'll either give it to them, or I'll find a resource that can—this includes things like money, supplies, clothes, and food.

My final two slides are for my students. I put a slide up with four questions they need to answer verbally by getting up and going to someone they don't know or normally hang out with. The questions are about their families, pet peeves, favorite things, and weekend or after-school activities. This whole experience loosens them up to be open for the final task of completing a worksheet about themselves that they only share with me. Getting a jump start on knowing my students and memorizing the information they share with me is the Golden Ticket for me as their teacher. And when I go first, they follow suit.

Given what you've learned, respond to the following reflection questions.

WHAT WOULD YOU DO?

Reflecting ON TEACHING AUTHENTICALLY

How real and authentic are you with your students?

What gets in the way of being real and authentic with your students?

What steps might you take to increase being real and authentic with your students?

*Visit **go.SolutionTree.com/teacherefficacy** for a free reproducible version of this reflection.*

Scenario: You're not sure how to tell whether what you're doing is authentic

The following sections describe how each teacher type approaches this scenario in their classroom.

Teacher Type: Caring Connector

I would say that this is affirmed by two different factors: (1) my mental state surrounding teaching and (2) the interactions with my students.

When I was a new teacher, I was so concerned about student performance and achievement that I was in a constant state of stress and anxiety surrounding the job. I had difficulty sleeping at night, which would leave me exhausted and only increased my anxiety in the classroom. I focused on planning to utilize every minute of class time to maximize the students' academic growth, but I was going about it all wrong. Jamming as much instruction and review into class as I possibly could only increased my stress and led to overall student disengagement. The learning wasn't meaningful for the students because I hadn't taken the time to connect with them on a personal level. Also, I was pretending to be this strict and regimented person that I'm truly not.

Once I reflected on this, it changed my whole approach to the teaching profession. I opened up about my own life and started being more vulnerable with the students. I started to make more of my signature dad jokes and showed my real personality. I slowed down on the content of lessons and really focused on how to make them meaningful and engaging. I learned more about the students and their interests to create lessons that would connect to their experiences. I realized that when you relax and have fun learning and growing together, the lessons themselves become more memorable for the students and lead to improvement in their academic achievement as well.

My mental state began to completely shift. I was sleeping better because I was looking forward to going into the classroom in the morning. I felt more confident in delivering lessons because the students were buying in. I was having fun doing my job for the first time. I would even get excited watching the news in the evening because I'd see a current event that would lead to a great discussion the next day.

My interactions with students were completely different. Instead of fighting with them to pay attention or to get to work, I was laughing and learning with them. They were starting to open up to me about their own lives, sharing about their weekends, or even coming to me for advice. I saw that by letting down my guard, they felt safe doing the same. By being myself, they felt that they could be themselves as well.

Teacher Type: Gentle Giant

I can really tell that things are aligned when I get going on what my students refer to as TED Talks. They are not lectures but stories of meaningful experiences that help connect content to the real world. Students often ask, "Why do we need to learn this?" I answer them honestly from personal situations. Sometimes our class loses half the class time just talking about life lessons related to the lesson plan; before I know it, the bell rings and students are ready to leave. It's moments like that where time doesn't matter to you as a teacher; you'd prefer if the bell didn't ring because your students are so engaged, and an interruption seems like a waste of knowledge being shared. These are always funny moments, too, because stragglers will often wait until the last second to finish their thoughts before running to their next class.

These types of connections are the things that make teaching feel less like a job and more meaningful. To have students leading the conversations, asking questions, and being genuinely curious is more effective when it comes to engagement. Sometimes it means thinking outside the box and putting the lessons and questions in terms that the students can visualize.

Teacher Type: Nurturing Narrator

Though I start our morning coffee talks, students quickly take over. I teach the humanities, which lends itself to a more adaptable nature, and some days our talks take us into journaling, script writing, or even current events. I remember when I was going through university and my professor for social studies told me, "A student who is sitting in your class should never be able to tell which political party you align with." That resonated with me—that our jobs as history and social studies teachers are not to form students' minds but to guide their minds to their own reasonings. I carry this with me when interacting with students. I authentically can be many versions of myself, because each day I teach isn't about me. I leave my own "baggage" at the door. When I walk through my classroom door, it is a cleansing, and I remind myself each and every day to meet students where they need me. On these days, when I leave, sometimes my baggage is waiting for me outside, and other days, it has disappeared. I encourage educators to take a day off when you cannot leave your own stuff outside. We need this, people need this; it is not a sign of weakness to take time off. And making plans for a substitute—though a pain—is not impossible. Looking back on all you created in your year, you will not remember your one missed day of curriculum, but you will remember the day you had to puke in the bathroom or cry or the day the kids saw you fall. If you cannot be authentically who they need you to be, give yourself a day of rest and come back ready for them.

Teacher Type: Perceptive Pragmatist

You would think this would be a lot easier to tell than it actually is. There have been many practices through my career that seemed like good ideas but didn't survive the test of time. Introducing new practices, or maintaining old ones, requires a lot of continual reflection. There are, for sure, times when an idea elicits an immediate gut reaction of no, but other times it takes a few attempts, or even years, before asking, "Why am I doing this, and is this the best way to fill that need?"

I also find that one of the quickest tests for whether something is aligned to who I am is asking myself, "If I had to justify this to a parent, colleague, or administrator, could I do that unwaveringly?" If the answer is yes, I know it is a decision I have made from my core; if not, it's time to do some re-evaluating or fine-tuning.

At the end of the day, if I go home feeling good about decisions I've made, I know those decisions are authentically aligned to who I am. If they occupy my thoughts, or if I am questioning myself, then I need to listen to that nagging feeling and fix it.

Teacher Type: Warm Demander

You can feel it—it's hard to explain but easy to know. When I'm teaching authentically, there's passion that comes through in my words. I feel excited, exhilarated, and I'm sure I seem as if I'm entertaining a crowd. It also feels easy instead of forced.

Given what you've learned in this chapter, respond to the following reflection questions.

WHAT WOULD YOU DO?

Recognizing WHAT AUTHENTIC TEACHING FEELS LIKE

Have you had the experience of feeling like what you are doing is aligned with your authentic self?

- What did you notice about your thoughts and feelings?

continued →

- What did it feel like in your body?

Have you had the experience of trying to be like someone else or doing something the way you thought you should, but it felt misaligned with who you are?

- What did you notice about your thoughts and feelings?

- What did it feel like in your body?

Visit ***go.SolutionTree.com/teacherefficacy*** *for a free reproducible version of this reflection.*

Wrapping Up

Being real and authentic with our students increases the trust they have in us and their willingness to engage in our classes. It helps them see us as fellow humans and improves the relationships we have with them. When we are authentic, it also gives them permission to be authentic. Discovering who we are as authentic teachers can take years and requires frequent reflection on ourselves and how our students respond to us. One powerful tool to help us become more authentic is to anchor into how our bodies feel when we are in alignment with our deeper true selves versus when we are not.

Chapter 3 Book Study Questions

As a staff, explore the concepts presented in this chapter and reflect on how they are evidenced in or might impact your school culture. As you read each of the following questions, think about how you would respond based on your individual role. If you are an administrator, think about these questions as you reflect on how you support your staff. If you are a teacher or support staff member, think about these questions as you reflect on how you support students.

1. What (real or perceived) personal barriers do you experience that prevent you from being authentic (beliefs, fears, how you were raised, childhood traumas, personality, past experiences, and so on)?

2. What (social or systemic) barriers within your school prevent you from being authentic (shoulds, should-nots, norms, policies, student clientele, and so on)?

3. What schoolwide expectations are there for staff members? Is there space for autonomy and authenticity within those expectations?

4. Are staff encouraged to be authentic in your school? What does that look like for you?

5. What does it look like in the classrooms of teachers who are being their authentic selves? What kind of relationships do those teachers have with their students?

6. What's your wish list that would allow you to be able to do activities or lessons with your students that would accentuate your authentic self?

CHAPTER 4

Increasing Student Engagement

It can be one of the most frustrating aspects of our jobs when students don't engage in our classes. In fact, studies show that low student engagement is one of the leading contributing factors to teacher burnout (Byrne, 1994; Junker, Donker, & Mainhard, 2021), which is one of the top reasons teachers leave the field (Brasfield, Lancaster, & Xu, 2019; Harmsen et al., 2018).

In this chapter, we dig into what student engagement is, what factors influence it, and how we might increase it. We explore factors that influence student engagement, barriers to engagement and ways to address them, and how to create real-life connections to content. Then, we practice flipping the script through self-reflection activities. We end the chapter by hearing how the five teacher types respond to two common scenarios related to increasing student engagement.

Looking Outward: Themes in Research and Practice

When you imagine a student who is engaged, what do you see? You probably envision a student sitting attentively at their desk, their eyes focused on you, actively listening, raising their hand to ask questions, and working diligently on whatever activity you ask them to do. I (Rebecca) used to think this is what engagement looked like until one day when I was observing another teacher's class. We were implementing a new social-emotional learning curriculum, and I was there to observe how the teacher was doing and how the students were responding to it. I noticed a boy sitting toward the front of the class on the left side of the room. As the teacher went through the lesson, the boy was looking down at his shoes, then looking down at the desk, then fidgeting with his pencil, and moving around in his seat. He didn't look engaged at all. But then the teacher paused and asked if there were any questions. This boy raised his hand and asked a very deep question that indicated he had not only been listening to the teacher, but he'd also been thinking critically about the content and how it pertained to his life. That experience shifted my understanding and perspective about what engagement can look like. A student doesn't have to be looking at us and sitting still to be learning and processing what we are teaching. The following section breaks down engagement into three types.

Most of the time, when we think about engagement, we think about what students are doing (behavioral engagement), but there are two other types of engagement that are equally important and strongly influence behavioral engagement: (1) cognitive engagement and (2) emotional engagement. *Cognitive engagement* includes how students understand and think about what they are learning, and it is connected to their intrinsic motivation (Fisher & Frey, 2021). *Emotional engagement* includes how connected students feel to us and the school as well as their levels of anxiety, interest, and happiness in school (Fisher & Frey, 2021). Both cognitive and emotional engagement impact behavioral engagement. That is why positive relationships, creating an environment where students feel like they belong, and making our content relevant to students matter so much when we want to increase engagement. In the following sections, we dig into some of the factors that influence students' cognitive and emotional engagement, because if those are high, most of the time behavioral engagement will follow.

Factors That Influence Student Engagement

When it comes to student engagement, teachers sometimes feel they must put on a show to engage students. We'd like to propose that we shift our thinking about engagement and think of it more as motivating students to learn and participate in class activities and assignments. We can't force anyone to do anything, but we can motivate students to choose to do something on their own. To understand how to motivate our students, we need to understand several things.

- What motivates people, in general but also in terms of adolescent development—what motivates students at that age and what gets in the way
- How meeting or not meeting human needs impacts motivation
- What roles self-efficacy and hope play in student motivation

Let's look at each of these in more detail.

Human Motivation

What motivates us as humans? Until the 1960s, psychologists thought the best way to motivate humans was to reward good behavior and punish bad behavior (Pink, 2018). It was believed that we were motivated by external rewards and punishments and that control, threats, and coercion were needed when leading others (Pink, 2018). When humanistic psychology emerged in the 1950s and '60s, psychologists began to realize that we have shared human needs—not only safety and survival but also psychological (connection, belonging, and competence) and self-fulfillment needs (Maslow, 1999), which impact our levels of motivation. In fact, a 2021 research study shows that performance does not increase when student motivation is driven by trying to avoid punishment (Howard et al., 2021).

In *Drive: The Surprising Truth About What Motivates Us*, author Daniel Pink (2018) explains that researchers identify three psychological needs that impact our motivation more strongly than reward and punishment approaches: (1) connection, (2) competence, and (3) autonomy. When we are asked to do an activity and we feel connected to our leader or a group of people who are also engaged in the activity, we are more motivated to engage in it. We are also more motivated to engage in something if we have at least some hope that we will be competent enough to succeed at it. How often are you highly motivated to do something you feel completely incompetent at? Probably not very often. Finally, we are more motivated when we are given some level of autonomy. That doesn't mean we don't have clearly defined parameters or expectations, but we are also allowed to be who we are and bring our own thoughts and ideas to the work. Pink (2018) acknowledges that sometimes the tasks we ask our employees (or students) to do are not that interesting, and they may not be very motivated to do them. However, motivation will increase if we can explain why a task is important, acknowledge that we know our employees (or students) may not want to do it or that it might be boring, and then we allow them to have autonomy in how they complete the task. Positive deviant teachers excel at this. I've often seen them say some version of this: "Here is what we are doing. I know this might seem boring, and you aren't excited about doing it. I would have felt that way too when I was your age, but this is why it matters." And then they explain why it is important for students' real lives. This approach motivates students to engage when they might not have otherwise (Knighton, 2022).

Think about your own life and what motivates you. Are you more likely to be motivated to do something your leader asks of you if you feel connected to them? Are you more likely to want to engage in something when you feel at least somewhat competent? And are you more motivated to engage when you are given some level of autonomy?

Many students with a history of not succeeding in school, either academically or behaviorally, don't believe they are competent. They don't believe they can succeed, and they need teachers to believe in them. For those students, it feels easier (and safer) to avoid engaging in an activity than to risk failure. Punishment and reward systems aren't enough to motivate these students to engage, as you've probably seen. However, when they feel connected to their teachers, they become more willing to risk trying (Knighton, 2022). When teachers design activities and lessons that scaffold well enough that these students do feel competent, it increases their motivation even more. And when students have autonomy in the way they complete tasks and demonstrate learning, it meets the human psychological need for autonomy, something that is especially important for adolescents as they are in the process of discovering who they are.

Take a moment to read and answer the following self-reflection questions.

WALKING IN OUR STUDENTS' SHOES

Reflecting ON MOTIVATION

Think about a time in your life when you felt like you couldn't succeed at something. It could be a personal or professional experience.

- How did you feel when you were asked to do that task or activity?

- How motivated were you to do that task?

- What did you think about as you prepared to engage in that task or activity?

- Did you compare yourself to others who seemed more capable?

Visit ***go.SolutionTree.com/teacherefficacy*** *for a free reproducible version of this reflection.*

Some people have high self-efficacy and a growth mindset and will jump into tasks and activities even if they don't think they can succeed, because they trust they can learn and improve. Others, especially people with fixed mindsets, avoid what makes them feel incompetent. Disengaged students tend to fall into the category of avoiding what makes them feel incompetent.

I (Rebecca) encountered that feeling of incompetence four years into my dissertation. I handed in the first draft of two of my chapters to my supervisors. I'd put a lot of time into researching how to write a qualitative dissertation, but both of my supervisors were quantitative researchers. They had stylistic disagreements with how qualitative researchers believed dissertations should be written, and they told me that I did it completely wrong. I now agree with them and am grateful they made me change it, because it is so much better than it would have been. At the time, however, it was rough. It felt like every time I submitted revisions, they gave me a longer list of additional things to change without indicating that anything had improved. I felt like I received list after list of what was wrong. I am sure they were just being efficient in their replies to me to move things along more quickly, but all I heard in my mind was the repeated message, "You're not good enough." I began to think, "Maybe I am really just not mentally capable of writing this." I wanted to quit because I honestly didn't believe I could succeed. Even if you've never written a dissertation, I'm sure you can recall a time in your personal or professional life when you didn't think you were capable of succeeding and wanted to give up or avoid the situation. Luckily, my husband talked me out of quitting, but not everyone has someone to support and reassure them when they face seemingly insurmountable obstacles.

Now think about your students. When they struggle in school or are told by teachers that they aren't measuring up, *it affects the development of their identity.*

When they struggle in school or are told by teachers that they aren't measuring up, *it affects the development of their identity.*

If we don't show them that we believe in them, if we only tell them what they need to improve, what they hear is, "I'm not good enough." I was forty-six years old when I concluded I wasn't good enough during my PhD, even though I had self-reflection skills and emotional maturity. How can we expect adolescents—whose brains have not fully developed, whose identities are still forming, and who have less experience with self-reflection—to come to different conclusions?

In schools, it seems like our policies, procedures, and even beliefs continue to operate under the assumption that we have to control, threaten, and coerce students or they won't engage in school. However, as humans, we have an innate desire to learn (Moreno, 2022). If you've ever been around a four-year-old, you'll know they ask a lot of questions as they try to learn about the world they live in. People aren't born disengaged. We are born curious and wanting to learn, but something happens along the way to quiet that desire.

People aren't born disengaged. We are born curious and wanting to learn, but something happens along the way to quiet that desire.

Gallup polls show that student engagement decreases as students move through our education systems (Hodges, 2018). That isn't because older students don't want to learn anymore. They just need us to think differently about how to engage them. We can start by thinking about how we align with the science of human motivation, as well as address the adolescent developmental needs we talked about in chapter 2 (page 53). How do we build connections in our classes and with our students, making sure to build in time for peer connection? How are we being real with our students while accepting and respecting them so they trust us enough to try harder in our classes? How do we scaffold our lessons carefully to build competence, especially for those students who don't believe they can succeed, while also making content relevant to real life? How do we share control and give students autonomy as we facilitate their learning? It also helps to think about two additional factors that impact adolescent engagement: (1) human needs and (2) the roles of self-efficacy and hope in motivation to engage.

Human Needs

I'm sure you've heard "Maslow before Bloom" when it comes to supporting students in school and increasing engagement. This phrase refers to how important it is to address a student's human needs before they can engage in the cognitive skills outlined in Bloom's taxonomy. Abraham Maslow was a prominent psychologist in the 1940s who explored and wrote about human needs (Maslow, 1999; McLeod, 2018). In Maslow's hierarchy, there are five levels of needs divided into three categories: (1) basic needs (physiological and safety), (2) psychological needs (belonging and esteem), and (3) self-fulfillment needs (self-actualization). Maslow also points out that we have deficiency needs and growth needs. *Deficiency needs* are those that meet a basic or possibly psychological need, such as food, safety, or feelings of belonging. *Growth needs* help individuals meet their full potentials and come from a desire to grow, such as cognitive, creative, and personal growth needs and the need for beauty and harmony.

Maslow's hierarchy is well-known in the field of education; however, often only his first two levels (physiological and safety needs) are emphasized. My study shows that positive deviant teachers meet student needs at all five levels of Maslow's hierarchy. When students hadn't slept all night, teachers gave them space to take a nap (with the agreement that the student would make up the work and work harder the next day). They designed their classrooms and class cultures so that students felt safe. If students were hungry, they gave them food. They connected with students, created a sense of belonging, and helped students feel valued. They scaffolded their lessons so that students' confidence, esteem, and self-image improved. And they met students' self-actualization needs by encouraging students to be themselves (by seeing, accepting, and not judging them), guiding self-reflection, encouraging students to discover their interests and passions, and showing them that their lives had more possibilities than they once believed (Knighton, 2022). The former students in my study said they tried harder for their positive deviant teachers. In part, this was not only because it made students feel cared about and valued when teachers did these things, but also because they saw how much effort their teachers were putting into them, and they didn't want to let their teachers down (Knighton, 2022).

Self-Efficacy, Hope, and Locus of Control

Some of our most disengaged students have a history of adversity or trauma. When students grow up in these types of situations where they feel powerless, they can develop the belief that they have no power in the world. This can be seen in their lack of self-efficacy, an external locus of control, and low hope for the future, all of which impact the motivation they have to engage in our classes (Dixson et al., 2017; Phan, 2013; Sujadi & Aulianisya, 2020). *Self-efficacy* is the belief that we will be successful if we attempt to do something (Bandura, 2006). *External locus of control* is the belief that everything that happens in your life is due to external factors and that nothing you do personally will change your life path (Sujadi & Aulianisya, 2020). Lack of hope for the future is one of the primary reasons students drop out of school, whereas having hopeful thinking is associated with increased engagement and academic achievement (Marques et al., 2015; Rubens et al., 2020). When students don't think they will succeed, believe that nothing they do will impact their lives, or have little hope for their futures, it decreases motivation to engage, because they don't see how their efforts will make a difference in their lives. Who loves to do something they are sure they will fail at or that they think won't matter?

When we see students who won't try, we feel frustrated and helpless, but what we aren't seeing is that underneath that apparent apathy is a student who doesn't believe they will succeed, doesn't think their actions can positively impact their lives, or doesn't know how to reach a goal or believe they can do so. Sometimes these students are battling all three of those beliefs at the same time.

Take a moment to read and answer the following self-reflection questions.

Reflecting

ON SELF-EFFICACY, HOPE, AND LOCUS OF CONTROL

WALKING IN OUR STUDENTS' SHOES

Think about a time when you didn't think you could succeed at something or were hopeless that something would work. It might have been trying to lose weight, changing a habit you didn't like, repairing a relationship that had turned south, or surviving the loss of a loved one.

- What happened for you when you faced that seemingly insurmountable struggle?

- How sustainable were your efforts to tackle it?

- Did you do it on your own or did you need help?

continued →

- Did you start to try and then give up? Why? If you didn't give up, what helped you persevere?

Visit ***go.SolutionTree.com/teacherefficacy*** *for a free reproducible version of this reflection.*

When we don't think we can succeed at something or we don't have hope that something will work out, we are significantly less likely to do something about it. This is what happens for our students. Sometimes we look at our students, and we think, *They just won't even try.* We label them the "students who won't" and compare them to the "students who can't." "Students who won't" are often facing an insurmountable struggle with the belief that they will not be successful in school or in life, so they don't try. Oftentimes this lack of hope exists because of the extreme life struggles these students have gone through. That is when our job as teachers becomes so much more important. We need to believe in our students until we can lead them to believe in themselves.

We need to believe in our students until we can lead them to believe in themselves.

We can help our students change those beliefs. We can increase their self-efficacy through careful scaffolding so they do succeed, and they start to believe they can succeed.

One of the biggest gifts we can give our students is to shift their external locus of control by helping them self-reflect and begin to see that their actions do impact their lives—in good or bad ways. The assistant principal mentioned in chapter 2 (page 53) was able to do this through drawing a map on his window of the chain of events that led a student to his office. When students realize they do have some power to influence their life path, it can have a huge impact on the trajectories of their lives. We can help students develop hopeful thinking by teaching them the skill of sequentially thinking through the steps to reach a goal and providing opportunities for them to achieve even small goals so they begin to believe there is hope for their futures. See appendix C ("Realistic Goal Setting," page 265) for an example of how to do this. Finally, increasing students' self-efficacy by meeting them where they are and carefully scaffolding lessons can transform a student's academic self-concept. Appendix B (page 239) is one example of how my coauthor, Jessica, helps her students shift from thinking they are incapable of writing to being confident language arts students. These shifts in thinking will increase students' engagement in our classes and their success in life.

Barriers to Engagement and Ways to Address Them

Sometimes we can get stuck in a rhythm of adhering to the processes, systems, or policies in our classrooms or schools without stopping to think about the bigger picture of why we are there, which is to facilitate students' learning and growth. Sometimes our processes, systems, or policies inadvertently create barriers to student engagement and learning, and sometimes a student's own beliefs about themselves create these barriers. When we slow down and begin to ask *why* a student isn't engaging, it can help us identify and address the barriers they are facing.

If a student is not working in your class, struggling with attendance, or resisting what you ask them to do, there is a reason. When you pause and ask yourself, "What is the barrier that might be leading to that behavior?" it helps you do two things: (1) feel less frustrated with the behavior because you are seeking to understand it and (2) start a process to removing the barriers that prevent engagement. Let's look at a few examples.

- A student is disrupting class because they have an academic gap they don't want their peers to see. Once you understand that, you can better provide scaffolding or interventions.
- A student doesn't believe that school adds value to their life, so they don't engage. You can show them how what they're learning connects to real life, examine what they want in their future, and ask guiding questions that illuminate how school is a gateway to that.
- A student doesn't show up to school or consistently arrives late because they have to care for family members. You can explore adjusting their schedule so they don't miss anything or partner with the family to find another option that meets their need so the student can help them and still get to school on time.

- A student struggles with mathematics and becomes easily overwhelmed. You can reduce the number of problems the student is assigned to complete so they can be successful.

As teachers, we influence the trajectories of our students' lives. We can either remove barriers and support the love of learning or we can ignore barriers and stifle it. I (Rebecca) had a student who was gifted at mathematics. She loved the challenge of finding solutions to the mathematics problems in her head and she often solved them differently than how the teacher was showing the class to do it. In the middle of seventh grade, this student came to me and told me she hated mathematics. She explained that having to show her work on every problem was taking away what she loved most about the subject. I explained to her that as mathematics gets harder, it starts to take pages of work to solve, and you must be able to write down the steps. Her teacher just wanted to make sure she knew those steps so she would succeed at higher mathematics levels once she got there. But not wanting to kill this student's passion for learning, I suggested that we see if the mathematics teacher would work with her on this. Maybe we could find a way for this student to solve some of the problems in a way that was challenging and fun for her while showing her work on some of the other problems to demonstrate her thinking to the teacher. The teacher agreed to this arrangement and the student started to love her classwork again.

Alternatively, another middle school student who was highly gifted at mathematics experienced a different outcome when his barriers were not explored and addressed. This student didn't complete his homework because it wasn't challenging and because he consistently earned around 98 percent on tests; it seemed like a waste of time to him. Instead of asking him why he wouldn't do his homework, his gifted and talented mathematics teacher punished him for it and removed him from the program, taking away one of the things he enjoyed about school. His engagement in school steadily declined and he eventually dropped out. Before dropping out, he scored a 1580 on the SAT without any preparation or studying. Here was a highly gifted student who was completely disengaged. If his teachers had thought to ask *why* he wouldn't do his homework and then given him more challenging and relevant homework instead, his educational trajectory might have been very different.

The positive deviant teachers I studied were highly skilled at both anticipating and addressing barriers (Knighton, 2022). Many of them reviewed their students' cumulative files prior to the start of the year to get an idea of what supports they could implement immediately. One high school social studies teacher implemented alternative assessments for his students, many of whom were multilingual learners and whose English skills would have prevented them from succeeding in essay-based assessments and would not have been an accurate reflection of what they learned in their social studies class.

Sometimes engaging our most disengaged students requires us to think creatively to find outside-the-box solutions because they haven't been succeeding with the typical classroom approaches. When we know our content standards and where we need to take our students, it's OK to be creative about how we get there. If what we do meets the standards, it's often OK for it to be unconventional.

Take a moment to read and answer the following self-reflection questions.

Reflecting ON BARRIERS TO ENGAGEMENT

WALKING IN OUR STUDENTS' SHOES

Remember a time when you attended a class or conference session and you felt disengaged.

- Why did you feel disengaged?
- What thoughts, feelings, or reactions contributed to that disengagement?
- Were there any external factors (something about the teacher, the environment, other participants, and so on) that contributed to your disengagement?

continued →

- If you could have changed two things about that class or conference session that would have increased your engagement, what would they be?

Visit ***go.SolutionTree.com/teacherefficacy*** *for a free reproducible version of this reflection.*

JESSICA'S VIGNETTE

Sometimes we just need to meet individual students where they are, despite needing them to meet particular benchmarks. Besides teaching skills, our job is to have evidence of students hitting content standards, so sometimes we need to get creative about how that may look for certain students, whether they are in a gifted program, have an individualized education program (IEP), or don't have a specific educational plan.

I had a very intelligent student, Lance (not his real name), who was autistic and had an IEP. My students were writing an essay about who was the most influential person in the book *The Outsiders*. After the second day out of five in which students had class time to begin writing, Lance hadn't done a thing except read the entire period. I asked him what was up. Was he feeling OK? Would he like me to help him get started? He answered me by saying that essays were stupid, and he wasn't going to do it. Here's how the rest of the conversation went.

Me: I totally understand your feelings, Lance. Here's the thing: I need each of my students to show me they can organize their thoughts according to a topic. If you're willing to work with me, I'm also willing to work with you to create something besides an essay for this topic. What would you like to do instead to show who was the most influential person in *The Outsiders*?

Lance: I want to make a stop-motion movie with building bricks.

Me: Great! That sounds so cool! I would love to see what that would look like. Would you be willing [this allows him to feel like he's in control] to fill out a six-panel scene planning page where you draw a picture and tell me in one phrase [I specifically refrain from saying "sentence"] for each panel?

Lance: (*Reluctantly*) I guess.

Not only did I get Lance to write on the paper planning page, which was also evidence of his organized thoughts, but he also was engaged in the assignment because he got to use his imagination to answer the prompt. Asking Lance what he wanted to do was a game changer. As teachers, we don't always have to be the ones coming up with personalized assignments. If what we've created isn't working for all students, ask *them* what they want to do instead. In my experience, they have much better ideas than I do anyway!

Lance's stop-motion building-bricks movie showing how Dally was the most influential person in *The Outsiders* was amazing, very thoughtful, well planned out, and harder to show in actions than in words. It was also a refreshing change of pace for me as the teacher because grading essays is so repetitive.

Here's the takeaway: A big "hill to die on" as a teacher should always be doing what's best for students. If you can defend your professional choices—choosing to meet a student where they are—to your principal, superintendent, board of education, and beyond, then do it! We're told to differentiate for each student. As long as we can show how it meets the standards we're teaching, let all evidence be allowed.

Real-Life Connections to Content

Nelson Mandela identified the goal of education this way: "Education is the most powerful weapon which you can use in order to prepare our youth for their role as leaders of tomorrow" (GBH News, 1990). Can we achieve that goal when we get lost in the details, facts, and figures associated with our content area and forget what the larger picture is (why students need to know what we are teaching and how that knowledge or those skills will help them in life after school)? When students understand how our content area and the associated knowledge and skills pertain to and are relevant to their lives, they are more willing to engage in learning it (Shernoff, Csikszentmihalyi, Schneider, & Shernoff, 2014). When they don't see the point, they resist.

I (Rebecca) remember running into this trying to teach science to middle and high school students. I could probably retire if I had a dollar for every time a student asked me, "Why do I need to know this?" They didn't understand how knowing the biological structure of viruses and how they spread mattered to their lives unless they planned to become a doctor. They didn't realize that having a basic understanding of immunology and illness could help them if they were to become parents and their babies were sick. I made my lessons interactive, interesting, and engaging. I had students moving around the room acting out DNA replication, but did I do a good job of helping my students understand how learning my content applied to their lives? Did I teach them how learning to think critically would help them navigate the world more effectively in all settings? Probably not. We lose an opportunity to help our students build life skills that transcend our content areas when we focus too much on the content itself and not enough on why it matters or how it connects to deeper life skills.

We lose an opportunity to help our students build life skills that transcend our content areas when we focus too much on the content itself and not enough on why it matters or how it connects to deeper life skills.

Understanding and communicating the *why* of what we teach increases student engagement. How often have you sat through a staff training at your school or district and thought to yourself, *Why am I here? How is this going to help me in my classroom?* Students sit in your classroom asking themselves the same thing. As humans, we are motivated to do what we are being asked to do when we see value in it. Simon Sinek (2009) says it best, "People don't buy *what* you do, they buy *why* you do it." Though he was talking about businesses and customer sales, he communicated a truth about basic human motivation. When we share someone's vision, we are motivated to do what they ask us to do. This is true for educators, but it is also true for students.

Sometimes in schools we lose track of our individual and collective why. We get lost in the day-to-day stresses and expectations, and we forget why we became teachers in the first place. We forget why learning our content matters in the world outside of school. What life skills or lessons can our content areas provide for students? How can we use our content areas to help students understand what it means to be good humans and highly functioning adults who can navigate the world well? How can we use our content to help our students better understand themselves and others so they can contribute positively to their families and to society?

For example, if you teach physical education, your *why* might be teaching teamwork or how to work with others you may not know or understand outside of that setting. If you teach social studies, your *why* might be understanding what motivates leaders of countries or how to critically evaluate sources of information to determine whether those sources are credible. If you teach English language arts, your *why* might be teaching students how to structure a paragraph so they can communicate well with others; we don't learn to write essays just to know how to write essays but to communicate ideas effectively.

Not understanding the deeper *why* of what we teach makes it harder to connect with and engage students, especially at the secondary level. Sometimes we can get lost in the weeds when designing our lessons. We can get caught up in what we think we should do. Instead, we find it helpful to take a wider view. Step back and ask yourself, "Who are my students (what do they need, what is their content knowledge, and what is their skill level)? Where do I need to take them (what skills and knowledge do I want them to learn)? How can I guide them from where they are to where they need to be?"

Looking Inward: Flipping the Script

In this section, you will have the opportunity to engage in two activities, shown in figures 4.1 (page 137) and 4.2 (page 140). These activities are designed to help you understand yourself better and develop some of the skills discussed in this chapter.

Given what you've read in this chapter, remember back to when you were in middle and high school. Then reflect on the following questions.

1. Describe the teacher you worked the hardest for. What was it about this teacher that motivated you to work for them? (What did they do? How did they interact with you?)

Figure 4.1: Reflecting on motivation in school.

continued →

2. Describe a teacher you were not motivated to work hard for. What was it about this teacher that decreased the motivation you felt in their class? (What did they do? How did they interact with you?)

3. Think about what motivates you now. Are there any similarities between that and what motivated you as an adolescent?

Now, think about your students, what motivates them, and you, as a teacher. Reflect on the following questions in the space provided.

1. Think about the type of teacher you are. Do you share any of the qualities or approaches of the teacher you were motivated to work the hardest for?

2. Do you share any of the qualities or approaches of the teacher you weren't as motivated to work for?

3. In thinking about what motivates humans (connection, competence, and autonomy) and in thinking about human needs (physiological needs, safety, belonging, esteem, and self-fulfillment), what are two things you do well to motivate and engage your students?

4. Remember a lesson or activity you led that students did not seem motivated to engage in like you'd hoped. Based on what we've talked about in this chapter, what would you change about that lesson or activity that might increase your students' motivation and engagement?

Visit ***go.SolutionTree.com/teacherefficacy*** *for a free reproducible version of this figure.*

Part 1

We have all experienced a barrier to learning at one point or another. It might have been our own internal barrier (negative self-talk, distraction by difficult life events, disinterest in the content, and so on). It might have been an external barrier (the classroom environment, the way something was taught, and so on). Or it might have been a combination of internal and external barriers (your relationship with the teacher; cultural or religious incompatibilities; or too wide of a gap between your knowledge, skills, and abilities and what was being taught). Consider the following questions about barriers.

- Remember a time in school (or as an adult) when you were not engaged. What were the barriers for you?

- What do you wish your teacher would have done to either remove the barrier or help you overcome it?

Part 2

In this section, we are going to practice anticipating a student's barriers and thinking creatively about how to remove those barriers or help that student overcome them. Choose option 1 or 2 to engage with this activity.

Option 1

Think about a student you've had or currently have who is disengaged in your class.

- What does their disengagement look like? (What are they doing or not doing, saying or not saying?)

- Based on what you know about this student, what external barriers might be contributing to this student's disengagement?

- How might you think creatively to address these barriers and support this student's engagement in your class?

Option 2:

This activity pertains to a seventh-grade male student whose father left him, his three brothers, and his mother. A few years later, this student's father ended up in prison. Due to these events, he has a severe sense of abandonment and has a difficult time trusting others, let alone showing them respect. This student has a seven-year reading and writing gap. He comes into every class, goes to his seat, and puts his hood up and his head down on the desk. He won't talk to the teacher or his peers and refuses to answer any questions, let alone participate in anything happening in class.

- What internal barriers might be contributing to this student's disengagement?

Figure 4.2: Anticipating, accepting, and addressing barriers.

continued →

- How might you think creatively to address these barriers and support his engagement in your class?

Visit ***go.SolutionTree.com/teacherefficacy*** *for a free reproducible ver-sion of this figure.*

Learning From the Five Teacher Types

This section presents two common scenarios. For each scenario, the five positive deviant teachers you met in the introduction describe how they navigate these scenarios in their practice. The first is how to connect class content to real life, and the second is how to engage a student who rarely participates in class. As you read through these examples, highlight, underline, or circle the parts you relate to.

Scenario: You're not sure how to connect class content to real life

The following sections describe how each teacher type approaches this scenario in their classroom.

Teacher Type: Caring Connector

I teach high school social studies as my main subject area, which allows me to regularly and organically connect content to real life. It is helpful to do some of the legwork early in the semester. You read in chapter 1 (page 39) that I typically begin each new course by giving every student a questionnaire that they can fill out with information about themselves (favorite movie, hobbies, part-time job, favorite subjects, and so on). Knowing about their interests allows me to gauge the different interests represented among these students so I can connect the curriculum to their lives in a more meaningful way.

For example, when I teach grade 10 social studies, the focus is on to what extent we should embrace globalization. In the first unit, which focuses on how globalization impacts identity, I give a culminating project in which students choose any cultural phenomenon they are interested in and answer the big questions from the unit by researching that phenomenon. I have had students present on video games, fashion, dance, sports, social media, religion, and many other topics. They are typically very engaged with this project because they chose the topic, it is something they are passionate about or interested in, and they realize the content we are learning in class has a direct impact on their real life and identity.

Teacher Type: Gentle Giant

Being a physical education teacher is awesome for connecting content to real life. Pretty much every activity in class can be discussed through so many different lenses.

We talk a lot in class about the different roles and responsibilities we take on in sports and games and how those relate to our social responsibilities in regular day-to-day events. Vulnerability is another huge talking point. We discuss in class how being willing to fail is sometimes necessary. This is helpful in explaining that learning new skills is a process; for example, learning to throw a perfect spiral will take practice, or driving a car may not come naturally or easily to each student. We use physical education to help students develop an understanding of growth mindset, confidence development, and character building—ideas that easily relate to real-world situations.

Teacher Type: Nurturing Narrator

Students will often come into social studies class with a predisposition of "I hate history" or "I am not good at it." Oftentimes, though, they don't realize that they don't hate history—they just haven't had the chance to truly understand it yet. I am lucky to teach Worldviews in Conflict, which has so many dark undertones it grabs students' attention almost immediately. Students, like most adults, have a call to the dark side of human nature. Presenting history in this way gives them an avenue to understanding. I have found in my time that students of all walks want to be told stories by their teacher. As we take an immersive journey through the curriculum, we also explore many asides; sometimes it takes an entire class for us to come back to where we started. Oftentimes in social studies, I let students guide our path—and I am honest when I don't know the answer. I tell them I am not an encyclopedia, and we look up answers together. Students connect social studies to real life through the passion of their teacher; the textbook is only a supplementary resource in my class. Students learn the content through acting, role playing, and direct lecture. I walk through the rows, call on students to help me act out historical scenarios, have deep discussions, and engage students through their own interests. Students who connect social studies to the untapped dangerous potential of humans pretty quickly stop asking me, "When will I ever use this?" because we build an understanding that we're living it. I always tell my students, "To the victor goes the pen," and that is as real today as it was a thousand years ago.

Teacher Type: Perceptive Pragmatist

It's inevitable that at some point a student is going to ask, "When are we ever going to need to know this?" I used to make sure I had a response to the real-world application of everything we did. However, the reality is that there are many things we learn in school that don't apply directly to real life. Instead, my answer has shifted over the years. Are my students ever going to complete the square on a quadratic equation to find the dimensions that offer the maximum area for their yard? Probably not, but what they will encounter is a problem in their life that needs solving, and they need to think about all the tools and strategies at their disposal that can help them resolve the problem. So instead, I help students reframe the question to ask, "How does this grow our brain?" or "How will this kind of thinking help us in the future?"

Teacher Type: Warm Demander

The first two questions I ask myself about any lesson I'm going to are, What is the real-world relevance? and How does that relate to my students? Many times, I have to dig deep for the answers, but once I do, I know I can present a reason for why they need to learn the material. Secondary students always need to know the why *before they decide it's worthy of their time. If it's not something that they think they need to know, no teacher will be able to actively engage them, and the learning process will never get started.*

My second step is to determine what my attention-getter is going to be. If I were a teenager, what would interest me? A video with great graphics? A catchy song? A movie clip? Role playing? A visual demonstration? An activity that gets everyone up and moving? A quick game? A teamwork activity that involves candy? Kahoot!? A scavenger hunt? I've done them all. These days, we teachers have the awesome availability of material online, so I often start there. I then take what I find and tailor it to my lesson's needs.

When beginning my Family and Consumer Sciences class each semester, I need my students to understand the importance of teamwork and sharing the load, because when they're in their kitchens following a recipe, they need to each have a role and do that job well for the food to turn out correctly. If I don't start with this, each kitchen will have one student who does nothing except eat the food at the end. My "Do Now" for the start of class is a YouTube video called "Teamwork With a Cause," which is an excerpt from the movie Here Comes the Boom (Miller, 2013). *On the surface, this video has nothing to do with cooking in a kitchen, but the underlying message can be applied to any situation. After watching the three-minute video, my students do a two-minute turn and talk at their tables to discuss the answer to one question: How does this video connect to cooking in a kitchen with their tablemates? They choose the best answer from their table and each table quickly shares out their group's answer to the rest of the class.*

The lesson starts by going over our daily agenda, which includes the real-world relevance (RWR) and the day's fun fact. For this lesson, the RWR is this: In practically any job you have, it'll be important to have strong teamwork, a plan before starting, and specific roles assigned to share the workload and reduce mistakes, missed deadlines, and possible injuries. The fun fact is this: The most common injuries in the kitchen are burns, fires, and cuts.

From there, I teach a student-centered lesson where each kitchen group comes up with how burns, fires, and cuts could happen in the kitchen and how to avoid them. Students make a list of the possible roles they think will need to be assigned when cooking and baking. They write a description of duties for each role, which will be on a rotation basis, and everyone signs the paper as a group contract commitment. Finally, students come up with consequences for any team member who doesn't meet the contract's expectations. Each student signs their name again to show they understand their responsibilities. I enforce these agreed-on consequences.

When students lead and create anything, they feel ownership and a responsibility to hold each other accountable—more so than I ever could because I'm overseeing thirty students at once. This leads my students and sets them up for fair group scoring and self-scoring themselves for each future activity in class.

Given what you've learned in this chapter, think about and answer the following reflection questions.

Connecting CLASS CONTENT TO REAL LIFE

WHAT WOULD YOU DO?

Think about how you make your content relevant to your students.

- Do you currently connect your content to real life? In what ways?

continued →

- Do you have any internal resistance to connecting your content to real-life, real-world relevance? If so, where does that resistance come from? Why is it there?

- Based on what you've read, what ideas do you have for connecting your content to real life?

*Visit **go.SolutionTree.com/teacherefficacy** for a free reproducible version of this reflection.*

Scenario: You have a student who rarely engages in class

The following sections describe how each teacher type approaches this scenario in their classroom.

Teacher Type: Caring Connector

This is a common issue that arises in a social studies classroom. Since we are often discussing political or other controversial issues, students will be afraid to voice their perspectives, particularly if it differs from the other students. So, it is best not to completely rely on full-class discussions; you might only hear from the few loud personalities in your room. What I like to do is give students time to chat about issues with their friends or other students sitting around them while I roam around the room and ask questions to these smaller groups. Most of the time, they are way more comfortable sharing their thoughts in this type of low-pressure scenario.

If a student is still not engaging after this, I try to have a one-on-one conversation with them. Typically, if they aren't engaging at all, they either don't understand the task or expectations or something is going on with them outside of school. Usually, due to the connections that I build with the students at the beginning of the semester, they are often willing to share with me what the issue is. If it is too difficult, I will simplify the task or clarify the instructions. If there is something going on at home, I can give additional time or refer them to our wellness team. If it is an issue of interest, I will try to connect the task to their own life and collaborate with the student to brainstorm ways to make the work more interesting and relevant to them.

Teacher Type: Gentle Giant

This is a tricky one. I am concerned that the student is disengaged, especially since engagement in a class activity is paramount. The best answer I have for how to navigate this is trust *and* encouragement.

Students in physical education disengage for so many different reasons: fear, peer pressure, inability, lack of confidence, feeling sick, being tired, disinterest, and so on. Typically, the best way through any of these issues is to encourage and cheer on the student. Many students just need that vote of confidence from me that I believe in them, and they should too! Over time, modeling this allows other students to do the same. We work hard to make classes community focused, and often other students will do the work for me. They invite others to play, assist with skill learning, and develop groups to include all members of the class.

As the year goes on, we try to reiterate the importance of social responsibilities; we talk about how to be involved in games and activities in different capacities. An example may be a student who doesn't want to play soccer. Maybe I have them referee with me. Sometimes they keep score. Heck, I even let them announce the games, if they are willing.

My goal is to show students that there are so many different opportunities, outside of being the star athlete, to be successful in physical education and, ultimately, in life.

Teacher Type: Nurturing Narrator

Students sometimes need to be able to unlearn their own negative self-talk before they can find new success in class (especially in a class they hate). The very first thing I do each year is assign a written personal narrative that I use to intentionally "cook the books" (start them out with higher grades and boost their confidence). I often will scribe for students who are more challenging, as this gives me a lot of insight into their lives. What they're willing to share with me sets me up to know what they need from me. Once students hand in these personal narratives, I give them high marks—because honestly it is difficult to mark personal narratives on content. I always tell them we will focus on grammar later, but for now, I just want them to write. Positive reinforcement isn't the only strategy in this; it also incorporates students' interests, gives them choice and autonomy, and helps build relationships. I also keep these submissions. I put them in a binder behind my desk, and I intentionally read them a couple times throughout the year. I will touch base with students privately about what they wrote. Maybe on their way into my classroom one day, I will stop them and say, "Thank you so much for trusting me with your journey so far; you have a beautiful voice behind your writing." Students don't always respond, and in this strategy, you also need to be prepared for what students may write to you. I do this personal response other times throughout the year, and as their trust in me grows, so does my access to some of the more difficult parts of their lives. Any time a student trusts me with sensitive information, I always follow up, and in my early years of teaching, this was very uncomfortable for me. The years and experiences have not made some of these conversations any less intense, and learning how to leave some things at school is important. When the baggage is really heavy, I remind myself to leave it here—it'll be waiting for me the next day. Crying privately at home for students' struggles and resetting is so critical. The weight of the connection is still there the next day, but each day it is less daunting.

My approach to all strategies starts with relationships. I find once students trust me and know that we are on the same team and that their success is my number one priority, having them engage is a lot easier. This doesn't mean challenging students are going to be raising their hands and getting honor roll, by any means, but it does mean I can give them breaks, walks, or flexible seating arrangements, and they always come back. I can set clear goals and expectations, and the students don't push back as strongly, outright refuse, or leave. We work together as often as possible. I have a table attached to my desk where students come and sit during independent work periods. Once the groundwork is established for trust, I never have enough seats—they are always filled first with my students who historically have had the most challenging behaviors.

Teacher Type: Perceptive Pragmatist

Before discussing any strategies, I want to establish what I consider participation to be in my class. As a student (and honestly, still as an adult), I hated *being called on to answer a question or read aloud when I wasn't volunteering. Based on the number of students who write something similar on their "getting to know you" sheets I give at the beginning of the semester, it is something that is incredibly anxiety-inducing for many. I have always made it a rule for myself that I will never do this to students, and I tell them so right off the bat. Their audible sigh of relief always reassures me that this is the right decision. In my class, participation means you can be as quiet and reserved as you want, but you must be alert if I'm instructing and be productive if it's work time.*

When I have students who rarely participate, it usually comes up during work time. The strategy I am going to address is for students who won't attempt anything on their own and are resistant to accepting help. My first goal is not to get them engaged with the content, but to connect.

When I have a withdrawn student, most often they don't have a group of friends to work with and are generally hesitant to accept help right off the bat. I actually avoid making our interactions about schoolwork at the beginning. I take some time to connect with them in small ways: making sure I am saying hi every day; asking about what they're reading; or commenting on their doodles, the shirt they are wearing, or some other personal detail. I also make sure that these are done in ways that are respectful of the fact that the student is reserved and doesn't want a lot of attention drawn to them. Not only does it give the student a chance to see me as a human who cares about them and not just their productivity, but it also allows them to trust that when I offer help, I'm genuine about it and am going to offer it in a way that works for them. I find that after having just a few genuine moments of connection, these students are comfortable enough to work with me and even take the initiative to ask for help.

The other type of student who frequently is disengaged is the class-clown type. These students are not afraid of having attention drawn to them and are usually fine with some banter. I find that often these students use their humor and disruption to get out of doing the work they perceive as their weakness. My strategy with these students is to get them participating in nonacademic ways and to make sure humor is at the center of most of our interactions. I say things like, "Hey, since you're not doing any math right now, anyway, do you think you could help me bring this stack of textbooks to the library?" I have never had a student not jump up at the opportunity to help with a special job. I make sure that I go with them as an opportunity to have a normal conversation about sports, video games, or other interests. By the time we get back, I can usually get them working by saying something like, "Thanks so much for your help! Do you want to pull up a chair, and maybe I can help you get a few questions done?" This isn't usually enough to get them to permanently turn over a new leaf, but frequent relationship building typically results in them enjoying coming to class, which makes them way more likely to engage in the future.

Teacher Type: Warm Demander

First, I need to figure out why students aren't engaged. When it comes to secondary students it's usually one of two things: (1) either they don't want to make a mistake in front of their peers, so they act like they don't care and won't try, or (2) it's because they truly don't have the skill set to do what is being asked, and there's no way they want their peers to know that either. The only way to get them to do anything is to create a safe place for them to try, which begins by building trust with the teacher.

I always ask myself, "What do I know they can do successfully, right now?" The simplest answer: I start by giving them a job. Every student can run an errand, pass out papers, and sharpen pencils. It just so happens that every school I've taught in has incentive school bucks that I can give to students for a multitude of reasons. I make sure to give out a lot of them and *make them worth things that students want, but don't cost me money. Some examples are sitting where they want for the day, being teacher assistant, sitting at my desk, being king or queen for the day, and so on. However, I realized I was so focused on teaching and watching my room that I'd forget to pass them out, so I gave the job to one of my students who didn't participate. These are usually the students who other adults don't trust one lick, which is perfect for me. I can use both the lack of participation and trust as a platform to not only build trust with that student, but also build their confidence level enough that the combination of the two create a safe environment for the student to* try.

Being transparent and honest up front is the absolute key to this method. Here's an example of a private conversation between me and a student, Ryan (not his real name).

Me: Hey, Ryan, I was wondering if you could help me with something.

Ryan: What?

Me: Well, I've been so busy walking around teaching and asking questions that I forget to pass out Pride Tickets. I was hoping you'd be willing to walk around during class discussions and give one Pride Ticket to anyone who answered a question—right or wrong—or made a comment. Number one, this would take a load off my plate and help me immensely. Number two, it would get you up and walking around, because I know how much you need movement. So, can you help me out?

Ryan: Yeah, I guess.

Me: That's terrific. Now, what would most people be afraid you might do with the Pride Tickets since you have a stack of fifty of them in your hands?

Ryan: They'd think I'd steal them.

Me: Right, which I know you won't do. What else might they think you'd do with them?

Ryan: Probably think I'd give extras to my friends.

Me: Exactly, but again, I know you won't do that. What do you think would happen between you and me if you did either of those two things?

Ryan: You'd be mad.

Me: Not mad. Disappointed? Yes. But what would happen with our relationship?

Ryan: It would be bad.

Me: Because . . . ?

Ryan: You wouldn't trust me anymore.

Me: Correct. And what would happen if I didn't trust you anymore?

Ryan: You wouldn't let me do anything.

Me: Like what?

Ryan: Like go to the bathroom or get a drink of water.

Me: Right. I wouldn't be able to let you out of my sight because I wouldn't be able to trust you. Anything else?

Ryan: I wouldn't get to pass out Pride Tickets anymore or sit by my friends when I ask.

Me: Correct. And I know you know I don't want to have to be like that with you. You're a great guy. But now you know the level of control and power you have by taking on this job for me. I'm giving you the privilege and permission to go into my top desk drawer every day to grab the Pride Tickets and then at the end of class to put them back without me watching you because I trust you fully. Are you still willing to help me out?

Ryan: Yes.

Me: Perfect! I knew I could count on you! Thank you so much, Ryan.

You may be thinking to yourself that the content of this conversation is a given; of course, they know all this. However, assumptions get us nowhere real fast. Students frequently tell me they've never had such a straightforward conversation with a teacher. We also need to remember that the adolescent brain requires frequent reminders. We feel like a broken record, but that's developmentally where our students are, so we need to meet them where they're at. Talking out a thought process and what the consequences will be allows students to relax because we've removed the unknown for them. The conversation stays with them later when they are pondering doing the wrong thing, and because of this, they will usually stay on the straight and narrow because we took the time to explain the repercussions of their decision making and how it affects others.

And finally, having gained the students' trust and respect by having the conversation and giving them a job, I can now ask them to attempt one or two questions on an assignment that I know they can do, even if it's just writing their name and choosing two questions to verbally answer with me. Taking baby steps helps students feel successful, so do not start by asking them to complete the entire assignment.

It's also important that we remember that adolescent students are very hormonal beings; we shouldn't get unduly concerned when they backslide. Life happens and life is tough—for everyone. Be patient, give them grace, go back to the first step, and build them back up again.

Given what you've learned in this chapter, think about and answer the following reflection questions.

WHAT WOULD YOU DO?

Reflecting ON STUDENT DISENGAGEMENT

Think about how you normally try to engage a student who rarely participates in class.

- When you have a student who rarely participates in class, what are your initial reactions and thoughts?

- What are your emotional responses when this happens? Does it trigger you?

- How might you have responded in the past?

- Based on what you've read and the previous examples, how might you respond now?

*Visit **go.SolutionTree.com/teacherefficacy** for a free reproducible version of this reflection.*

Wrapping Up

Engaging adolescents can be challenging. Because of where they are in their development, they need to understand the real-world relevance of what we teach. Engagement is also more effective when we understand both what motivates them and what barriers they might be facing. When we can build connection with our students; design lessons that help them develop self-efficacy and competence; give students options to have autonomy in our classes; and anticipate, accept, and address the internal and external barriers to engagement that they may be encountering, we can increase their motivation to participate and learn in our classes.

Chapter 4 Book Study Questions

As a staff, explore the concepts presented in this chapter and reflect on how they are evidenced in or might impact your school culture. As you read each of the following questions, think about how you would respond based on your individual role. If you are an administrator, think about these questions as you reflect on how you support your staff. If you are a teacher or support staff member, think about these questions as you reflect on how you support students.

1. Reflect on each of the three types of engagement (cognitive, emotional, and behavioral). How do you, or how might you, address all three for your students?

2. What is your school culture when it comes to being creative or thinking outside of the box about addressing student barriers? Is there something you would like to try, but are hesitant about? Why?

3. What is an engagement strategy you've seen someone else do, learned about at a conference, or read about in this book that you want to try? Describe what that might look like.

4. Are the factors that motivate people (connection, competence, and autonomy) present in your school? Are they present in your classroom? What might you change to increase the presence of these factors?

CHAPTER 5

Navigating Student Conflict and Behavior

One of the most difficult aspects of our jobs as educators is how to effectively manage student behavior and conflict. It is also one of the most common barriers to developing positive relationships and creating safety and connection in our classrooms. We know that students who have positive relationships with their teachers are more likely to have higher engagement and achievement in our classes (Roorda et al., 2017), fewer behavior incidents, and improved high school outcomes, such as graduation rates and post-secondary plans (Romero, 2015), than students who don't. We also know that how we navigate conflict with students impacts our well-being, job satisfaction, and motivation (Aloe et al., 2014; Spilt & Koomen, 2009). But it is hard to have a positive relationship with someone when there is constant struggle and neither party feels like the other person cares about them. Our jobs as educators would be so much easier if all students were naturally engaged and easy to relate to, if all we had to do was facilitate learning, but with so many students coming into our classrooms with a history of trauma or other complicating life factors, it just isn't our reality.

In this chapter, we share strategies positive deviant teachers use that make them highly successful at navigating student behavior and conflict. We explore topics such as recognizing the cycle of negative teacher-student relationships, managing student conflict, leading and motivating students, and common classroom management myths. Then, we practice flipping the script through self-reflection activities. Finally, we end the chapter by hearing how the five teacher types respond to two common scenarios related to navigating challenging behaviors and conflict with students.

Looking Outward: Themes in Research and Practice

Maybe one of the biggest problems with how we approach unwanted student behavior is that we think we should be "managing it." The idea of managing behavior implies that we can somehow control how our students behave. When we let go of trying to control students, we can shift instead to a model of leading and motivating them. Let's dig into what perpetuates negative teacher-student relationships, how we navigate conflict, and how we might shift our approach from managing students to leading and motivating them.

Recognizing the Cycle of Negative Teacher-Student Relationships

When I (Rebecca) was working on my PhD, I read a lot of research about teacher-student relationships, teacher stress and burnout, and student behavior. The research reflects what many of us have experienced: a cyclical dynamic between relationships, behavior, stress, and burnout. When we are faced with frequent student behavior struggles and chronic student conflict, and if we feel ill-equipped to navigate it, it creates feelings of stress and helplessness (Chang, 2013; Spilt & Koomen, 2009). When that happens, we are more likely to use punitive and reactive forms of discipline, such as office discipline referrals (Eddy et al., 2020). These forms of discipline tend to damage teacher-student relationships, which, in turn, increase the likelihood that students will have higher rates of unwanted behavior and decreased engagement. This creates a negative cycle where student and teacher behavior negatively impact one another. Figure 5.1 (page 159) illustrates this cyclical dynamic.

We've all been there. Certain student behaviors trigger us when others don't, and how stressed or burned out we are impacts how patiently we navigate those conflicts. So, what do we do about it? We must understand what factors contribute to

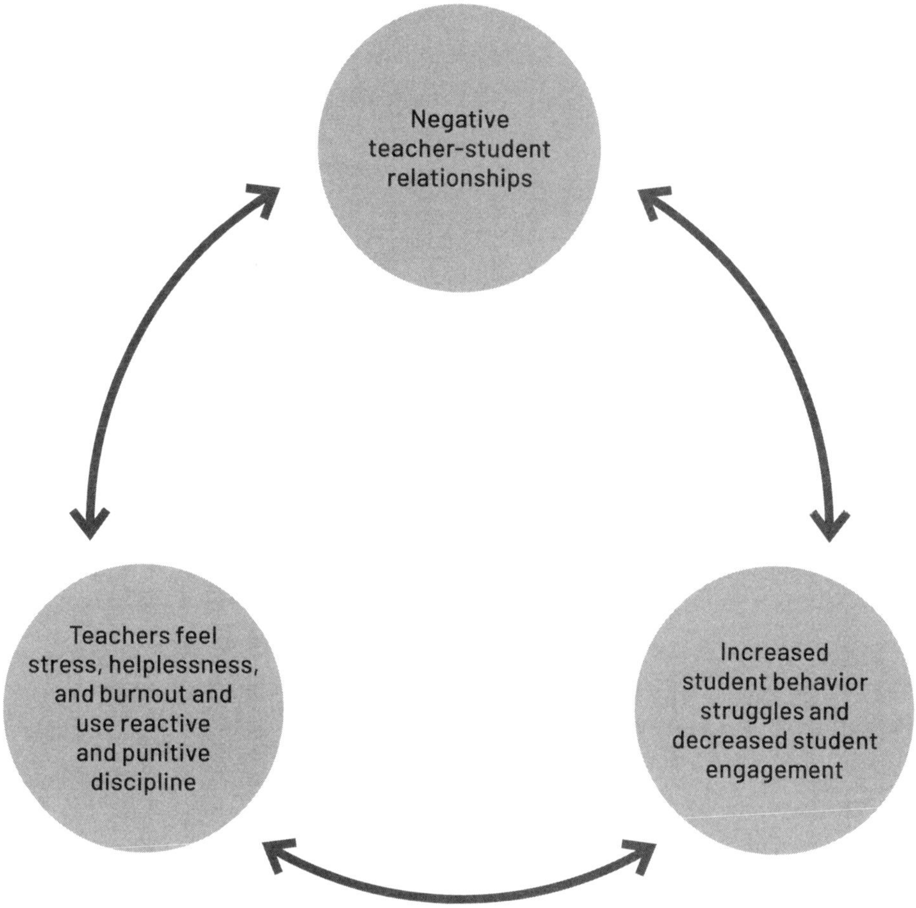

Source: Knighton, 2022.

Figure 5.1: Cyclical dynamic of negative teacher-student relationships.

teacher-student conflict, understand why we respond to certain student behaviors the way we do, and figure out how to minimize unwanted behaviors and respond to them more effectively when they do arise.

Managing Student Conflict

There is always something going on underneath the surface leading to challenging student behaviors. The more empathy and curiosity we can have for why students exhibit specific challenging behaviors, the more effectively we can manage the conflicts we find ourselves in. Remember, they are fellow humans and share the same human needs we all have (safety, belonging, sense of purpose, feeling seen and understood, finding and expressing their authentic voices, and so on). If they resist doing something we ask them to do, it is most likely because it pushes against a human need.

Additionally, when teachers find themselves triggered and react to student behavior with anger, students respond to and match that anger. The more teachers can understand why certain behaviors push their buttons, the more they will be able to control their responses to those behaviors. These are opportunities to both preserve the relationship and model how to effectively navigate conflict.

Remember, they are fellow humans and share the same human needs we all have (safety, belonging, sense of purpose, feeling seen and understood, finding and expressing their authentic voices, and so on). If they resist doing something we ask them to do, it is most likely because it pushes against a human need.

There is a lot of guidance out there about the importance of teachers regulating their own emotions when students' emotions are elevated. It's true. We can't resolve a conflict with a student or help them regulate their own emotions if we are also in an elevated state. It is also ineffective to fake it, to be outwardly calm while internally still livid. Students can sense that and won't be responsive, especially if they come from homes or communities where their survival depends on reading people. When we are emotionally elevated, it is incredibly difficult to talk ourselves out of it and be both outwardly and inwardly calm and present. So, what do we do? We are human and have our own emotional reactions to people and situations just like everyone else.

To navigate student conflict in a manner that leads to positive relationships and increased engagement and achievement for students and greater job satisfaction for us, it's helpful to remember two things we mentioned earlier in this book. First, it is important to gain greater self-awareness of our own internal responses to student behaviors (which are most likely tied to our core beliefs and assumptions about why students do what they do). Second, we become less reactive when we seek to truly understand why students are behaving the way they are—through examining the factors that influence students' reactions to us, our content, and school in general, such as adolescent development, exposure to AELEs (trauma, neglect, bullying, chronic toxic stress, and so on), and students' beliefs about their abilities and lack of hope for the future. Let's look at each of these more closely in the following sections.

Understanding Our Core Beliefs

Often our reactions to student behaviors result from core beliefs we have about ourselves, the world, how individuals should behave in the world, how students should behave in school, and what student-teacher relationships should look like. Core beliefs are formed early in life and often from modeling or messages we receive from our parents or other influential people in our lives. We believe that they are *the one way* to be human. These beliefs form the lenses through which we see, understand, and judge others. The experiences that led to our core beliefs, however, may be vastly different from the experiences that are forming how our students see, interpret, and interact in the world. We may have a core belief that if a student cares about our class, they will focus on what we are teaching and be compliant when we ask them to do something. This belief may cause us to assume several things about a secondary student who talks to the person next to them, pulls their hoodie over their head and face during class, or disrespectfully refuses to engage when we ask them to do something. We may assume that this student doesn't care about learning, doesn't respect us, or doesn't care about our class. If we hold this core belief, then we will be upset when students engage in those behaviors.

However, there are other possibilities for why students don't seem to pay attention or comply with our requests. A student who is talking in class instead of listening may really care about your content, but sitting next to a friend has their need for peer connection overriding their desire to pay attention. A student may pull their hood up and appear not to listen because they are having a difficult time at home or in their personal lives, and engaging at that moment feels too overwhelming. A student who disrespectfully refuses to engage might have low self-efficacy in your class, and rather than allow anyone to see them fail, they just refuse to work. It doesn't mean they don't want to learn. It means they think they can't. Each of these examples offers one of many possible valid causes of the student's behavior. Being curious about the reason a student behaves a certain way, rather than assuming the student doesn't want to learn, opens opportunities for us to shift a limiting core belief and begin to truly understand and connect with that student.

Our core beliefs help us interpret what happens around us, but they also lead us to make assumptions and judgments about others that may not be accurate or fair. When we become aware of our reactions to students' behaviors and examine how the core beliefs we hold might be causing us to interpret their actions in inaccurate ways, then we can be more open to understanding our students and less quickly triggered by certain behaviors. Both of the Looking Inward: Flipping the Script activities in this chapter (page 172) will help you begin to explore your internal responses to student behaviors.

Understanding Why Students Behave the Way They Do

It is also helpful to understand why students behave the way they do. If we remember that adolescents are seeking to understand themselves and how they fit into the world, then we can learn not to take it personally if they push back on what we ask them to do or who we expect them to be. That doesn't mean we don't have expectations for them, but it does mean we explain why we are asking them to do something, and it also means we give them space within those expectations to have autonomy and be themselves. Remembering that adolescents are biochemically preoccupied with status and respect and that they trust people that they perceive to be part of their "inside" group and distrust those who are in the "outside" group (Hutchison, 2019; Tschannen-Moran & Hoy, 2000) is helpful to understanding why we need to build connections with our students. It also explains why sharing power and respect and approaching teacher-student conflict through the lens of collaborative problem solving goes a long way.

Remembering that adolescents' brains are still developing, and their inability to anticipate the long-term consequences can lead to questionable choices and behavior, helps us see errors in judgment and challenging behavior as opportunities to facilitate growth and help them form new neural connections rather than see these as personal attacks. Sometimes students are trying to antagonize us, but often that is not what motivates the behaviors that drive us crazy.

It is also helpful to remember that students who have experienced AELEs (bullying, abuse, neglect, poverty, or exposure to violence, and so on; Hambrick et al., 2019; Koplan & Chard, 2015) are predisposed to struggling in school in two ways. First, those experiences can cause neural pathway changes in their brains that affect impulsivity control, emotional regulation, and thinking through sequential steps to accomplish goals (Hambrick et al., 2019; Hashimoto et al., 2015). These are all skills students need to succeed academically and behaviorally in school. Second, they are more likely to have developed low hope for the future and low control beliefs (low self-efficacy and an external locus of control), leaving them to believe that life happens to them, and they don't have any control over the direction their lives will take (Sujadi & Aulianisya, 2020). I've had countless conversations with students who consistently exhibit challenging behaviors. When I ask them about what they want for their futures, and they tell me, "My future is already set, and there is nothing I can do about it." The behaviors we're most likely to see when students have low self-efficacy, an external locus of control, and low hope for the future are disengagement and disruption. They want to avoid looking "stupid" in front of their peers, and they also may believe school doesn't matter for their futures because they have no hope. It makes sense. Why would students try when they believe they will fail and don't believe their efforts or achievement will matter anyway?

When we can examine our own thoughts and reactions to student behaviors and remove our judgments about what certain behaviors mean and instead seek to understand why students behave the way they do, then we take their behavior less personally, are less triggered by it, and are more equipped to navigate it. When we seek to understand why students engage in certain behaviors, it can help us both have empathy for them and come up with effective solutions to those problematic behaviors. Understanding ourselves and our students increases how effectively we manage student conflict and challenging behavior.

Take a moment to read and answer the following self-reflection questions.

JESSICA'S VIGNETTE

I had a student who was freaking out about charges made to his savings account from a video game app company. He would not focus on anything else and kept asking me if he could call his bank to figure it out. Our school had a no cell phone policy for both teachers and students, but I also knew he wouldn't hear a single thing I was teaching until this matter was cleared up.

Here's how my conversation went with this student.

Me: OK, I understand this is causing you great stress, so I'm going to help you. But I need something too.

continued →

Student: OK. What?

Me: I will let you go out into the hall by the boys' bathroom, and you can call your bank. However, when you come back into class, what do you need to do?

Student: I need to focus on my work and do what you tell me to do.

Me: Yes. And what happens if you don't do those things?

Student: You won't ever let me call my bank again.

Me: Not quite. It's not about calling your bank. It's about using your phone when our school doesn't permit that. So, if you don't come back in and get the work done, I will never let you use your phone for whatever emergency you might have, and our mutual trust will be broken. Do you understand?

Student: Yes.

Me: Just to make sure we are both understanding things, please tell me what you have to do when you return to class.

Student: I have to get my work done, or I will break your trust and never be able to use my phone again for an emergency.

Me: Perfect. Now, go call your bank.

While that situation worked out well and he did come back in and did his work, the next day was another challenge. He was messing around and distracting other students, so I pulled him aside and said how I felt like such a fool right now because I worked with him to solve his problem yesterday and here he was causing a problem for me today. I said, "I let you go deal with what you needed to yesterday, and now you come in today and are distracting other kids. How do you think that makes me feel?" He said, "Not good." I replied, "Exactly. So please go back in the room and do the right thing." He walked back in and was more focused than before our talk. I needed him to "see" me and my feelings for him to develop empathy and think about how his behavior affected me.

And though he continued to have daily behavioral challenges, I kept coming back to him, saying that I gave him what he needed in that moment, and I needed him to give me the same respect of giving me what I needed too. In a nutshell, it's the theory of "I've got your back, and I need you to have my back too." Developmentally, this is the single most important trait for adolescents; that's why it works.

WALKING IN OUR STUDENTS' SHOES

Reflecting ON CONFLICT

Think back to a time in your life when you had a boss, teacher, or coach who managed conflict with you well. Did that influence how you felt about them and how you responded when they asked you to do something?

Now think about a boss, teacher, or coach who did not manage conflict with you well. Did that influence how you felt about them and how you responded when they asked you to do something?

- Did you feel respected? Did you respect them?

- Did you trust them? How did that impact your relationship with them?

continued →

Now think about yourself as a teacher. Reflect on your current approaches to managing student conflict. How might students feel about those interactions and their relationships with you? How might that influence how they respond to you and how they engage in your class?

Digging in deeper, reflect on a recent interaction with a student. You can choose an interaction that either had a positive or negative outcome. Be specific about what happened.

- What did you say?

- What did they say?

- How did each of you navigate any emotions that came up?

- What did you say or do that eased or generated more conflict?

- How did you feel after the interaction?

- How do you think the student felt after the interaction?

- What did you learn from the experience that you did or could apply to future student interactions?

Visit ***go.SolutionTree.com/teacherefficacy*** *for a free reproducible version of this reflection.*

Leading and Motivating Students

Trying to control our students creates power struggles and conflicts with them and increases stress and burnout for us. Thinking we can somehow control anyone else goes against what we now know about humans and motivation (Pink, 2018). We can certainly influence how our students respond to us and the environment we create, but unless they are motivated to behave in a certain way, there is nothing we can do about it. Even leadership styles that focus more on control and coercion acknowledge that one's behavior reflects one's motivation (Pink, 2018).

Student engagement increases more when we create safe environments, build positive relationships (Gregory & Kaufeldt, 2015), *and* focus on the internal factors that motivate students (Deci & Ryan, 1985) than it does when we try to use the outdated control and coerce model (Pink, 2018). This is especially true for adolescents, who have a developmental need for autonomy as they discover who they are in the world (Allen et al., 2013). However, it seems like many school policies were developed based on the outdated understanding of human motivation—that young people will not be motivated to do the right thing unless they are controlled, directed, and threatened with punishment. We can see examples of this in our discipline matrices that assume punishment is the best way to change unwanted student behavior. We also see this in that many teachers underestimate how much our students want to take ownership of their own learning. As a result, teachers feel like it is their responsibility to control the students in their classrooms. But since that approach isn't the most effective way to motivate humans, trying to control thirty-plus students who all have different ideas about what they should be doing at that moment is incredibly stressful. Research shows that for the control and punishment model of motivation to be effective, we must vigilantly watch our followers at all times to ensure they are doing what we want them to be doing (Pink, 2018). That is exhausting! If we want to decrease our own stress and improve our student relationships and engagement, we have to acknowledge that students are their own human selves, that they inherently want to learn (Deci & Ryan, 1985), and different factors impact their motivation and participation at any given moment. So how can we tap into what motivates them rather than think we can somehow magically control them?

Take a moment to read and answer the following self-reflection questions.

WALKING IN OUR STUDENTS' SHOES

Reflecting ON RELATIONSHIPS AND MOTIVATION

Think about a teacher you had in middle or high school who you had a good relationship with and who you worked hard for. What was it about that teacher that motivated you to work hard for them?

- How did they interact with you?

- How did you behave in their class?

- Did you have a teacher you did not work hard for or in whose class you did not behave well? What contributed to the differences in how motivated you were or how you behaved in those two classes?

- What were the differences between those two teachers?

Visit ***go.SolutionTree.com/teacherefficacy*** *for a free reproducible version of this reflection.*

When I (Rebecca) was teaching the elective class for students struggling with unwanted behavior, I felt extreme pressure to control their behavior out of fear that my administrator would walk in and see them being rowdy. These were not the types of students who were going to sit quietly at their desks and do exactly what I asked them to do. They were the students who would advocate for themselves (what others might call "talking back"), talk to each other a lot, and walk around the room often. They were the students who found themselves in the office regularly and who didn't feel like they belonged at school. My class was about helping these students gain the skills that enabled them to succeed in school, skills like self-awareness and reflection, self-regulation, goal setting, and organization. These skills helped them feel competent in school for the first time. My class also provided a safe space where they felt like they belonged. I could not have accomplished those goals if I had tried to control these students or threatened them with punishment. I accomplished those goals by providing a space where they felt connection and autonomy and had the chance to develop competence. The same could be said about all of the positive deviant teachers who share their strategies in this book. They create environments where students are motivated to participate rather than environments where they try to control their students.

Busting Common Classroom Management Myths

Through our experiences, conversations, and observations, we've encountered several misconceptions about how teachers lead their classrooms that contribute to the stress they feel and how well they navigate teacher-student conflict.

Myth 1: There Has to Be a Power Struggle

There is a misconception among many teachers that when we run into a conflict with a student, we must show the other students that we are in control and have the power or we will lose their respect. In reality, when it comes to adolescents, exerting power over one of their peers actually decreases the respect the other students feel for us as teachers (Knighton, 2022). Showing a student respect earns us respect not only from that student but also from their peers.

Myth 2: We Have to Do It All

We seem to have developed the belief that we have to manage all aspects of everything that happens in our classrooms. We may have learned by example from our teachers when we were in school, or maybe it was something we were taught in our teacher preparation programs or modeled by colleagues. But the truth is, adolescents don't want us to manage everything for them. In fact, they have a developmental need to be respected by adults (Allen et al., 2013), and one of the best ways to do that is to let them help manage aspects of the class by assigning them roles. For example, maybe you give one student the role of reading the learning target to the class each day, and you give another student the job of paying attention to who is raising their hands during class discussions. Another role might be to ensure that the iPads are all neatly returned to their assigned locations. The more we can share these types of roles with students, the more respected they feel and the more it frees us up to focus on who needs additional one-on-one support during class.

Myth 3: Students Don't Want to Learn

In reality, students would learn if they could. Humans are inherently curious and want to learn (Shin & Kim, 2019). If they aren't participating, there is a reason. In addition to sharing roles with students, we can share the responsibility of their learning with them. We think we have to micromanage and control students in order for them to participate and learn. We don't trust that they have an internal desire to learn and succeed. Think about a time in your life when someone was micromanaging you. Did you feel more motivated to work hard, or did you feel less motivated? Research shows that autonomy and a sense of competence are two of the most important factors in human motivation (Pink, 2018), and that respect and autonomy are developmental needs of adolescents (Hasel & Grover, 2017). How might we focus on respecting our students, helping them develop competence, and giving them more autonomy rather than trying to manage every aspect of learning in our classrooms?

One important mindset that positive deviant teachers all shared in this study (and that former students reported made a substantial impact on how motivated they were to engage) was the belief that students "would if they could" (Knighton, 2022). When positive deviant teachers encountered students who were disengaged, rather than assume the student did not want to learn, they tried to figure out what the barrier to learning was. Was it a student's belief that they could not succeed? Were they lacking the skills needed to complete the task? Was it that the student hadn't eaten all day and needed a snack? Discovering what the barrier was often took a combination of leaning on the knowledge you had of who the student was, what they cared about, what their abilities were, and what they struggled with *and* taking the time to have a collaborative problem-solving conversation with the student. Simply asking a student what they need and what they are struggling with can go a long way. Figuring out the source of the student's resistance enables us to help that student resolve the barrier and, in most cases, student engagement and achievement will increase.

Myth 4: You Can't Connect With Hard-to-Reach Students

When we hear that we are going to have a student who tends to get into conflicts with teachers, disrupts class frequently, or won't engage in class, we might feel a sense of dread about how challenging it might be and how much harder our jobs will be in that class. One of the things that positive deviant teachers do with this information is view it as a challenge. They try to learn all they can about who the student is, what they care about, and what supports they need to be successful. They might look through the cumulative folder or talk to colleagues. They thrive off figuring out how to connect with this student. They know that if they win this student over, then they will have won the whole class over (Knighton, 2022). Having a positive relationship with these students prevents them from disrupting our classes, and they tend to have a strong sense of loyalty to the people they trust. They can also serve as leaders in our classrooms to help other students stay on task and follow our expectations.

Keeping these myths in mind, as well as seeking to understand both our own reactions to students and why our students behave the way they do in our classes, can be incredibly helpful in shifting how we navigate both challenging behavior and conflict with students.

Looking Inward: Flipping the Script

In this section, you will have the opportunity to engage in two activities, shown in figures 5.2 (page 172) and 5.3 (page 174). These activities are designed to help you understand yourself better and develop some of the skills we have discussed in this chapter.

Our life experiences shape the lenses through which we see the world. We then make assumptions about other people based on what we see through those lenses.

- What kind of student were you? (For example: Did you sit still and follow directions well? Did you chat with your friends when you were supposed to listen? Did you do your homework and turn it in? Did you avoid certain classes or activities?)

- How did you interact with your teachers? (For example, were you respectful? Did you follow their directions well? Did you rebel? Did you avoid them?)

Based on your own experiences in school, what are some beliefs you have about how students should and should not behave in school?
• How *should* students behave?   • How *should* students *not* behave?
Our core beliefs are formed from our experiences and influence how we think the world should operate. We think others share our core beliefs and that can lead us to misinterpret others' actions based on assumptions we make about their motivations.
• What are some of your own core beliefs (about yourself, school, teacher-student relationships, power dynamics between adults and adolescents, people in positions of power, and so on)? For example, do you believe that young people should respect adults unconditionally? Do you believe that students should always do what the teacher tells them to do? Do you believe that students have trust issues and teachers need to earn trust?

Figure 5.2: Examining core beliefs.

continued →

- How might those core beliefs influence how you feel about certain student behaviors?

- How might they influence how you react to certain student behaviors? (For example, do some behaviors cause you to judge students as "bad" or disrespectful? Do you assume some students don't want to learn? Do you consider some students to be "good students?")

Visit ***go.SolutionTree.com/teacherefficacy*** *for a free reproducible version of this figure.*

If we want to remain calm when students are pushing our buttons, then we need to understand our own triggers and reactions. Usually, our triggers surface when a student's behavior challenges one of our core beliefs, if we feel like we will lose something we care about, or if we feel like that behavior threatens one of our human needs (safety, competence, belonging, or security).

Sometimes we react to students or student behaviors because they push on a wounded part of our younger self—for example, if you were bullied in school and you have a student who reminds you of the person who bullied you. As humans, we all have wounded younger parts of ourselves, and it's important to remember that the part of us that reacts to those triggers isn't our current teacher self.

We all have triggers, whether it is because behaviors challenge our core beliefs, threaten a human need, or push on a younger wounded part of ourselves. What we do with them makes all the difference. The first step is understanding which behaviors trigger us and reflecting on why.

Part 1: Understanding Your Reactions to Student Behaviors

The first step in transforming our triggers is to understand what behaviors push our buttons, what we think and feel, and how we respond when they do.

- What student behaviors trigger you? What causes you to lose your cool? Make a list of the student behaviors that trigger you and then choose one to focus on as you complete the rest of the activity.

- Why might that behavior trigger you? (What core belief docs it challenge? What need might not be met? What might you lose? Are you afraid of something?) Take some time to reflect and identify what threat that behavior creates for you. (Does it threaten your place of authority over the class? Does it threaten your job security? Does it exist in conflict with one of your core beliefs about how humans should behave in the world?) Try to identify why that specific behavior bothers you and describe it.

- What assumptions are you making about a student's beliefs and values because of that behavior? (Do you believe the student doesn't want to learn? Do you believe the student doesn't respect you? Do you believe the student doesn't care about the other students in the class?) Describe what you believe about a student's beliefs and values when they engage in that behavior.

Figure 5.3: Understanding and transforming your triggers.

continued →

Part 2: Transforming Your Triggers

Now that you understand a little more about your reactions to and thoughts and feelings about that behavior, let's dig in and try to understand why that behavior creates such a strong emotional reaction for you.

Step 1: Think about a specific type of student behavior that drives you crazy. Remember how it makes you feel when a student does that. Try to feel the emotions that come up for you when this occurs. Don't rationalize how you should or should not feel, just be with the feeling.

- How does your body feel?
- What do you think?
- What emotions come up?
- Write down what the behavior is and how you feel when you encounter it.

Step 2: Ask yourself, "Why does that behavior upset me so much?" Don't try to analyze it. Let the answer come to you. Whatever pops into your head first is probably the answer.

Step 3: Say to yourself, "OK, but why does that upset me?" (Again, let the answer come to you and don't try to analyze it or rationalize it away.)

Step 4: Keep repeating step 3 until you get a clear answer. You might experience a moment of realization: "Aha! Of course, that is the deeper reason why this bothers me so much."

Once we understand the root of why something bothers us so much, its strength decreases, and those behaviors often don't upset us as much. This enables us to manage conflict with students more effectively and use behavioral missteps as opportunities to guide growth as students develop into adults. This also helps us find effective solutions to prevent or correct a behavior because we are less emotional about it.

Given your new understanding of why that behavior upsets you so much, how might you respond the next time you encounter it?

Visit ***go.SolutionTree.com/teacherefficacy*** *for a free reproducible version of this figure.*

Learning From the Five Teacher Types

This section presents two common scenarios. For each scenario, the five positive deviant teachers you met in the introduction describe how they handle these scenarios in their practice. The first is how to navigate a situation when a student is talking to a friend in class, not engaging in class, and ignoring the teacher's first attempt at redirecting them. The second is how they navigate a situation where a student has been reminded by the teacher to put their phone away for the second time and still refuses to do so. As you read through these examples, highlight, underline, or circle the parts you relate to.

Scenario: A student is talking to a friend in class rather than engaging in the lesson and ignores your first attempt to redirect them

The following sections describe how each teacher type approaches this scenario in their classroom.

Teacher Type: Caring Connector

I would likely try a conversational approach like the following.

Me: Hey, guys, what's up? How's the assignment going?

Student: Fine.

Me: I just noticed that you were having a pretty good chat and wanted to make sure that you heard me when I asked you to get back to work.

Student: Yeah.

Me: Are there any questions you have? Or is there any way that I could help you out with it?

Student: No, I'm good.

Me: OK, well, just know that if you're ever having trouble with a project, I'm happy to help. I just want to make sure that you both have enough time to complete it in class.

Student: I just don't see the point. I don't care.

Me: I see. Well, I promise you that I will never make you do a project for no reason. I'll let you take a break for today, but just make sure you aren't distracting your friend; they need time to work as well. I'm happy to explain why we're doing this after class.

(At the end of class, I pull the student aside.)

Me: Hey, is everything all right? It isn't like you to push back against doing an assignment like that.

Student: Yeah, I know. I had a rough fight with my parents last night, and I just couldn't do it today.

Me: I totally understand that. When I have a rough night it can make it hard to focus on other things. Is there anything I can do to help you out? And do you really not see the point in what we are doing?

Student: No, I do. I'm just having trouble thinking of a topic and got overwhelmed. Could I maybe have an extra day or two to finish it?

Me: Absolutely you can. Next time just come and talk to me. I'm always flexible, and I know that school isn't the only thing going on in your life. You're big into anime, right? Why don't you focus your project on the genre itself? Or a specific show that you love? That way you can use something you're interested in to show your understanding of the impact of globalization on the world.

Student: I never thought about doing that! Sounds good. I will try to have it narrowed down by tomorrow. Thanks!

Me: Awesome! I can't wait to see what you come up with. Let me know if you want to go over any ideas with me.

Obviously, I made the scenario pretty specific, but my approach to teaching is rooted in building relationships with my students and showing genuine interest in their lives. That's why I spend a lot of time at the beginning of each new semester making sure I build those connections; they end up paying major dividends in the end. There is also the added bonus of creating more genuine engagement, and these relationships build a more positive, comfortable classroom environment where students are more willing to step outside of their comfort zones and try new things. Without these relationships, I don't believe that this approach would be effective, because the student wouldn't be comfortable telling me about the fight with their parents, and I wouldn't have a good suggestion to try and re-engage the student in the classwork.

Teacher Type: Gentle Giant

Teaching in a gymnasium really makes this a unique situation. On one hand, community building and communication are imperative in physical education. On the other hand, distractions and lack of focus derail an entire class faster than anything else.

Generally, the most common time for this to happen is during the first few minutes of class during direct instruction. When students do happen to ignore the lesson to chat with each other, I handle it quite simply. I generally ask the students to stop interrupting and explain how their talking over top of me is unfair to those around them. I challenge students to think of their actions like a stone thrown in water . . . how far does your behavior reach? Whether it is good or bad behavior, we invite others to do the same. This can be good and bad—when the ripples become so big the negative behaviors are unmanageable and take the enjoyment out of class. When the behavior and focus is on point, the engagement in class is exceptional.

I like to be real with adolescent students. They hate being told no but can accept the answer when it also comes with a why not. Simply explaining to them how interrupting a conversation or not being able to "read the room" will lead to others forming opinions and lasting impressions. I like explaining how developing strong communication skills can lead to less stress and better relationships. Another strategy I often use when students are distracted and disengaged is to invite them to finish their conversation in private. I know they are going to talk one way or another, so this way allows them to have more autonomy and self-awareness.

Here's an example to illustrate how I would respond to students John and Jeff (not their real names) talking during direct instruction.

> **Me:** John and Jeff, if you need a minute or two to finish your conversation, please feel free to do that in the hallway. It will be easier for each of us to have our conversations if we are not talking over each other. You will miss some instructions, though, so it will be your responsibility to catch up once you've returned.
>
> **Students:** Really?
>
> **Me:** Yes. (To whole class) I understand wanting to be able to say the thing that is on your mind, and sometimes you have to do just that. I just ask that you are respectful and self-aware enough to know where and when is a good time for that conversation.

This typically works so well. Students appreciate the freedom to leave the space to finish their conversations, but more often than not, they will put a pin in their thoughts and re-engage in the lesson.

More commonly, my struggles in physical education come from lack of engagement during the activity. In these cases, encouraging participation becomes more challenging. I often ask students to find specific ways to get involved. Rather than ask them to play soccer, I'll challenge them to take the ball away from at least three players in class. Or I might make a dodgeball game that requires guards who do not have to throw, builders who cannot be hit, and so on. Creating different roles within the games allows students autonomy and usually helps with engagement. Ultimately, showing students that I care enough to let them choose how to engage results in a trust between us that leads to success.

Being proactive and knowing when to give an inch goes a long way too. I'll often notice students who group together and like to do everything together. Rather than fight this and separate them, I encourage them to be on the same teams and work together. Our strongest support systems are the people closest to us, so if we can get one nonparticipator to rethink their level of engagement, chances are they will influence others to do the same!

Teacher Type: Nurturing Narrator

The first attempt I always make is a general guide from afar to avoid highlighting the behavior or engaging in a power struggle. I refer to students by nicknames (especially students with highly challenging behavior) that usually develop naturally over time from greeting them at the door each day.

For example, the first attempt would probably be from my desk, casually and simply, "Ms. Jones, would you kindly focus on my assignment, or if you must tell your story, you can come tell it to me as I, too, love a good tale."

If this didn't work, I would then move myself into the conversation as opposed to moving the student to me. I often use body language to control the narrative of where we're going. I sit on a desk near them, crouch down, or put my hand on the desk of the student who is exhibiting the behavior, depending on our relationship. I also take my time getting over to the student, making my way through the classroom and touching base with other groups or students to suggest I am doing a general check-in as opposed to coming to engage with the undesirable behavior. As I get to their level, I ask about their night or their family. As I shared in a previous chapter, I get to know students' caregivers early in the year and foster that connection over time.

Once I approach the student, here's how the conversation might go.

Me: Mr. Smith, did you get to the skatepark this weekend? I know Stacy [mom] had mentioned you loved going there.

Student: No.

Me: Oh, too bad, what did you end up doing?

Student: Nothing. Watched TV.

Me: I love TV. Did you watch the new Housewives of Potomac?

Student: Uhhh, no, I watched YouTube.

Me: Right. That makes more sense. But if you did want to watch any of the Housewives shows, I am always standing by ready to discuss it with you.

Student: Yeah, OK.

Me: In fact, while I was trying to watch my favorite Housewives, my husband would not stop asking me questions like, Who's that? Why is she yelling? and Is that the same girl from last year? Which, I have to tell you, Mr. Smith, I did not at all care to be distracted and did have to send him away. Now, I know that you're not intentionally distracting Ms. Jones, but you can see how chatting may be difficult to focus through. And since you've already admitted to me you are not discussing a show that I can contribute to the conversation in, I am wondering how the assignment is going.

Student: It's fine.

Me: Perfect. Can you show me what you've done so far?

(Student shows no work is done.)

Me: Some of this can be tricky. Do you mind if I sit down, and we can work on a bit of it together? Ms. Jones is welcome to work with us, should she prefer.

I will sit and work with a student to guide their learning and help them get started. Once they've started working, I will casually stand up.

Me: Guys, I am so impressed with the work you're doing. You obviously don't need me here, but if you find yourselves lost again, just pop up to my desk. Thanks for the chat!

On my way back, I will again stop and touch base with other students. This not only suggests to the disruptive students that they're not the only ones who might be struggling, but it also tells the rest of the class that I am invested in their work and not just highfliers.

I would not address the behavior with a student after class for a first offense. If this behavior became a regular occurrence, I would first move their seat closer to my desk. Proximity is a great tool; it provides easy verbal check-ins and support. I also always keep snacks in my desk that all students know are there. I'll often just point at the drawer and students will nod or shake their heads to indicate hunger. This is easiest for the students who are placed closest to me. Putting the student closer to me makes them choose me often as their chatting partner, and then I control the narrative of when we can tell stories, when I can redirect them to work, and it helps me identify signals to when I need to help guide their learning. These small desk conversations help me gain a true understanding of the student—what they like, what they don't like, and who they are. Students who know you care about them will always make teaching them easier for you.

Teacher Type: Perceptive Pragmatist

In a high school classroom, I see this scenario often, especially during work time. While I encourage working together and expect there will be a certain level of visiting while working, it can very quickly turn into a situation that isn't conducive to being productive. I generally take the approach of either sitting in an adjacent desk or crouching to eye level and opening the conversation with, "How's it going over here? I notice you don't have any work done. Do you have any questions?"

Typically, the response I get is: "No, we're good."

The route I take next depends on how I perceive the nature of the conversation between friends. If it seems serious, agitated, or like there's something significant going on for the student, my next line is usually: "Is this something you need to go discuss in private and come back when it's resolved?" or "Do you need to talk to someone who can help?"

Alternatively, if the conversation seems like they've just gotten carried away with visiting, I say, "I don't mind visiting, but you also need to get some work done. Why don't you try and get three questions done before you continue with your conversation? Then, alternate visiting time with work time." At this point, the students either admit they need some help with the assignment, or else they generally start working on their own.

Both routes tend to accomplish the same outcomes. Either the student genuinely needs help with an issue (or the assignment) and is prompted to get it, or the student refocuses on the task at hand while avoiding a power struggle.

Teacher Type: Warm Demander

Sometimes a student just isn't in the space to think, and they need something besides class time with an assignment. If they seem off, I will have a conversation with them, just the two of us; I always preface that they're not in trouble, because I don't need to add to their struggle. Here's one of those conversations.

Me: You're not in trouble, but can I see you for a minute out in the hall?

Student: Yeah.

Me: I've noticed you're not acting like yourself because you usually don't ignore me when I'm talking to you. What's going on?

Student: Nothing.

Me: While I know that's not true, I understand not wanting to talk about it. So instead, what can I do to make my class better for you today? What do you need from me?

Student: I don't know.

Me: OK. Would you like to know what other students have told me when they're feeling this way?

Student: Sure.

Me: Here are three common options. One, you can put your head down and take a break for the rest of class. Two, you can work on the assignment with me, and I'll write down your answers for you. Or three, you can go into the cave (this is under one of my teacher tables, which has many body pillows) and give your body and brain some rest for the rest of class. Would you like to do any of those things?

If they choose option one or three, I respond by saying, "Great. Since you are getting what you need today, what do I need from you tomorrow?"

Student: Get all my work done that I miss today.

Me: Correct. And what will happen if you don't get all your work done tomorrow?

Student: I won't get to use the cave or put my head down again.

Me: Perfect! Does that sound like a deal you can agree to and keep your word about it?

Student: Yes.

Given what you've learned in this chapter, think about and answer the following reflection questions.

WHAT WOULD YOU DO?

Redirecting STUDENTS

Imagine yourself in a situation where a student is talking to a friend in class, not engaging in class, and ignores your first attempt at redirecting them.

- What would you be thinking?

- What would you be feeling?

- Would this push on any of your own triggers?

- How might you have responded in the past?

- How might you respond now?

Scenario: You've reminded a student to put away their phone for the second time and they still refuse to do so

The following sections describe how each teacher type approaches this scenario in their classroom.

Teacher Type: Caring Connector

Haha! If I had a nickel for every time I've experienced this scenario in my classroom! Phones can definitely be a major source of frustration from a teaching perspective, but they also present many opportunities for learning.

I work at a school that does not have an overall policy guiding cell phone use, which can present a lot of challenges regarding the individual classroom restrictions that you put in place. You might get the old "but my other teachers let me do this . . . " response. Also, confiscating cell phones from students can cause a variety of adverse reactions from both students and parents. In my first year of teaching, I made the mistake of trying to take a phone from a student who I didn't have a solid connection with yet, and his refusal led to a confrontation as neither of us wanted to back down. He didn't want to give up his personal device to a teacher he barely knew, and I didn't want to lose face as an authority figure in front of the other students. Another time, taking the phone away led to an angry email from the parent, as they claimed they needed to be in constant contact with their child, regardless of whether they were in class or not. After experiencing these two "failures," at least from my perspective, I knew that I needed to adjust my approach to proper use of technology in the classroom.

Usually, I try to be as proactive as possible regarding cell phone use. I talk about how it is important to start practicing self-regulation regarding technology. I remind students that in the future, there won't be anyone around to tell them to put their phone away. I mention that cell phone addiction or dependence can negatively impact their personal relationships and their ability to find meaningful employment. However, I also follow this up with a "time and place" discussion. I don't mind if students use their phones for research, or in some cases, even for typing up their work. (Many students don't have solid typing skills and can work more efficiently on their phone. I know, it seems crazy to me too!) Also, I don't mind if they use it after their work is complete, as I don't want to punish them for being on task (of course, the work must be up to a certain standard). Often, I will encourage them to look up something we don't have the answer to or to find a current event for discussion to try and engage them in the class but also to show them that there are uses for this technology besides entertainment alone.

However, if a student refuses to get off their device altogether, there is usually an underlying issue that is causing this behavior. Consider the following possibilities.

- ***Finding the work too challenging:*** *In this case, with my teaching style I would focus on using the connection we have or trying to disarm them with humor. "Wow, your Snapstreak must be breaking records right now!" Then, I would follow up by asking them how they are doing on the assignment and if there is anything that I can do to help. If they do ask for help, great! If not, at this point I can clearly see whether they have been completing the work. If they have done little to none, I will ask the student questions about the task. If they can't provide any responses, I will prompt them, show them how to find the information they need, or try to break down the assignment into simpler terms. Then, I will ask them to complete the task, and they can continue to use their device once they finish. In my experience, this usually solves the issue for the time being, and I learn something about the student to engage them in the future while still upholding classroom expectations.*
- ***Experiencing social-emotional stress:*** *We've often heard the term* digital pacifier *related to student use of smartphones. If anything becomes overwhelming for them, they turn to technology for something comfortable that takes them out of their current situation. This can also relate to my first point, as challenging schoolwork can also cause stress. However, often it is something completely out of the context of the classroom that is leading to the behavior. In this case, it is important to again approach with empathy. "How is everything going? Is there anything I can do to help?" Often, when it is a social or emotional issue, this won't get much of a response, they will reply with no or even nothing at all. In this case, I would ask, "Is everything ok? I just noticed that you are on your phone a lot more than usual today." Hopefully, if I have a solid connection with the student, this will start a conversation. Sometimes, the conversation is enough to get them to a place where they can re-engage; other times, they may need to just take a break for that period. You have to judge based on the student themself, and their current circumstances, regarding how to handle it in their best interest. Sometimes, this may lead to encouraging them to connect with our wellness team of counselors at the school.*
- ***Battling a technology addiction:*** *Rarely, in severe cases, students will refuse to get any work done at all. Or they will only work when you are directly hovering over them, taking out their device as soon as you turn your back. In these cases, I find trying to take the device to be the worst*

> *possible response, as you will be met with a visceral reaction. What I would do at this point is contact their parents. I try to always approach these conversations with a positive attitude, making sure that you let the parents know that you are connecting with them because you care about their child, and that you only want to come up with a plan to help them become more successful in class. There are very few parents who don't want their child to be more successful, so typically we make a plan together. Often, this leads the parents to regulate their child's use (not bringing the phone to school or keeping it in their locker during class) or even teaching self-regulation in the home, as these behaviors often exist there as well.*

These three categories don't cover all the potential scenarios related to cell phone use but are definitely some of the most common experiences I have had in my classroom. It is a complex issue that doesn't look like it is getting any simpler with the addition of AI technologies like ChatGPT, but in my experience, we need to adapt our teaching practices to them as they are going to continue to advance and change. We need to continue to find new ways to keep our learning environments relevant to the lives of our students while still teaching them the value of hard work and respect for others.

Teacher Type: Gentle Giant

Cell phones in class, any class, are a major distraction. In physical education, they are irrelevant and unnecessary 99 percent of the time. In situations where a device is an issue in class, I often handle it in a way that brings very little attention to the student or the device.

Early in the school year, we set our expectations and boundaries. We preface the idea that all devices should be put away for physical education. This can be through a bunch of options: left in a locker, put in the cell bin or bag, or even left unseen in a pocket. I like to remind students that I, too, have a cell phone and take great pride in leaving it alone during the school day. Fighting this issue from an authoritarian perch leaves me frustrated and overwhelmed. In comparison, reasoning with like-minded people, showing them how to be present in the moment, and demonstrating control over urges to check notifications leaves me feeling proud of my own ability to disconnect.

If I have a student who is having engagement issues due to a device, I usually start the conversation with humor.

Me: Hey, I notice you have your phone out . . . I was just going to ask you what time it is. You must have read my mind. [Alternatively, you can say:] How are the stock markets today? Is the DOW up or down?

Student: No, I wasn't checking the time [or the stock markets].

> **Me:** OK, then you wouldn't mind putting your phone in the bag [or bin or pocket] for the rest of class so it isn't a distraction.
>
> **Student:** (starts putting phone in pocket.)
>
> **Me:** Thanks for doing that. If I could suggest . . . putting it in the bag would be safer. You won't accidentally break it or lose it during class, and you'll know where it is at all times! It's a pretty expensive thing to be responsible for!
>
> **Student:** Yeah, I guess so.

It doesn't always go this way, but it has certainly helped reduce the escalating behaviors that come from just taking the phone away. Again, this interaction only works when trust is established. I hold myself accountable and stay off my phone during school hours; students don't see mine, and I ask that I don't have to see theirs.

There will always be those kids who fight against expectations and push boundaries. I remind myself all the time, the lesson is to teach them to respect boundaries and other people, not to reprimand the use of devices.

Teacher Type: Nurturing Narrator

Cell phones are, and have been, an ongoing and predominant issue in our classrooms, so we try to set expectations early regarding phone usage in our school. Here's how I address this with my students.

> **Me:** I ask that each day, when coming into my classroom, you make a conscious effort to leave your phone in your locker. This is for two reasons: one, your phone is gross, and you take it everywhere with you, so the thought of having to confiscate it from you makes me feel ill. Trust me when I say, no one, no one, wants to take your phone less than I do. So, to avoid this, it is better left where neither of us are in a position where I have to touch said disgusting phone, and you don't have to lose said disgusting phone.
>
> The second reason is because your phone calls to you. I love teaching middle school, but have you been in a classroom when a teacher has to engage in this power struggle over a phone? You have. We all have. And suddenly, the beautiful middle school student turns into some creature of the lagoon when it comes to that phone. It is reasonable to think you can sit in my class and have your phone in your pocket, but the reality is, once it buzzes—once it signals to you that something has happened—you must check it. And like The One Ring to Gollum, suddenly you cannot focus on anything but the phone. It burns in your side, until the notification is checked. You cannot focus on my entirely interesting and engaging social studies lesson because you are distracted. So—what do you do? You check the phone. Maybe subtly at first, but it doesn't end there. You need to respond to the moment, and it is a dangerous game. Suddenly, the Snapchat or the "TikyToky," or whatever else you do, is a new priority, because it called to you

and you opened it. Now, we are down the rabbit hole. Thus, bringing me back to the previous point of not wanting to touch your phone.

One year, I had all my students put their phones on their desks and turn on their notifications. At the front of the room, I had a tally chart. In two periods, we recorded every single sound that came from the whole class, so in two blocks, ninety-six minutes, do you know how many notifications went off in this room? Three hundred and seventy-eight. How can you be asked to focus on social studies when your phones are calling to you that often? You cannot. So, to avoid all of this and for the benefit of all of us, please don't bring it. Trust me—I will let you know when you need it.

Inevitably, this doesn't always work. I have a visual reminder at the front of my room of the steps. If a student has their phone, and I have noticed it is a distraction to them—I very quietly walk to their desk and simply tap it and give them "the look."

With the second offense (in the same class period), I will ask students to put it in the phone chart, which is by my desk so I can make sure no one is grabbing perhaps what isn't theirs, or I offer to lock it in my desk. I remind them that they are welcome to have it back at the end of class, but it has become a problem today.

When they outright refuse to give up their phone is when it gets tricky. When this happens, it unlocks a whole new level of behavioral management. I give students options in these moments, and the conversation does have to be quiet. I will go over to them, get to their level, and give two choices.

Me: Your success is the most important thing in my day here, so in order for me to make sure you can complete this assignment, the phone cannot be out. You can either give it to me by simply placing it on your desk, and I will come back and take it, or we can go put it in your locker, if you think that's better. I need you to know, I want you to be here, but if neither of those options are going to work for you today, you will have to work somewhere else until we can touch base later. I'm going to give you a couple of minutes to decide, and then I'll pop back over.

After class, I will ask the student to stay back.

Me: I know that you have so much going on, and I want to talk about it with you. Is there something specific today that you needed your phone for, or do you just prefer to have it?

It is always a case-by-case basis here, but generally they just want their phone.

Me: I understand that you're frustrated, and maybe we can come up with a solution for when a good time for you to use your phone might be. For example, while you're working isn't ideal, but if you finish your assignment, there is probably some room for you to pop out and check whatever you need to check.

But we need to be on the same team, so when I ask you to put it away, knowing that your best interest is my priority, I need you to respect me as much as I respect you.

These conversations usually end well, but they do take a lot of time and require a lot of alternatives to be at the ready. If I have to do this more than once in two weeks, I make sure to also include the student's adults in our conversations as well.

Teacher Type: Perceptive Pragmatist

Cell phones are (not surprisingly) one of the top issues I deal with on a daily basis. It is also an issue that I continually reflect on. It is increasingly difficult to institute a blanket no-phones policy in high school as students are often expected to be "on call" from external sources. They are responsible for pickup and drop-off of younger siblings, they have jobs, or, as my very first day of teaching taught me, their partner is pregnant and is approaching the due date. While that last scenario may be rare, it certainly helped shape my feelings about cell phones. We often have no idea why students may need access to their phones, and simply confiscating them will often send them into a panicked state, which won't make them any more receptive to learning. I think learning how to manage themselves with access to their phone is a life skill our students need.

In a scenario where a student has not put a phone away during instruction time, I usually stop the lesson and address the whole class. My aim is not to single out the student but to have a conversation about why the behavior is problematic and not just say, "put your phone away."

Me: OK, let's talk about this . . . if it was work time, and you came to my desk to ask me something, and I didn't even acknowledge you and continued to stare at my phone, what would you think?

Student: Well, that would be rude.

Me: Exactly. Do you realize that when you are staring at your phones while I'm teaching, you are doing that exact same thing to me? The lesson is almost done. I think you can all have your phones put away for a few more minutes. You will be able to check them soon.

Alternatively, if the student is glued to their phone during work time, I will usually approach them privately and say, "I can't help but notice that your phone is preventing you from getting work done. If there is something going on that needs your immediate attention, would you like to step out to deal with it in private?"

Occasionally, this is the case. Maybe it's not a crisis, but students need to make a quick call to work, finish a conversation with a parent, check on a friend, and so on.

Most of the time, though, they've just gotten carried away with their socializing. In that case, I would take the following approach.

Me: Look, I don't mind some texting while you're working, but you also need to get something done. Let's try to spend fifteen minutes focusing on your assignment, and then you can take a quick break to check your phone. Are you able to keep your phone out of sight, or would you rather put it at the front so there's no temptation?

Student: I can hang on to it.

Me: Perfect. Let's maybe put it in your bag so it's out of sight. You can even set a timer on it for fifteen minutes so you know when you can take it out again.

I've also used this strategy with the whole class—set timers to alternate between no-phone time and break time. Working with students to find a compromise tends to have students buy in a lot quicker than a hard and fast no-phones rule, while also teaching them some time-management and self-restraint skills.

Teacher Type: Warm Demander

In my experience, if a student is that tied to their phone, something upsetting is going on, which means I need more information instead of getting mad and demanding they hand it over.

Me: (With a smile and cheery tone) I wish I were that phone . . . to have all your focus and attention like that would be wonderful. So, I'm guessing whatever is happening on the phone must be pretty important.

Student: Yeah. Stuff's being said, and I have to know what's going on.

Me: So, is this happening between other students at our school?

Student: Yeah. And a few from another school.

Me: Are you just reading everything or are you actively responding?

Student: Both. It's just making me so mad.

Me: Look, I understand how important those things are in your life, but let me ask you a question. Is this something you can fix right now?

Student: No, but I want to know what they're saying so I can tell them they don't know what they're talking about.

Me: Why do you want to know what they're saying?

Student: Because if it's all lies, I need to know.

Me: Help me understand why you need to know if people are telling lies.

Student: It's not OK to lie about me or my friends.

Me: I agree. What would you do to fix the lies?

Student: I'm gonna tell them all what the truth really is.

Me: And will this make everyone believe you instead of the lies?

Student: Maybe. But at least I'm telling my side of it, which is actually the truth.

Me: Are you saying that you will feel better when you have your say?

Student: Yes.

Me: Have you been able to yet?

Student: Kinda. But really it's just a mess.

Me: Can I offer you a solution for right now?

Student: I guess.

Me: Well, since you and all your classmates know that our school expectation is that we don't use or look at our phones during class, what if you message everyone that you have to go because Mrs. May is walking over to you right now and will probably take your phone away and you're going to have to deal with this later during lunch? That means I'm the bad guy and you get a break from the stress of the conversation, then I can help you catch up on what you've missed work-wise. And afterward, if you'd like to, you and I can think through and brainstorm what you want to say later to everyone who's involved in this.

Student: I don't know. I just want to deal with it and be done.

Me: I get that. But you also know that I need to have you put your phone on my desk, right next to my own personal phone, for the rest of class because you understand that I follow and enforce our school rules.

Student: Yeah, I know.

Me: So . . . ?

Student: I'll send one more text while I walk my phone over to your desk. (Sigh)

Me: Excellent choice. I'm so proud of the maturity you are showing right now. Nice work.

Student: It doesn't feel good.

Me: I agree. But by choosing to handle it this way, you are making it easier the next time you have to put your phone away, which is something you will have to learn how to do—stepping away from things on your own—when you're an adult. So, what you're really doing is practicing the strategies you will need to use in the real world.

Sometimes it does take a chunk of time to talk them through their situation, but it's worth it because there will *be a next time, and I won't have to spend as much time dealing with it because I will make a reference to this first conversation.*

I have also found that it's so important when I name all their feelings and walk them through what they feel, *so they can begin to see how it's not really the end of the world or as urgent of a matter that they were caught up in. Saying things out loud is a powerful tool since it usually sounds a little preposterous or it's so validating that the power of the feeling is released.*

Finally, I learned from my own mother to always make myself the bad guy in any situation when it comes to teenagers; that way their friends don't get upset with them for ending the conversation or behavior. It takes the pressure off them.

Given what you've learned in this chapter, think about and answer the following reflection questions.

WHAT WOULD YOU DO?

Navigating CELL PHONE CONFLICT

Imagine yourself in the situation where you have a student who has been reminded to put their phone away for the second time and still refuses to do so.

- What would you be thinking?

- What would you be feeling?

- Would this push on any of your own triggers?

- How might you have responded in the past?

- How might you respond now?

Visit ***go.SolutionTree.com/teacherefficacy*** *for a free reproducible version of this reflection.*

Wrapping Up

Navigating challenging student behavior and conflict with students are two of the most stressful aspects of our jobs as educators. The more we can understand ourselves and why certain behaviors bother us, and the more we can seek to understand why students are behaving the way they are, the more easily we will be able to manage behavior and conflicts with students. Understanding how unmet human needs; adolescent development needs; and low self-efficacy, an external locus of control, and a lack of hope influence challenging student behavior helps us have more empathy for students, be less emotionally triggered by those behaviors, and come up with effective solutions to those behavioral problems.

Chapter 5 Book Study Questions

As a staff, explore the concepts presented in this chapter and reflect on how they are evidenced in or might impact your school culture. As you read each question, think about how you would respond based on your individual role. If you are an administrator, think about these questions as you reflect on how you support your staff. If you are a teacher or support staff member, think about these questions as you reflect on how you support students.

1. How might your classroom look and sound different if you switched your approach from managing your classroom to leading your students in learning? (What would you be doing differently? What would your students be doing differently?)

2. When looking at the list of classroom management myths, which one resonates with you the most? Has your thinking around that changed? In what way?

3. What are the biggest behavioral challenges you face in your school? As a staff, brainstorm why you think that might be. (What staff and student factors contribute to this problem?)

4. Are your school's behavior policies effective for students who exhibit the most challenging behaviors? If so, what about them makes them so effective? If not, how might incorporating some of what you learned in this chapter improve their effectiveness?

5. Are your school's policies and procedures developmentally appropriate for adolescents? Do they honor the adolescent needs of respect, peer connection, and autonomy?

CHAPTER 6

Flipping the Script

In the previous chapters, you've seen some examples of how students' scripts influence how they perceive the world—especially their potential in school and their relationships with teachers and peers. You've also had an opportunity to explore some of the scripts you may have that impact your relationships with students and their engagement in your classes.

In this chapter, we take a closer look at the concept of flipping the script. We explore what research and practice show about how to do that, such as recognizing scripts that limit students and teachers, encouraging authenticity and hope, and using scaffolding. Then, we practice flipping the script through self-reflection activities. Finally, we end the chapter by hearing how the five teacher types respond to two common scenarios related to shifting students' self-concepts.

Looking Outward: Themes in Research and Practice

Remember, each of us has scripts that impact how we interpret what happens to us (Erskine, 2018). Our own scripts influence how we understand, relate to, and guide our students, and our students' scripts influence how they engage in our classes.

Our own scripts influence how we understand, relate to, and guide our students, and our students' scripts influence how they engage in our classes.

Let's take a deeper dive into these scripts and how they impact us. To make sense of how scripts show up in our lives, I categorize them in two ways: (1) externally focused and (2) internally focused.

Our *externally focused scripts* influence how we see others and what we expect from them. They lead us to judge others, be annoyed by their behavior, or misinterpret their actions. These scripts come from messages and expectations (and sometimes modeling) from our parents. So how and why do we write them? As humans, we all crave love and acceptance. Our survival depends on belonging to a group of people, and rejection from that group feels like a threat to survival, especially when we are young. To fit in with the families, schools, and communities that raise us, we sometimes have to bend who we are to fit into the boxes of what is accepted. The pain of stifling who we are, and pretending to be someone we aren't, is less threatening than the fear of exclusion.

But when we do this, we close the doors to the possibilities of who we could be. These experiences of adopting someone else's scripts for our lives play out in how we interact with our students and our children. We tend to impose on them the same stifling demands to fit into boxes that were imposed on us without thinking twice about it or remembering how painful it was to be on the receiving end of that when we were young. We don't question whether what we are doing or the boxes we ask students to fit into are the best way to be or to live life. We are just playing out the scripts we adopted when we were young. This is not to say that we should cease to provide guidance to

The pain of stifling who we are, and pretending to be someone we aren't, is less threatening than the fear of exclusion.

students as they develop into adults or that we should stop trying to instill strong values and skills. It just means that maybe we step back and question if we are giving space for students to also discover and be their authentic selves at the same time as we are giving them guidance on how to develop into an adult.

Our *internally focused scripts* are written as a result of experiences we had when we were young (often painful or traumatic) and modeling from our parents and communities (Erskine, 2018). These scripts make us believe things like *I'm not lovable* or *I'm not able to succeed.* They limit how we show up in the world and what we think is possible for us. These are the scripts we want to help our students flip. These are the scripts that cause our students to think, *I can't succeed, so why try?* These are the scripts that make them believe there is no hope for their futures or that their lives are already predetermined. These are the scripts that enable students to buy into harmful stereotypes that limit who they think they can become. Our internal scripts don't lead us to judge others as much as they cause us to judge ourselves.

Recognizing Scripts That Limit Students

Students who have never been successful in school are operating under the script that they are not capable and will never be able to succeed. As mentioned in a previous chapter, struggling students often carry the belief that they have no power to change the trajectories of their lives. Why would they do something difficult, like do the work in a class they struggle with or regulate their emotions when someone threatens their friend in the hallway, if they think it won't matter one way or another?

Students' scripts can, and often are, influenced by their families and the environments they've grown up in. Students sometimes assume they are destined to become the parts of their parents that they struggle with (living in poverty, abusing their children, battling addiction, and so on). When students have this script, they assume that becoming their parents is their fate. Because of this script, they may struggle with feeling depressed and stuck. They may not try hard in school, and they may not really step into their strengths or even consider that they might have anything to contribute to the world around them. I (Rebecca) have also seen students whose parents do not value school and have a family culture of "we aren't school people." These students have a deeply held belief that if they tried hard and did well in school, it would somehow separate them from their families, their people, so why would they want to do that? This may be difficult for us, as educators, to comprehend, but it is a very real barrier for some of our students.

Another important script has to do with the stereotypes about their identities that students see in the media, experience in their surroundings, and hear from adults in their lives (sometimes even from their teachers). Students experience these stereotypes and may internalize them as part of their identity. This script influences how hard they try in school, what their peer relationships look like, and what careers they think they are worthy of.

I (Rebecca) have also seen students whose parents do not value school and have a family culture of "we aren't school people." These students have a deeply held belief that if they tried hard and did well in school, it would somehow separate them from their families, their people, so why would they want to do that?

There are many other scripts that prevent students from succeeding in school and eventually in life. We have an opportunity to help our students flip the scripts that limit them. Students have told me that when a teacher really sees them and takes the time to show them that the scripts that had been guiding their lives weren't real, it completely changed their self-concept and identity and even changed what they thought was possible for their adult lives (Knighton, 2022). This is the power we hold. We can reinforce these scripts (you aren't capable, you will grow up to be just like your dad, you have no power in your life to change things), or we can help our students discover that those scripts aren't true. They are capable. They aren't just like their parents or the stereotypes they see on TV. They can do things now that will change the path of their lives. But to help our students flip their scripts, we need to understand, and sometimes even flip, some of our own scripts.

Recognizing Scripts That Limit Teachers

We've spent time in the previous chapters exploring the scripts that guide our decisions and our actions, prevent us from being authentic or trusting ourselves, prevent us from truly seeing our students or believing that any student can succeed, and keep us stuck in the cycle of adult-adolescent power struggles. These types of scripts can create unintentional barriers to building relationships and engaging students.

These unconscious beliefs—our programming—can override our intentions. I (Rebecca) have seen teachers who fully believe in the power of positive relationships to mitigate the impacts of trauma on youth. They show a genuine desire to create safe learning environments, but then in the next moment, they turn around and yell at a student because they felt disrespected. The script that *youth should not "talk back" to adults* overrode their intention to create a safe learning environment for a student who had an incredibly difficult home life. These teachers believe in helping students and giving them grace and guidance to grow, but the scripts inside of them that say *students should not talk to adults that way* or *a student who disrupts class is personally attacking me* override their intentions. This leads them to call a student out in front of the class or send them to the office without any attempt at redirection, creating an unsafe learning environment and further damaging the teacher-student relationship. So often, the scripts we operate under—the subconscious programming about the role of a teacher and what teacher-student or adult-youth dynamics should be—govern our decisions and reactions in the classroom. These scripts override our intentions as educators when it comes to our expectations for adolescents and how we interact with them.

These deeper beliefs, our scripts, often come from what was modeled for us—what we saw our parents, caregivers, and teachers doing. We form core beliefs about what certain relationships should look like (adult-youth or teacher-student), and those beliefs (sometimes unconscious) govern our thoughts, feelings, and reactions. If we don't take the time to reflect on ourselves and our interactions, we often don't realize we are replicating patterns that don't serve our purposes.

If we don't take the time to reflect on ourselves and our interactions, we often don't realize we are replicating patterns that don't serve our purposes.

We play out the scripts we learned from our parents, caregivers, or teachers, and it can cause us to act in ways that are in opposition to what we now believe and who we want to be in the world (Gujral & Kaur, 2018). We need to identify the scripts that prevent us from evolving into who we want to be. What scripts guide our actions? Then the question becomes, how do we flip them? In the Looking Inward: Flipping the Script section later in this chapter, you'll engage in an activity that will help you explore this.

Encouraging Authenticity and Hope

We've seen throughout the book how important hope is to student engagement. Hope is also important if we are trying to help our students flip their scripts and step into a more fulfilled and authentic life. Research shows that hope and self-actualization are intimately linked (Snyder, 2002). That means when someone is living a life in which they are being an authentic expression of who they are, they have greater hope, and when that is stifled, they have lower hope. In communities where individuals are not encouraged to discover and express their authentic selves, there are much greater rates of hopelessness and depression (Snyder, 2002). In my research study, I interviewed a woman who had been a struggling student in her youth and who had a couple of positive deviant teachers. She explained that the trauma she experienced caused her to shut down her authentic self. She described it as the light deep within her going out. She told me that because her positive deviant teachers were *authentic* themselves and because they were trying to help her see a future she had not imagined possible, the authentic part of herself began to light up and vibrate again. Her relationships with these teachers countered the damage the trauma had done (Knighton, 2022).

No one can know the right path for someone else. Each of us must learn how to listen to our hearts, how to connect with who we are, or how to embody our deeper selves when making decisions. Helping our students learn how to do this is more important than telling them who we think they should be. As teachers, we have to learn how to balance teaching students the social norms of how to behave and interact with others and how to be successful in the workforce while judging students and giving them the opportunity to be authentic, think for themselves, ask questions, have autonomy, and explore future life path options based on who they are, what their skills are, and what they care about.

Two prominent humanists, Carl Rogers and Paulo Freire, explain that one of the goals of being human is to discover our authentic selves, and to do that, we must free ourselves from the distortions of the self from outside influences (O'Hara, 1989). These scripts we carry are distortions; self-reflecting and learning how to feel if something is congruent with our authentic selves are skills we can learn that help us flip those scripts. These are also things we can teach our students to do. Rather than taking on the role of the expert and someone who knows what path our students should take or who they are, we take on the role of expert question-asker. We teach students how to reflect and listen with their hearts, their guts, and their subconscious. We ask them questions when they are faced with a decision that helps them feel what is right, true, and resonant with who they are. That is the most valuable gift we can give someone—helping them connect more deeply with who they are and how they can contribute to the world.

We can contribute to the world in more powerful ways when we live authentic lives connected with who we really are and use the skills and attributes we have. We contribute less when we try to be someone we aren't, both because we aren't as good at being someone else, *and* because when we aren't authentically us, we are more prone to hopelessness. And no one functions best when they are suffocating under the weight of hopelessness.

Helping Students Flip Their Scripts

There are several things we can do to help students flip their scripts. It begins with having a trusting relationship in which the student knows that you have their best interest in mind. This is vital because we are asking students to change who they think they are. We are asking them to try when every fiber of their being is convinced that they won't succeed. This takes courage on their part, and they may only be brave enough to try if they trust that we have their backs.

The Importance of Believing in Students

In my study, I interviewed adults who'd had a positive deviant teacher so I could understand, from a student's perspective, how these teachers made a difference. Almost every person talked about how their teachers opened their minds to new possibilities for their futures. Several Latino students told me about the racism they'd experienced and how those messages, coupled with negative stereotypes they saw in the media, colored who they thought they were and what their futures could be (Knighton, 2022). Their positive deviant teachers showed them that the stereotypes and racial slurs were not true and that, not only could they be doctors, but also that their communities needed them to step into larger roles so their voices could be represented.

We are asking them to try when every fiber of their being is convinced that they won't succeed. This takes courage on their part, and they may only be brave enough to try if they trust that we have their backs.

So often, our students who are chronically disengaged don't believe in themselves, or they don't have hope for their futures (Rubens et al., 2020). Positive deviant teachers believe in their students, even when students don't believe in themselves. This is one of the most important things we can do for our struggling students. We have to believe in our students, and we have to hold their hope for them until they can hold it for themselves.

Through lessons, activities, and intentional scaffolding, we can create experiences where students succeed when they didn't think they could. This, coupled with our belief in them, helps them to believe in themselves and begin to hope that their futures could be different from what they imagine.

Take a moment to read and answer the following self-reflection questions.

We have to believe in our students, and we have to hold their hope for them until they can hold it for themselves.

WALKING IN OUR STUDENTS' SHOES

Reflecting ON OUR SCRIPTS

Remember a time when you had a self-limiting script about your ability to succeed at something (related to school or life).

- What was that belief?

- How did that belief impact how you approached doing that thing?

- Did other people in your life help you succeed when you didn't think you could? What did they do that helped you?

- How might you support your students who don't think they can succeed in a similar way?

Visit ***go.SolutionTree.com/teacherefficacy*** *for a free reproducible version of this reflection.*

Intentional Scaffolding

Research shows us that low self-efficacy is one of the primary reasons students don't engage (Ouweneel, Schaufeli, & Le Blanc, 2013). Often our disengaged students are those who don't believe they can succeed, so they don't try. Sometimes their identity is *the student who is not good at school and is always in trouble* or their identity might be *someone who can't do mathematics* or *someone who can't write an essay.* To help these students flip those scripts, we need to change their academic identity. Intentional scaffolding is an excellent way to do that. When we truly seek to understand and accept what our students know and what they can do, we can design lessons that meet them where they are *and* carefully guide them to where we need them to be.

Positive deviant teachers are masters at scaffolding. They never say, "students *should* know this already." Instead, they seek to understand what their students do know and are able to do and then they adjust their lessons to meet students where they are at. Imagine if you went into a class where you were expected to read and understand a passage in German and you'd only learned twenty vocabulary words. Without some help learning the additional vocabulary, there is no way you would be able to understand or succeed in reading the passage. This is how some of our students feel. If they walk into our algebra classes without a strong foundation of basic arithmetic, they will be completely lost. Or if our students walk into a ninth-grade language arts class and their vocabulary is at a fourth-grade level, it will be extremely hard for them to understand what we are reading.

Scaffolding is something we all learn about in our teacher preparation programs, but it is more complicated when we have students in our classes who are three or four years below grade level, and we have to balance teaching our standards while also trying to help them catch up. Jessica is a master at this and consistently sees two or more years of growth in her students because she scaffolds so well.

JESSICA'S VIGNETTE

Middle school students hate writing essays because they always say they don't know how or where to start one, and they don't know what to write in each paragraph. Years ago, my co-teacher and I realized that our students all had the same questions about each step of the essay writing process, so we decided to create a packet that said all the specific things we would remind them of for each part they were writing (you can see what our packet looks like in appendix B, page 239).

We chose to break it down first by page and then by sentence; this way students would feel less overwhelmed, and it would help them understand the format and structure of an essay. The secret benefit of this idea is that it builds self-confidence, as revealed by this story of my student named Kenzi (not her real name).

Kenzi had an IEP for processing and writing. She had great anxiety about doing things wrong, so she was very dependent on me, asking at least one question every step of the way. I reassured her and the rest of the students in her class (made up of eight more students with IEPs and low readers in a class of twenty-seven) that I created a five-page packet to set them up for success in writing their first five-paragraph essay in my class. I reminded them that I'd be with them every step of the way; I wasn't just handing out the packet and letting them fend for themselves. I also refreshed their memories that they had mastered writing great individual sentences in the last two months and now they were simply putting all those skills together into the essay.

We worked on one page per day, one sentence box at a time; their confidence level was that low. Each of the five days we worked on it, Kenzi would ask, "When are we going to start writing our essay?" I kept saying that they had already started—that's what they'd been doing each day in bite-sized chunks. She couldn't quite wrap her brain around what I was saying and what she was doing, but I patiently kept reassuring her, and the others, that she was writing her essay each day because I knew when we started the sixth day, it would finally click.

Day 6—The Big Reveal.

> **Me:** All right, guys, you should have your packet in front of you. Stand up if you have a sentence written in every box on the Introduction page.
>
> (*All students stand up. I repeat this for the Body Paragraph #1, Body Paragraph #2, Body Paragraph #3, and Conclusion pages.*)
>
> **Me:** Congratulations! You've just written a five-paragraph essay!
>
> **Class:** (*Crickets*)
>
> **Me:** Your five days of focused writing in your packet created a full essay. (*I pause for think time.*) Each page of your packet equals one paragraph of the essay, so five pages equals a five-paragraph essay. (*I pause again for think time.*)
>
> **Kenzi:** But, Mrs. May. I don't know how to write an essay.
>
> **Me:** Did you complete your packet?
>
> **Kenzi:** Yes.
>
> **Me:** Then you already wrote your essay.
>
> **Kenzi:** What?! *I wrote an essay*?
>
> **Me:** Yes! It's all done! Now you just copy down what you wrote in paragraph form on the Rough Draft page. That's why I told you I was setting you up for success, something I always do for all of you. I told you that you could do it! I told you that you had the skills! Now do you believe me?
>
> **Kenzi:** (*In silent shock for a second*) Wow. That wasn't as hard as I thought it would be.

> **Me:** Kenzi, and all of you, I want you to remember this moment. Remember how you're feeling right now. You *can* do hard things. Look back on this and realize the importance of taking all tasks one small step at a time.

Breaking complicated tasks into small steps is a helpful way to flip the script in a student's head about the skills they don't think they have. Activities broken down into the smallest steps create success, which creates self-confidence. Developing assignments that break down big skills is offered to all my students, no matter who they are or what educational plan they may or may not have.

When we think about scaffolding for students, it involves more than the academic scaffolding we learned in school. We also need to scaffold based on what they can handle emotionally. If their dog died the night before, they may need to have their workload adjusted that day, or they may need some space to regulate their emotions before they can engage in content. If a student has a history of AELEs and is struggling with self-regulation, coping skills, sequential planning, flexible thinking, solving problems when they encounter barriers, or goal setting, we may need to scaffold for those skills too. These are the skills that many students who have experienced AELEs struggle with and lead to the development of scripts that tell them they can't succeed in school, that they have no power to effect change in their lives, and that there is no hope for their futures. Designing lessons or giving students activities in class that specifically build these skills is an incredible way to help students change the trajectories of their academic and adult lives (see appendix C, page 259).

Intentional scaffolding is more challenging, and it takes creativity, but it is possible. In this chapter's Learning from the Five Teacher Types section (page 214), you'll be able to read about how our five positive deviant teachers use intentional scaffolding with their students. You will also find an example of how to scaffold writing at the middle and high school levels in appendix B (page 239).

Looking Inward: Flipping the Script

In this section, you will have the opportunity to engage in two activities, shown in figures 6.1 (page 211) and 6.2 (page 213). These activities are designed to help you understand yourself better and develop some of the skills we have discussed in this chapter.

What personal scripts (beliefs that influence how we perceive the world and operate within it) do you have that might be getting in the way of connecting with and engaging your students, that prevent you from being fully present with them, and that cause you to make assumptions about their behavior?

Here are some helpful hints for identifying a script.

- A script will be a belief you think is *the one right way to be* (for example, prepared for class) and that tends to make you frustrated with students when they don't do that.
- A script may cause you to make negative assumptions about why students behave the way they do.
- A script may cause you to judge others.
- A script may be a replication of something you saw or heard a caregiver do or say when you were younger.
- A script will limit you from being able to be fully present and see your students without assumptions or biases.
- A script may limit you from being the full essence of who you are.
- When you are caught up in a script, your body may feel tense or uneasy; you think you are right and feel less open to alternate perspectives; your actions and words may not align with your intentions and values; and you may shut down, leave the room, or raise your voice.

Step 1:

Identify an external script you have that may create barriers to building relationships with your students. To identify a script, you can think about the preceding bulleted list, think about what assumptions you tend to make about a specific student behavior that is challenging for you, and then think about what belief might be leading you to make that assumption and to respond in the ways mentioned in the previous list.

1. Describe that belief here. What is the script? What does it cause you to think? What does it cause you to feel? What does it cause you to assume about other people?

Figure 6.1: Flipping our own scripts.

continued →

2. How did you develop that script? Where did it come from?

3. How does that script tie in with your identity (what you believe about yourself)?

4. How does that script influence what you believe about others and the world?

Step 2:

Create a list from your experience that shows you evidence that this belief is not always accurate. The following is an example:

Your script
Evidence that this script is not always accurate

Example: Students who don't bring a pencil to class don't care about learning.

Johnny did not bring his pencil yesterday but asked very good questions during the lesson, which showed that he wanted to learn.

Step 3:

As you go through your days over the next few weeks, notice when you find yourself caught in that script, and then ask yourself, "Is this true?" Feel the answer from the deepest part of yourself.

*Visit **go.SolutionTree.com/teacherefficacy** for a free reproducible version of this figure.*

Based on everything you've read, the reflection you've engaged in, and the teacher type examples, write a description of *your* teacher type. You may want to read through Learning from the Five Teacher Types (page 214) before you engage in this activity. You can either create your own or combine aspects of the five teacher types in this book. Consider the following guiding questions to help you.

1. What are two qualities you consider central to your approach to life that influence your teaching style and how you relate to students the most? Choose two words to describe yourself and then explain what those words mean to who you are as a teacher.

2. How do you or can you use your two qualities to develop relationships with, build trust with, and create safety for students?

3. What would it look like and sound like for you to be authentic as a teacher? What would you be doing? What would your students be doing?

4. How can you use your two qualities to engage students?

Figure 6.2: Developing your teacher type activity.

continued →

5. How can you use your two qualities to navigate challenging behaviors and conflicts with students?

6. How can you use your two qualities to help students believe in themselves?

Are there any additional details about your teacher type you'd like to capture? Write them here.

Visit ***go.SolutionTree.com/teacherefficacy*** *for a free reproducible version of this figure.*

Learning From the Five Teacher Types

This section presents two common scenarios. For each scenario, the five positive deviant teachers you met in the introduction describe how they navigate these scenarios in their practice. The first is how they use intentional scaffolding to show students that they are more capable than they thought they were, and the second is to describe a moment when they saw a student's self-image shift. As you read through these examples, highlight, underline, or circle the parts you relate to.

Scenario: You are trying to use intentional scaffolding to show students they are capable when they don't believe they are

The following sections describe how each teacher type approaches this scenario in their classroom.

Teacher Type: Caring Connector

At my school, we have put heavy emphasis on the idea of developing a growth mindset. This is the idea that, despite certain strengths and weaknesses that we all have, every person can grow and improve. Whether it be learning a brand-new skill, improving an existing one, or even mastering something, we all have the capability of doing so. When a student says something like "I just suck at math," I just say, "No, you just might take a little longer to learn it." I use driving as an example of a growth mindset and common ability to learn. Usually, students are motivated to learn to drive because it gives them freedom from their parents, allows them to get places faster, hang out with friends more easily, and facilitates part-time work. This motivation makes it easier for them to push themselves to learn and improve. There are many drivers who are better than others (we don't all have a car on an F1 circuit!), but most humans have the ability to drive safely in our society. I use this idea to demonstrate to students that if they are motivated to put in the effort, they can learn in any subject, even if that learning may go slower or never achieve the same success as others. They have to decide what success looks like for them and not base it on those around them.

In a classroom context, I always try to start the semester with relatively simple tasks. This allows students to experience initial academic success and helps to build their confidence in themselves. As assignments get more involved and challenging, I ensure that they know about all the supports that are in place for them: due-date flexibility, ability to get feedback and resubmit projects and tests, extra help after school, simplified instructions, and clarified expectations. When students know they have access to these things, they are more likely to take risks and not fear failure because they know they always have another chance. All of these supports help to facilitate a growth mindset and foster learning in the classroom.

Teacher Type: Gentle Giant

Scaffolding is something I love to use in my class and allows me to guide students through the learning process step by step. By breaking down complex tasks into smaller, more achievable goals, students can develop their skills incrementally. This approach prevents students from feeling overwhelmed and gives them the opportunity to master each skill before moving on to more advanced concepts. Instead of presenting students with a large amount of information all at once, scaffolding allows me to introduce concepts gradually, building on previous knowledge and experiences. This step-by-step approach makes it easier for students to understand and retain information.

By breaking down larger goals into smaller, achievable steps, scaffolding shows students that progress is possible and encourages them to continue working toward their goals. This sense of accomplishment boosts students' confidence and motivation, leading to greater overall success in their learning journey. This support gives students the confidence to tackle new challenges and persevere in their learning.

Teacher Type: Nurturing Narrator

Scaffolding is a great technique to set students up for success as they learn to trust themselves. Students who have more challenging behaviors will often look for ways to escape the work, whether that be physically, by disappearing during independent work periods, or by heightened behaviors that offset their inability to access the curriculum. Students who struggle to read by the time they're in grade 8 very rarely want that pointed out, so it is a lot easier to "be bad than to be stupid." I give students the opportunity to access learning in many different ways as we warm up to each other, oftentimes at the beginning of the year giving up my preparation time and lunches to read quizzes and assignments to individual students after the rest of the class has written it. I also connect with their adults pretty quickly off the hop and find out what has worked—or equally importantly—what has not worked for their child. I use direct instruction a lot *in my class. Students are on their own mostly for supplementary learning, but even in grade 8 during our novel study, I read the entire book out loud to them. Although I give the option for students to go read in a quiet area instead, 99 percent of students snuggle in and will listen for up to two full forty-eight-minute periods in a day. I also go through individual support plans with students after I have written them. Scaffolding, like chunking, questioning, pre-teaching vocabulary, choice, interactive activities, cueing or prompting, and access to technology are all helpful strategies. Giving students the language to advocate for their experience is also powerful. I believe asking them for guidance on their learning is one of the most helpful tools I have, and this is even more powerful with behavior support plans. When I have to write a behavior support plan for a challenging student, I always sit down with them and we go over what they need, as opposed to what I need from them to be in class.*

Teacher Type: Perceptive Pragmatist

The most regular place I use intentional scaffolding is when students are working on an assignment. Students who struggle are more likely to ask for and accept help when something is "for marks." Also, since several days of learning occurred before the assignment, a greater number of students can work independently, which gives more opportunity for individual help for others. The students I try to target here are the ones who feel so lost they don't even know where to start. I sit with students either one on one or in small groups and work through questions together. It starts out extremely guided, and we work as slowly as needed so they're with me at every step. This manages to help student confidence in a couple ways—students know they will at least get a few marks on the worksheet, so they don't feel like failing is inevitable, and with the individualized, step-by-step instruction, they are usually willing to at least try some questions on their own.

Teacher Type: Warm Demander

Brooks (not his real name), one of my eighth-grade boys, had a very colorful vocabulary. On my first day with students, when I share my "backpack"—an "All About Mrs. May" slide deck, which shows me as a person, not a teacher. I let all of them know that one of my pet peeves is swearing in school. I also tell them that I, too, in my personal life, use foul language, but never at school and rarely in public. I go on to say that I'm there to help teach them and prepare them for their workplaces as adults, which includes either refraining from that language or choosing inventive words as a replacement; another way to look at this form of teaching is scaffolding. My word of choice at school or in public is shootfire*; it gives me the* sh *and the* f *sounds and mouth structures, yet it won't get me in trouble and I am able to keep myself professional.*

Well, Brooks used the "f" and "s" words like commas, so I knew I had my work cut out for me. I worked hard to create a good relationship with him first before discussing his language. However, every time I heard him swear, I would simply say a one-word replacement: shoot, shucks, frick, frack, *and so on.*

After a couple of weeks of talking about his interests and dislikes of school, I knew it was the right timing to have a brief conversation with him about his word choices. I started by saying what an amazing young man he was—extremely smart and witty, passionate, loyal, and he has great ideas and comments in class. I explained to him that even if he ends up working somewhere that doesn't frown on swearing, quite a lot of people are offended by that language, including doctor's offices, hospitals, government agencies, religious buildings, public events with families, and so on. I pointed out the importance of being able to be a shapeshifter, at the drop of a hat, for any environment or group of people according to the location, the surroundings, and the audience. Sadly, there is also still a belief out there that swearing means you're uneducated, poor, and not worthy of being listened to because using repetitive swearing appears to others that the person has a limited vocabulary.

I then told him that I feel extremely awesome and mature that I am a shapeshifter in this way. And when I do choose to swear, it has a bigger impact when used appropriately. To say it all the time loses its power. I suggested that he should agree to let me help him master this skill each day in class because it was a tool that would never make anything worse for him, only better.

You could see the wheels turning in his mind and he chewed on this new way of thinking. Then, he agreed to let me help him. From then on, I continued to remind him with one-word responses, but very frequently, I would explain how he could say it differently so he could hear the difference it made.

As time went on, he started to correct himself and then apologize to me. I would always tell him how proud I was of his progress. He even began to correct his friends and other peers in class. Don't get me wrong, though, when he was really ticked off talking to me one on one about something that happened, I would let him go off because I knew I was his safe place to vent. It was better he said that with me than with others in the building.

Toward the last six weeks of school, after I gave a one-word reminder to him, Brooks stopped, looked at me, and said, "You know, you're the only teacher in this school who's trying to help me stop swearing. No one else cares enough to do that. You're the best teacher in this building." I was touched. I thanked him and said that I appreciated his words and the work he'd done so far in class to make changes to his word choices.

Humans are like animals; we need repetition, consistency, and praise in order to learn a new habit. If we as teachers can keep that piece of information at the forefront of our minds, we tend to have more patience and compassion to hold the course.

Given what you've learned in this chapter, think about and answer the following reflection questions.

WHAT WOULD YOU DO?

Using INTENTIONAL SCAFFOLDING

Are you, or have you been, stuck in the trap of "students should know ________" that keeps you from meeting them where they are at? How does that impact your ability to effectively scaffold your content?

What factors influence how effectively you can meet students where they are at (testing pressure, pressure from administration, not understanding how a student can really be so far behind, fear of job security, or others)?

What would help you feel more comfortable with slowing down and meeting students at their current ability level?

Do you believe that all students can grow and learn if given the right supports? Why or why not?

Visit ***go.SolutionTree.com/teacherefficacy*** *for a free reproducible version of this reflection.*

Scenario: Describe a student aha moment that shifted their self-concept

The following sections describe how each teacher type approaches this scenario in their classroom.

Teacher Type: Caring Connector

I was teaching a grade 10 social studies class to our Knowledge and Employability students. The Knowledge and Employability program is an alternate path to high school completion in our province; it is a good fit for students who struggle with traditional academic work and need more hands-on and active lessons with practical applications. Typically, social studies requires a lot of reading and writing for both research purposes and to present your findings. So, this student, Paul (not his real name), came into my class with a lot of preconceived ideas about what social studies class was like.

He was very vocal, even confrontational, about his dislike of the subject, saying that it was boring, stupid, and had no purpose. I knew I had to get to the bottom of the reason for this disdain if I was going to engage Paul in the course work in any meaningful way. So, I had a conversation with him about it, and he was surprisingly willing to open up about his feelings. He mentioned that he hated reading, writing, and listening to lectures for long periods as he had a hard time focusing and sitting down for that long. He explained that was all that he ever did in every social studies class he had before this, so he never experienced anything but failure and got negative reactions from his teachers. I assured him that he would have a lot more opportunities to show me what he knows this time around.

While I still required some reading and writing from the students, I focused the course around mainly visual and oral components. I consistently tied the course concepts to pop culture phenomena, often watching movies and connecting those to the curriculum rather than doing worksheets. I shifted most of my assessments to informal means, just asking questions and interviewing students to find out where their level of understanding was. I dropped almost every formal test and assignment I had previously used. I also assured the students that if they missed an assignment or didn't understand the expectations, they could always resubmit.

Within the first two weeks of the course, I already saw a huge change in Paul's behavior and attitude. He was discussing the concepts we were learning with his friends (very passionately in some cases; I even had to rein him in sometimes). He was turning in videos of himself responding to questions, rather than writing, but was giving detailed and well-reasoned thoughts. He was even excited to find out what we were going to learn that day. Once when he came up to me and asked, "Hey, what are we learning about today?" I said, "We're going to talk about the impact of the internet on globalization." He was so excited that his enthusiasm was infectious.

Paul ended up with a final grade over 90 percent in the course and achieved a perfect score on the final culminating project. He went from hating a subject with a passion to being passionate to learn just because he was finally able to demonstrate his knowledge in ways that worked for him, and he experienced success because he was supported to take risks, fail, and improve. It really warms my heart to this day thinking about the turnaround that Paul was able to achieve.

Teacher Type: Gentle Giant

Aha moments happen pretty regularly in activity-based classes like physical education. The immediate gratification of performing a physical skill with confidence and increased ability is something I've witnessed a lot in my career, and I feel pretty lucky to witness these moments regularly. The ones that stand out the most, though, are the students who struggle at first. The ones that ask, "Why do we have to do this?" or provide multiple reasons why they can't try. These students provide opportunities to teach from the perspective of why. *With these students, it's not about locking in the information or rote memorization of curricular content, but about connecting dots to real-world experiences. In my career, I've taken on new challenges and have had the opportunity to teach high school mathematics. Just the other day I was blessed with one of these moments. My students are in lower mathematics-ability classes and are generally not too interested in math. Rather than plug away at textbook problems, we had a talk about real-world mathematics that we have to do in our little community. I had my students thinking about mixing feed ratios for their livestock, calculating distances and supplies for building fences, and creating proper ratios of gas and oxygen for welding, but the one that hit home was our talk about filling up our gas tanks! Students responded in a way that made me think,* wow, they really get it today! *I have found that aha moments are more effective when, as a teacher, I can relate to the struggles and stress of the problem. Sharing my strategies and then working with students to find solutions allows them to feel successful, supported, and confident that what they are learning has purpose.*

Teacher Type: Nurturing Narrator

My passion is teaching social studies, so I find myself very lucky to have been able to share history with students year after year. Students often come into the social studies classroom with a "Why does this matter?" attitude, and I start the year by asking them to forgive social studies, which they never quite know what to do with. It's something they have to chew on as I start the first of a series of lectures in this ten-month course. I do not ask students to take notes while I talk through our curriculum. I give students time after to complete notes and solidify the concepts through more traditional learning. Some days I will lecture for two full periods and students stay with me—because it is, of course, one of the greatest stories I am going to tell them. I deliver social studies through narrative, I walk the aisles of my classroom, I pull students up and re-enact moments, I stand on top of desks and I even go out and conquer other classrooms. I am not going to lie and suggest all students leave grade 8 social studies with a newfound love for the subject, but I will say students very rarely fail my class. Students, when they are immersed in the curriculum, can't help but absorb it. It isn't one aha moment, but it does feel pretty powerful when kids start passing a course they previously struggled with. I also mark each test by hand—because I enjoy it, and I'm old—and when I give them out to the students who start passing, I have them call their adults with their test scores. I get so excited to hand them their marks, so I wait for them to see it, I tell them how proud I am, then I tell them they have to go call their adults because this is a huge deal. If they don't have a reliable adult to tell, I have them tell our principal, and I call him ahead of time so he knows how excited to be. It isn't a movie—they don't come back with tears, thanking me, but that test never ends up in a garbage, and I guess that's the aha moment.

Teacher Type: Perceptive Pragmatist

I was teaching a grade 10 Knowledge and Employability mathematics class. We were working on some problem solving and the question was asking about how many tables would be required at an event with a certain number of people. We were discussing how we would solve the problem, but as soon as the word divide *came up, a student piped up, "Oh, well, I've never been able to do division, only multiplication." To which I responded, "Well, division is just multiplication" and went on to explain how. Immediately, his expression was pure shock, and he went, "*What*?! How did I never know this?! That's so easy!" That one tiny connection of dots for him was enough to change his attitude toward mathematics. It was such a small conversation—maybe five minutes—but it made him realize that maybe there were more concepts he thought he couldn't do that also just needed someone making a quick connection for him. In fact, the following year I taught him, he ended up being one of the top students in the class. He went from telling all his teachers that he was planning to just drop out at sixteen to finishing his high school certificate. Although his shift in attitude toward an education wasn't just from this one experience dividing, it was an accumulation of having a team of teachers who believed in what he could accomplish and having honest conversations about what it means to be a good person.*

Teacher Type: Warm Demander

Rolando, or Rolo (his real name, used with permission), was one of my seventh graders in language arts. I looped up with him and his peers to eighth grade for continuity since they were such an academically challenged group of students. Also, because they all had great reading and writing progress with me as seventh graders.

He and his friends, who were mostly Hispanic, would tell me they couldn't do what I was asking them to do because they were stupid. I worked to change their mindsets both as a group and as individuals during the first year I had them. The following year, as eighth graders, not only did they have me for language arts, but they also had me for a reading intervention.

This smaller class gave me the time to really work on skills that would give them the biggest bang for their buck, which in turn, gave them more confidence since they were small, doable steps. During the rest of the time, I taught them that they didn't need me in order to be successful in a class. What they could now do was because they possessed the skills, the power, to succeed. I pointed out that my belief in them this entire time was, of course, correct, but now I could see they were believing in their own abilities too! A few weeks later, the COVID-19 lockdown hit, and I never saw them in person at school again.

Fast-forward four years—I found out from my oldest son, Jonas, that Rolo was now working with him at McDonalds, and when he found out I was Jonas's mom, he freaked out, saying I was his favorite teacher and that I saved his life. A few months later, Rolo asked Jonas for my cell number. Rolo called me and asked if I would hand him, and six other friends from his class, their high school diplomas that May. I was so honored to be a part of his big moment, their big moment. But it got even better.

Rolo needed me to sign everyone's paperwork in order for me to hand them their diplomas, so he stopped by my house. As we stood there reminiscing and talking about life, I told him I was writing a "teacher's book" about building relationships and asked if I could share his story using his real name; he said yes. Then, I asked if he could explain to me why I made such a big difference in his life. With tears welling up in his eyes he said that I was the first teacher that didn't make him feel like a "stupid Mexican" (his words) and then said it was because I made him feel welcome in my class. Then we both started to cry. As we hugged, I reminded him that he has a superpower that my four sons don't have: the power of being 100 percent bilingual. You could see the wheels turning in his mind. As I spoke, he realized the huge difference it makes to feel welcomed, and that he could go out into the world and make others like him feel seen and welcomed as well. I reiterated to him that he's very intelligent; loyal; has a huge, loving heart with a great sense of humor, as well as a stellar work ethic. I finished by saying how much I loved him, how proud I was of him, and that I knew he would continue to do great things in life, which I couldn't wait to see unfold for him. I saw his light getting brighter, and then he walked back to his car.

Given what you've learned in this chapter, think about and answer the following reflection questions.

WHAT WOULD YOU DO?

Supporting STUDENTS IN SHIFTING THEIR SELF-CONCEPTS

As a teacher, have you experienced an aha moment when a student's self-concept shifted? Did you experience that yourself as a student? What happened?

What were the key factors (such as relationship dynamics or questions that were asked) that contributed to that shift occurring?

How might you replicate those factors for your students to experience those types of shifts?

Visit ***go.SolutionTree.com/teacherefficacy*** *for a free reproducible version of this reflection.*

Wrapping Up

If we want to help students flip the scripts that keep them from trying in school and keep them from attaining all that they can in life, then we must start by uncovering the scripts we have inside of us that prevent us from developing the safe, trusting, and supportive relationships we want to have with our students. This requires us to look for those deeper fundamental scripts that guide our lives and decisions. Once we uncover our scripts, we can begin to flip them and make decisions from a place aligned with our values and intentions rather than outdated patterns we carry on from our families or communities that don't serve us or our students.

Chapter 6 Book Study Questions

This section is an opportunity for you, as a staff, to explore the concepts presented in this chapter and reflect on how they are evidenced in or might impact your school culture. As you read each question, think about how you would respond based on your individual role. If you are an administrator, think about these questions as you reflect on how you support your staff. If you are a teacher or support staff member, think about these questions as you reflect on how you support students.

1. What are your reactions to the content in this chapter? Describe any aha moments, concepts you disagree with, and concepts that resonate with you.

2. Why do you think you reacted in the ways you did? How difficult is it discussing your scripts with your colleagues? What would make it easier?

3. What is a common script you see within your student body? What is needed to flip those scripts, and how might you work individually and together as a staff to successfully flip them?

4. What are some scripts you hold collectively as a staff that may create barriers to connecting with and engaging students? Where do you think those scripts came from? How might you work together to flip those scripts?

5. Of all the topics in this book, which ones made you feel most vulnerable? How do you see that vulnerability working to your advantage for you to flip the script for you and your students?

Epilogue

Not all of us realized when we started out as teachers that our jobs would be so much more than teaching mathematics, science, language arts, social studies, music, art, physical education, or other content areas. As teachers of adolescents, whether we like it or not, we play a role in our students' development as humans. We are influential adults in their lives as they form their identities and choose the paths they will follow into adulthood. We hold the incredible power of influencing the life trajectories of our students in positive or negative directions. The things we say to our students and how we respond to what they do and say impact how they feel about themselves and what they think they are capable of. We influence whether they will adopt the identity as the "student who is always in trouble" or "the student who can succeed at school." There is a lot of weight in the influence we have, but there is also great reward. There is nothing better than talking to a student years later and hearing that your class was the only place they felt safe when they were going through something difficult at home, that you were the reason they graduated high school, or that they became a doctor because you helped them break free from harmful stereotypes that led them to believe they would never amount to anything.

We wrote this book as a call to action for three reasons. The first reason is that we have heard, in all the schools and districts we've been in, that teachers know they need to build relationships with students but struggle with *how* to do so. The second reason is that, having been middle school teachers ourselves, we are tired of seeing students walk into our buildings in sixth grade and knowing with high accuracy who will eventually drop out of high school, end up in the criminal justice system, or end up struggling with substance abuse. These students need our help changing what they believe about themselves and what is possible for their futures. The third reason is that we've seen how exhausted, burned out, and stuck so many teachers feel, especially when they work in highly impacted schools, and we wanted to give them some strategies positive deviant teachers use that might help them get unstuck.

Positive deviant teachers are masters at building relationships with students, especially the ones who tend to push adults away and disrupt our classes. They are masters at helping students flip their scripts so that they begin to believe in themselves and see a future they never thought possible. And they have a high level of job satisfaction, sense of purpose, and greater well-being than teachers who struggle with student conflict, low student engagement, and lack of positive teacher-student relationships. It is our hope that the examples and activities in this book help you to develop the skills and perspectives that enable positive deviant teachers to succeed.

As we leave you, here are a few things to remember.

- When our students trust us, feel safe with us, don't feel judged by us, and feel like we have their backs and we believe in them, they will work for us.
- Think of student engagement as motivating students to participate and learn as opposed to thinking you must control students and force them to work. Humans are motivated by connection, competence, and autonomy. How can we design our lessons and our classroom environments so that our students feel connected to us, feel capable of succeeding, and have autonomy in how they complete work?
- The students who are most disengaged often struggle with low self-efficacy, low hope, and an external locus of control (they believe their lives are fated, and they don't believe their actions impact their lives or the lives of others around them). We can help our students shift those beliefs by:
    - *Anticipating* the barriers that prevent them from engaging or succeeding

    - *Creating* lessons where they succeed when they thought they couldn't
    - *Believing* in them when they don't believe in themselves
    - *Helping* them reflect so they see and understand that their actions do impact their lives
    - *Shattering* the stereotypes in their minds that limit them
    - *Holding* their hope for them until they can hold it for themselves
- To improve our relationships with students, increase student engagement in our classes, and help our students flip the internal scripts that limit them, we may have to flip our own scripts—the ones that keep us from truly seeing who our students are, what they need, and who they can become.
- We need to remember what it was like to be in middle and high school and what it was like to be an adolescent. This helps us have more compassion for what our students are going through, and it helps us feel less triggered by normal adolescent behavior.
- If we can accept human imperfection and see mistakes as opportunities for growth rather than character flaws, our health, well-being, and job satisfaction *and* our students' learning and engagement in our classes will improve.

We hope that this book will help you reimagine what your relationships with your students can be, and at the same time, help you feel greater job satisfaction and well-being. Some of you may be new to teaching, and we hope this book can help you move toward mastery quicker. For those of you who may have been teaching for a while and are beginning to feel stuck, frustrated, in survival mode, or even hopeless, we hope this book will help you feel inspired about teaching again.

Our call to action is that we all seek to grow, evolve, and transform. In his book, *The Four Pivots: Reimagining Justice, Reimagining Ourselves*, professor and author Shawn Ginwright (2022) writes about the need for transformation through reflection and healing as a path to sustainable change. That is what we need in the field of education. Flipping our own scripts will help us guide students to flip theirs so we can help more adolescents believe in themselves and see a future that they may not have thought possible. Only then can we stop the cycle of poverty, victimhood, and incarceration of disenfranchised youth and truly transform education and society.

APPENDIX A

Activities to Help Students Reflect

This appendix includes two concrete examples of how you might guide students to reflect on themselves. Feel free to use these as jumping-off points to create other reflection activities that match your own content and context.

I (Rebecca) used the "Self-Management Reflection" reproducible in an Advisory class when I was teaching students to develop skills that would help them succeed in school. At the end of each class, I asked them each to reflect on how well they managed themselves in the specific areas we were focusing on in class. I had the list of skills written out on a poster paper that always hung in the classroom. Sometimes we would reflect verbally all together, and other times I would ask them to fill out the following short form.

I (Jessica) use the "Life Wisdom Video Reflections" reproducible by searching social media for good videos with life wisdom that students need to hear from someone other than a parent or teacher (because they will take it more seriously when they hear it from someone else). I show these videos in class, and I always have four prompts they can choose from to write a response to the video. The prompts are leveled, and all four ask students to reflect on the message. The reproducible includes some examples of the slides I show them that list the prompts they can choose from. When using these in your classroom, you can let your students tell their elbow partners their answers verbally for a few weeks, and then you can ask them to write their answers down as you see fit after that.

Self-Management Reflection

Name: ______________________________ **Date:** ______________________________

Reflect on how well you set your own limits in the following areas:

On a scale of 1–5, how did you do in each of these areas today?

__ The beginning of class (arriving on time, completing warm-up, staying seated)

__ During whole-class discussions (raising hand, participating, listening, staying seated)

__ During independent work (trying hard, staying on task)

__ During group or partner work (helping your partner, staying on task)

What got in my way?

What would help me improve tomorrow?

Life Wisdom Video Reflections

DO NOW

BE LIKE BEES

EMERGING

List three things you noticed about the bees in the video.

PROGRESSING

Infer how our classroom and school would feel if we acted like the bees in the video.

MEETS EXPECTATIONS

Assess what it means to be an upstander like the bees.

EXEMPLARY

Connect how it would be beneficial in your life to act like the bees in this video

DO NOW

BE AN UPSTANDER

EMERGING

List three things you noticed in the video.

PROGRESSING

Infer how our classroom and school would feel if we fought for justice for *all* people.

MEETS EXPECTATIONS

Compare what it means to be an upstander in school.

EXEMPLARY

Connect how it would be beneficial in your life to fight for what's right for others.

DO NOW

SHOWING KINDNESS

EMERGING

List three things you noticed in the video.

PROGRESSING

Infer why the animals stayed in the car.

MEETS EXPECTATIONS

Draw conclusions as to why the little boy is doing this.

EXEMPLARY

Connect what you see in this video to something similar in your own life.

DO NOW

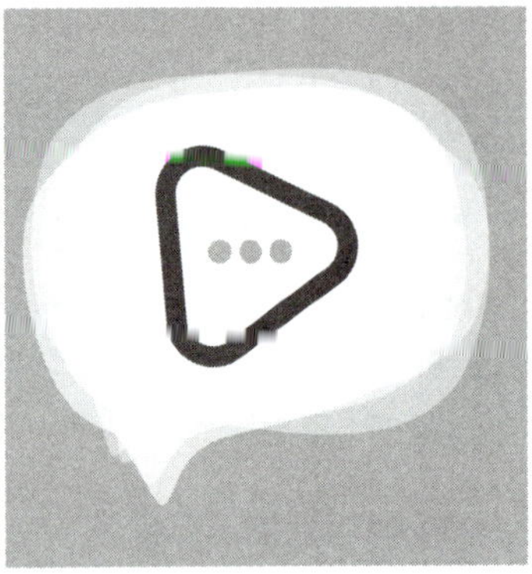

TURN AND TALK

- One thing you agree with and why
- One thing you don't agree with and why

BALANCING TOO MANY POTS AND PANS

DO NOW

LOVING ALL KINDS

EMERGING

Tell three things you noticed in the video.

PROGRESSING

Relate why animals want to be loved.

MEETS EXPECTATIONS

Draw conclusions as to what it means to "get back to our roots."

EXEMPLARY

Prove how you know that animals need love.

DO NOW

DIFFERENT KINDS

EMERGING

List three thing you noticed in the video.

PROGRESSING

Draw conclusions as to why dolphins did this.

MEETS EXPECTATIONS

Infer how the dolphins protected the mom and baby.

EXEMPLARY

Connect what you see in this video to something you've done in school for a peer.

Need a "Do Now" that takes under two minutes? For teachers who have extremely short classes, mainly elective teachers, creating an attendance question "Do Now" gets students talking to each other so teachers have time to take attendance. This is one of the most effective activities teachers can use to give themselves a breather from being surrounded by students, each wanting to ask a question as class is getting ready to begin. Finding questions is as easy as doing an online search for fun questions to ask teenage students. Tailoring questions based on the seasons, holidays, events, and trending topics makes this activity a quick and easy conversation that doesn't have to be led by the teacher.

DO NOW

ATTENDANCE QUESTION

Share at your table:

If you could only eat one type of food for the rest of your life, what would it be and why?

Mrs. May: Mexican food because I love every type of dish available, green chile on everything!

DO NOW

ATTENDANCE QUESTION

Share at your table:

What's your favorite show and why?

Mrs. May: *"The Big Bang Theory"* because their friend group makes me laugh a lot, which always makes me physically feel better!

DO NOW

ATTENDANCE QUESTION

Share at your table:

If you were given $1,000 for your birthday, what would you spend on?

Mrs. May: I would spend $840 on getting manicures for one year and the other $160 I would buy a concert ticket at Red Rocks.

DO NOW

ATTENDANCE QUESTION

Share at your table:

What's your favorite drink and why?

Mrs. May: Pepsi with ice. It's sweet and refreshing; plus, it always makes me think of my childhood drinking Pepsi with pizza.

APPENDIX B

Middle and High School Essay Writing Packets

Essay. The word all students dread. This appendix contains two entry-point examples for a middle school persuasive essay and a high school argumentative essay, which you can use with students who are struggling or resistant when it comes to writing an essay. The activity uses a claim, evidence, reasoning (CER) writing strategy to guide students in making a claim and providing evidence and reasoning to support that claim. Many students whose skills are below grade level need smaller, more defined steps to start and complete an essay. As teachers, we may think giving this much assistance to students isn't teaching them anything. However, students respond to this type of help. One, it gets them to try and complete *some* work. And two, these formats help build students' confidence and show them they *can* write an essay.

Middle School Persuasive Essay Writing Packet

Instructions: Have students use their notes to make the essay part easier and faster to complete. After reading a novel, or any other text, give them a packet where each page consists of one paragraph: the introduction format is on one page, the first body paragraph is on the next page, and so on. Have them complete one page each day, unless you have block classes. With students who struggle, instruct them one box at a time; don't move on until each student has a sentence in that box. They'll eventually reach the point where they have written a sentence in every box. When students finish the conclusion page, congratulate them for writing an entire essay! All they have to do now is handwrite or type each sentence from their packet, word for word, into paragraph form and then they're ready to turn it in. Students are usually shocked that the process was that easy! For more advanced students, talk about how they can write either a more complex, compound sentence using greater detail or write more than one sentence in each box by expanding on their statement using more details and specific content.

Prompt:
Who's the most influential character in The Outsiders?

Introduction Paragraph

Each of these parts make up a piece of your introduction! Write each of them together, **ONLY** indent part 1, then write the rest of the sentences behind it into one introduction paragraph. Remember, **do NOT use** the words *I*, *me*, *my*, or *you*. Write in third person.

Part 1: **Hook**	• Attention grabber, gets the reader's interest • Possible options include: ‣ Tell a story. ‣ Choose a quote from the book. ‣ Use a thinker statement. ‣ Use a cliffhanger.
Write your hook here:	
Part 2: **Summary of *The Outsiders***	Give the audience the foundation of the story! Introduce the characters, set the scene, establish the major conflict (problem), and include anything else the audience needs to know to understand the story.
Write your summary here:	
Part 3: **Topic Sentence**	State the topic in your own words (tell the reader the title of the text and who the most influential character is from the book).
Write your topic sentence here:	

page 2 of 9

Body Paragraph 1: Who Is the Most Influential Character?

Complete the following chart to have every aspect of your first body paragraph. You should follow the stoplight model (green, yellow, red)! **If you choose to add more than one piece of evidence, it must be followed with reasoning.** When you write them together, you will have your first body paragraph!

Claim **Green**	**Hint:** In one sentence, explain how the chosen character is the most influential person in the book.	
Evidence **Yellow**	**Hint:** The quote must **PROVE** the claim. Remember to include **who** said the quote (not **it**), the page number, and then the quote. Use phrases like: • According to the text . . . • One example includes . . . • For instance . . . • For example . . . **DON'T** use the words: "This quote proves . . ."	

Reasoning **Red**	**Hint:** This is the **MOST** important part! Explain **HOW** the evidence proves that the chosen character is the most influential person in *The Outsiders*. Use phrases like: • Clearly . . . • [The character's name] . . . • The impact of . . . • The effect of . . .	
Transition to the next paragraph **Green**	**Hint:** Use transition words to introduce how the character has another level of influence as well.	

page 4 of 9

Body Paragraph 2: How Else Is This Character Influential?

Complete the following chart to have every aspect of your second body paragraph. You should follow the stoplight model! **If you choose to add more than one piece of evidence, it must be followed with reasoning.** When you write them together, you will have your second body paragraph!

Claim **Green**	**Hint:** In one sentence, explain how the chosen character is the most influential person in the book.	
Evidence **Yellow**	**Hint:** The quote must **PROVE** the claim. Remember to include **who** said the quote (not **it**), the page number, and then the quote. Use phrases like: • According to the text . . . • One example includes . . . • For instance . . . • For example . . . **DON'T** use the words: "This quote proves . . ."	

Reasoning **Red**	**Hint:** This is the **MOST** important part! Explain **HOW** the evidence proves that the character chosen is the most influential person in *The Outsiders*. Use phrases like: • Clearly . . . • [The character's name] . . . • The impact of . . . • The effect of . . .	
Transition to the next paragraph **Green**	**Hint:** Use transition words to introduce how the character has another level of influence as well.	

page 6 of 9

Body Paragraph 3: Final Influential Factor!

Complete the following chart to have every aspect of your third body paragraph. You should follow the stoplight model! **If you choose to add more than one piece of evidence, it must be followed with reasoning.** When you write them together, you will have the third body paragraph!

Claim **Green**	**Hint:** In one sentence, explain the final big influence the chosen character has had on others in the book. If you want to discuss why some people may think a different character is the most influential, use this CER paragraph to write about the opposing view.	
Evidence **Yellow**	**Hint**: The quote must **PROVE** the claim. Remember to include **who** said the quote (not **it**), the page number, and then the quote. Use phrases like: • According to the text . . . • One example includes . . . • For instance . . . • For example . . .	

Reasoning **Red**	**Hint:** This is the **MOST** important part! Explain **HOW** the evidence proves that the chosen character is the most influential person in *The Outsiders*. Use phrases like: • Clearly . . . • [The character's name] . . . • The impact of . . . • The effect of . . . **DON'T** use the words: "This quote proves . . ."	
Conclusion **Green**	**Hint:** Use transition words to wrap up the influence of the chosen character.	

Conclusion Paragraph

Each of these parts make up your conclusion! Write each of them together, **ONLY** indent part 1, then write the rest of the sentences behind it into one conclusion paragraph.

<table>
<tr><td>Part 1:
Restate the topic</td><td>Restate the topic sentence in NEW words or flip it. Feel free to use Google (sites like WordHippo) to look up another word that means the same thing!</td></tr>
<tr><td colspan="2">Write your restated topic here:</td></tr>
<tr><td>Part 2:
Restate the thesis</td><td>Restate the thesis in NEW words or flip it. (What were the points you proved about the most influential character?)</td></tr>
<tr><td colspan="2">Write your restated thesis here:</td></tr>
<tr><td>Part 3:
Conclusion statement</td><td>Leave an impression! End STRONG!
Possible options include:
• Convince your readers.
• Summarize your proof.
• Choose a thinker statement.
• Choose a quote that can support, show, or demonstrate how the character you chose as the most influential is the most influential character in the book The Outsiders.</td></tr>
<tr><td colspan="2">Write your conclusion statement here:</td></tr>
</table>

page 9 of 9

High School Argumentative Essay Writing Packet

Instructions: After reading a novel or any other text, have students use their notes to make the essay part easier and faster to complete. Give students a packet where each page consists of one essay paragraph: The introduction format is on one page, first body paragraph is on the next page, and so on. For high school writing levels, you can add more boxes for more components of an essay, such as identifying and explaining the opposing view. For students who need extra time, set the expectation of only completing one page or paragraph each day, unless you have block classes. With student writers who really struggle, instruct them in one or two parts of the paragraph; don't move on until they have completed them. Then, turn them loose to finish the remaining content for that paragraph. When students finish the conclusion page, congratulate them on writing an entire essay, because all they have to do now is copy each sentence from their packet, word for word, into paragraph form on lined paper (or typed), and then it's ready to be turned in. They are usually shocked that the process was that easy!

Prompt:
Should students' cell phones be locked up in mesh pouches during the school day?

Introduction Paragraph

Each of these boxes make up a piece (sentence) of your introduction paragraph! Remember, **do NOT use** the words *I*, *me*, *my*, or *you*. Write in third person.

Part 1: **Hook**	• Attention grabber, gets the reader's interest • Possible options include: ‣ Tell a story. ‣ Choose a quote from an article. ‣ Use a thinker statement. ‣ Use a cliffhanger (stay away from asking a question because this writing is at a higher level than middle school).
Write your hook here:	
Part 2: **Summary of the chosen issue**	Give the audience the foundation of the argument. Introduce the issue at hand, explain both sides of the issue, and include anything else the audience needs to know to understand the issue you are writing about.
Write your summary here:	
Part 3: **Thesis statement**	State the claim in your own words (tell the reader which side you're on and the **three points** you will be writing about).
Write your thesis statement here:	

Body Paragraph 1: First Claim

Complete the following chart to have every aspect of your body paragraph. **If you choose to add more than one piece of evidence, it must be followed with reasoning.** When you write them together, you will have your first body paragraph!

Claim	**Hint:** In one sentence, explain that cell phones **should or shouldn't be** locked up during the school day.	
Evidence	**Hint:** The quote must **PROVE** the claim. Remember to include **who** said the quote (not **it**), the article title, and then the quote. Use phrases like: • According to the article . . . • One example includes . . . • For instance . . . • For example. . . **DON'T** use the words: "This quote proves . . ."	

Reasoning	**Hint:** This is the **MOST** important part! Explain **HOW** the evidence proves that cell phones **should or shouldn't be** locked up during the school day. Use phrases like: • Clearly . . . • The impact of . . . • The effect of . . .	
Transition to the next paragraph	**Hint:** Use transition words to introduce how **locking up or not locking up** student cell phones helps your next claim.	

Body Paragraph 2: Second Claim

Complete the following chart to have every aspect of your body paragraph. **If you choose to add more than one piece of evidence, it must be followed with reasoning.** When you write them together, you will have your second body paragraph!

<table>
<tr><td>Claim</td><td>Hint: In one sentence, explain that cell phones should or shouldn't be locked up during the school day.</td><td></td></tr>
<tr><td>Evidence</td><td>Hint: The quote must PROVE the claim. Remember to include who said the quote (not it), the page number, and then the quote.

Use phrases like:
• According to the text . . .
• One example includes . . .
• For instance . . .
• For example . . .

DON'T use the words: "This quote proves . . ."</td><td></td></tr>
</table>

Reasoning	**Hint:** This is the **MOST** important part! Explain **HOW** the evidence proves that cell phones **should or shouldn't be** locked up during the school day. Use phrases like: • Clearly . . . • The article's facts . . . • The impact of . . . • The effect of . . .	
Transition to the next paragraph	**Hint:** Use transition words to introduce how **locking up or not locking up** student cell phones helps your next claim.	

Body Paragraph 3: Final Claim

Complete the following chart to have every aspect of your body paragraph. **If you choose to add more than one piece of evidence, it must be followed with reasoning.** When you write them together, you will have one body paragraph!

Claim	**Hint:** In one sentence, explain that cell phones **should or shouldn't be** locked up during the school day. If you want to discuss why some people may believe the opposite is true, use this CER paragraph to write about the opposing view.	
Evidence	**Hint:** The quote must **PROVE** the claim. Remember to include **who** said the quote (not **it**), the page number, and then the quote. Use phrases like: • According to the text . . . • One example includes . . . • For instance . . . • For example . . .	

Reasoning	**Hint:** This is the **MOST** important part! Explain **HOW** the evidence proves that cell phones **should or shouldn't be** locked up during the school day. Use phrases like: • Clearly . . . • The author's name . . . • The impact of . . . • The effect of . . . **DON'T** use the words: "This quote proves . . ."	
Conclusion	**Hint:** Use transition words to wrap up how **locking up or not locking up** student cell phones helps the claim.	

Conclusion Paragraph

Each of these parts make up your conclusion! Write each of them together, **ONLY** indent part 1, then write the rest of the sentences behind it into one conclusion paragraph.

Part 1: **Restate the argument**	Restate the argument in **NEW** words or flip it. Feel free to use Google (sites like WordHippo) to look up another word that means the same thing!
Write your restated argument here:	
Part 2: **Restate the thesis statement**	Restate the thesis statement in **NEW** words or flip it. (What were the points you proved?)
Write your restated thesis statement here:	
Part 3: **Conclusion statement**	Leave an impression! End **STRONG**! Possible options include: • Convince your readers. • Summarize your proof. • Choose a thinker statement. • Choose a quote that can support, show, or demonstrate the **locking up or not locking up** of cell phones impact on others.
Write your conclusion statement here:	

APPENDIX C

Activities to Help Students Develop Social-Emotional Competencies and Skills

This appendix contains activities the authors have used to help students develop social-emotional competencies, such as reflection, goal setting, self-regulation, and empathy. It includes four example activities.

Social-Emotional Competencies Exam

This is an exam I (Rebecca) give students at the end of a quarter-long elective class where I taught them social-emotional competencies and how to understand their brains through the BrainWise curriculum (www.brainwise-plc.org).

Name: ______________________ **Date:** ______________________

There are *three typos* in this test. For each one you *find*, you will be given a piece of *gum*. *But not* if you talk during the test and tell other students where the typos are.

Part 1: Lizard Brain, Wizard Brain, and Red-Flag Warnings

Choose three of the following situations. For each one you choose, write about what red flag warnings you would feel in your body, and tell me how you would respond with your lizard brain and how you would respond with your wizard brain.

Situation	***Red-flag warnings in your body***	***How you would respond with your lizard brain***	***How you would respond with your wizard brain***
You forget your homework and your teacher gets calls you out in front of everyone.			

Someone who you think is your friend says something negative about you behind your back.			
Your mom forgets to pick you up after school.			
Someone shoulder checks you in the hallway.			
You mess up at something that matters to you.			

Part 2: Conflict Resolution

1. Describe a conflict you have (or have had in the past) with someone in your life.
    a. What is the conflict?
    b. Who is it with?
    c. What do you want?
    d. What does the other person whant?

2. Work through the following conflict resolution process.

    a. Think about what you need and what the other person needs. Conflict happens when people have different needs, and the goal is to find a solution that meets both people's needs.

What are your needs?	***What are the other person's needs?***

    b. What are some possible solutions that will help both of you meet your needs?

Part 3: Reflection on Class Skills

Look at the list of skills we were learning in class. Circle the two you feel you are better at now than before this class and give me an example of why.

- Self-expression
- Listening
- Knowing your strengths
- Expressing your needs
- Understanding your triggers
- Not being controlled by your triggers
- Conflict resolution
- Goal setting
- Creating a plan to reach a goal
- Setting your own limits—making good choices
- Being brave enough to share in the group

1. What is the first skill you circled?

2. Describe an example of using this skill and why you are better at it now than before.

3. What is the second skill you circled?

4. Describe an exampel of using this skill and why you are better at it now than before.

Realistic Goal Setting

Middle and early high school students can sometimes struggle to understand how to set a realistic and measurable goal. This series of activities can help them see the details that need to go into *actually* reaching a goal. Begin the unit by asking students to reflect on goals and their own experiences with them. Then share part 2 with them and teach them the details about how to set and work toward goals. Finally, give them part 3 to fill out, and spend the next few weeks working toward their goals and reflecting on them along the way. Students can easily complete this work without using the worksheets, so feel free to take the content here and adapt it to make it more interactive or customized to your context.

Part 1: Reflecting

This is the first activity in a series of three to teach students about goal setting. Use this activity to encourage students to reflect on past goal-setting efforts and break down the factors that contribute to the success of reaching goals.

Name: ______________________________

1. What is a goal?

2. Have you ever set a goal? What was it? Did you reach it?

3. What steps do you need to take to reach a goal?

4. In general, what things help you reach a goal?

5. Of those things you listed, which one are you best at?

6. In general, what things can get in the way of you reaching a goal?

7. Of those things you listed, what is the one you struggle with the most? What might help you overcome that struggle?

Part 2: Teaching the Steps to Actually Reach a Goal

This document is a guide and teaching tool as you help your students unpack and explore what a good goal is and how to reach it. Review the bullet points with students and give them concrete examples from your own life or student examples they can relate to.

Step 1: Set a goal.

What makes a good goal?

- It's specific. Don't say, "I'll be a better student." Say, "I will turn in my homework at least three times a week."
- It will challenge you but not so much that you give up because it's too hard.
- It is realistic for you. You have the skills or can gain the skills. You also have the time to do what you need to do to reach it.

- You want to accomplish the goal. It's not something you just think you should do.
- It has a deadline, and you can measure it.
- It has some flexibility. If what you set out to do isn't going to work, you can change it a little bit so it will work.

Step 2: Create a plan and reflect on it.

How do you stay on track with reaching your goal?

- Create a plan—think about the specific steps you need to take to achieve your goal.
- Reflect!
- Look at your plan and ask yourself, "Am I taking the steps I need to take?"

- Ask yourself, "Is what I'm doing helping me reach my goal, or do I need to change what I'm doing?"
- Ask yourself, "Do I need to learn how to do something more to help me reach my goal?"
- Ask yourself, "Do I need help from someone?"

- Forgive yourself—if you mess up and do something that gets in the way of reaching your goal, forgive yourself and start working toward it again.
- If you run into obstacles, come up with a solution to keep working toward your goal—it might mean you have to change your original plan.

Step 3: Celebrate achieving your goal.

How do you know when you reach your goal, and what do you do when you get there?

- Your goal should be specific enough that you know exactly when you reach it.
- When you complete each step in your goal plan, you should notice that and congratulate yourself.
- You should feel good about achieving each step and moving forward even when you run into obstacles.
- When you achieve your goal, celebrate! Feel good about what you've done and share it with someone.

Part 3: Creating a Goal Plan

In this third part of the series on goal setting, give students examples from your own life and from what you know about the students as they think through each step in the following goal-planning worksheet (especially the steps, strengths, and resources questions).

Name: ______________________________ **Date:** ______________________________

What is your goal?

(Be specific. Challenge yourself. Be realistic.)

Make sure your goal includes all of these:

__ Is it specific?

__ Is there a deadline?

__ Is it realistic?

Also consider the following questions:

__ Does it start slow?

__ Does it use your strengths?

__ Do you know how to get everything you need to reach it?

Now write a basic outline in the space provided. What steps do you need to take to reach your goal? (What do you need to do and in what order?)
1.
2.
3.
4.
5.

Now let's brainstorm about other resources you already have or need to gather to help you.

1. What strengths do you have that can help you do work toward and reach your goal?

2. What resources and support do you need to meet your goal? (What do you need to know or learn? Who might you need help from? Do you need any supplies?)

3. How will you know you've met your goal? (What will it look like? How will you feel?)

APPENDIX D

Activities for the First Two Weeks of School

In this appendix, Jessica shares unique and engaging activities she uses with her students, what she calls *boot camp*, to set expectations for her class during the first two weeks of school.

Boot Camp Activities

Day 1: I share my "backpack," an "All About Mrs. May" slide deck, which shows me as a person, not a teacher. I also pass out a worksheet called "All About Me" so I can learn who the students are both in and outside of school. They complete this (either as homework or in class) and I only count it as a Work Habit score. Some years I give students time to complete the worksheet in class because some schools don't give homework.

Days 2–10: I begin the "Trust and Respect" slide deck.

A few specific activities from these early days include the following.

- **Lip Syncing:** I choose three rowdy boys to be brave, put on boas and pink sunglasses, and learn to lip sync Aretha Franklin's "Respect" song by modeling it first. I teach the "audience" to be supportive by cheering and clapping for their classmates' willingness to display bravery in front of their peers. This teaches that vulnerability is encouraged because our classroom is a safe place to demonstrate that trait. It also shows how being silly and having controlled fun is acceptable in our room.
- **Role Playing:** To teach *The Four Agreements* (Ruiz, 1997), I choose brave students to help me role play the wrong way to act in class. This is an extremely popular and engaging activity because I tell the actors to go all out. Seeing the ways things shouldn't be and discussing how to make these mistakes right are huge teachable moments. I tell them I expect them to make mistakes and then I explain that it's what they do afterward that is the most important part of each scenario. Groups discuss people who are affected by the mistake (other students, the teacher, and so on) and then brainstorm what will make it right. It's a powerful activity.
- **Brain Breaks:** After thirty minutes of sitting down, the blood pools in your bottom and in your feet. Explaining this fun fact to my students gives me the opportunity to teach them three different brain breaks, which helps with better blood flow to their brains. I use them often when the class feels lethargic or before an assignment that requires sharp brainpower.
- **Writing Expectations:** I have students in groups writing answers on small whiteboards. I teach them that no matter when and what they write, I have expectations for One Good Sentence (OGS)—an updated version of the art of the sentence (Lemov, 2021)—using capital letters at the beginning, complete sentences that restate the question, and a period at the end. I also teach them CPUGS (capitalization, punctuation, usage, grammar,

and spelling, which a student of mine created in 2012). After each question, the whiteboard rotates to the next teammate. All other teammates need to make sure the writer did OGS and CPUGS correctly . . . no one can put 100 percent of the blame on the writer. This activity lets my students know my writing expectations for everything they do.

- **Money Demonstration:** This activity is a great visual for explaining equity versus equality. I hang two $2 bills (because most students haven't seen them, so they're novel) on a string with a paper clip, both are hanging at the same height, up quite high. Then I ask, "Who wants some money?" I purposely choose the tallest student whose hand is raised to volunteer. They walk to the hanging money. I tell them to grab either of the $2 bills. They grab one and I congratulate them for a job well done. Everyone claps and the student walks back confused at what they did so well. Then, I again ask, "Who wants some money?" I now choose the shortest student whose hand is up. I tell them to grab the remaining $2 bill. When they go to jump for it, I respond by saying, "No, no, no, no. You can't jump. The other person didn't have to jump to get their money." I've had kids try to grab a desk to stand on, recruit a taller friend to help, use something to throw at the money, and so on, but each time I stop them and remind them that the other student didn't have any help. At this point, the whole class is yelling that this is not fair because the other student is shorter and the money is too high for them. I remind them that they always want their teachers to be fair with everyone in class, and I'm just trying to be fair. They gripe about how that's actually unfair. I then ask them what the student needs to successfully accomplish the task. They always say they need to step up on something higher. I've previously planted a step ladder in my room, and I tell the student to look around to find something other than a desk because that isn't safe. All their peers are yelling and pointing to the stepladder, so they go get it and grab the money with lots of applause from the room. I then ask the class why I would do this demonstration and give away my money. What was the point? They can always name it: Not everyone can do the same thing; sometimes they need a little help or other type of support. I then show the slide explaining the difference between equity and equality. I also explain that sometimes they won't see the help and support I offer them, but sometimes they will; no matter what, I ask them to trust that I know what's best for each student so they can be successful. Then, throughout the year, when students start to think that something isn't fair, I point to the ceiling where we did this demonstration and remind students of the "money" activity. They immediately recall the reason I may be doing something different for a student, and the questioning and feelings retract. It's the greatest visual lesson, which I learned from my co-teaching partner.

References and Resources

Allen, J., Gregory, A., Mikami, A., Lun, J., Hamre, B., & Pianta, R. (2013). Observations of effective teacher-student interactions in secondary school classrooms: Predicting student achievement with the classroom assessment scoring system—secondary. *School Psychology Review, 42*(1), 76–98.

Aloe, A. M., Amo, L. C., & Shanahan, M. E. (2014). Classroom management self-efficacy and burnout: A multivariate meta-analysis. *Educational Psychology Review, 26*(1), 101–126.

Anderson, R. C., Graham, M., Kennedy, P., Nelson, N., Stoolmiller, M., Baker, S. K., et al. (2019). Student agency at the crux: Mitigating disengagement in middle and high school. *Contemporary Educational Psychology, 56*, 205–217. https://doi.org/10.1016/j.cedpsych.2018.12.005

Arain, M., Haque, M., Johal, L., Mathur, P., Nel, W., Rais, A., et al. (2013). Maturation of the adolescent brain. *Neuropsychiatric Disease and Treatment, 9*, 449–461.

Authentic. (n.d.). In *Merriam-Webster's online dictionary*. Accessed at www.merriam-webster.com /dictionary/authentic on September 30, 2024.

Balfanz, R., Herzog, L., & Mac Iver, D. J. (2007). Preventing student disengagement and keeping students on the graduation path in urban middle-grades schools: Early identification and effective interventions. *Educational Psychologist, 42*(4), 223–235. https://doi.org/10.1080 /00461520701621079

Bandura, A. (2006). Guide for constructing self-efficacy scales. In F. Pajares & T. C. Urdan (Eds.), *Self-efficacy beliefs of adolescents*. Information Age Publishing.

Bethell, C. D., Newacheck, P., Hawes, E., & Halfon, N. (2014). Adverse childhood experiences: Assessing the impact on health and school engagement and the mitigating role of resilience. *Health Affairs (Millwood)*, *33*(12), 2106–2115.

BrainyQuote. (n.d.). *Theodore Roosevelt quotes*. Accessed at https://www.brainyquote.com/quotes/theodore_roosevelt_140484 on February 27, 2025.

Brasfield, M. W., Lancaster, C., & Xu, Y. J. (2019). Wellness as a mitigating factor for teacher burnout. *Journal of Education*, *199*(3), 166–179.

Braveman, P., Egerter, S., & Williams, D. R. (2011). The social determinants of health: Coming of age. *Annual Review of Public Health*, *32*, 381–398.

Brooks, D. (2023). *How to know a person: The art of seeing others deeply and being deeply seen*. Random House.

Brown, B. (2010). *The gifts of imperfection: Let go of who you think you're supposed to be and embrace who you are.* Hazelden Publishing.

Byrne, B. M. (1994). Burnout: Testing for the validity, replication, and invariance of causal structure across elementary, intermediate, and secondary teachers. *American Educational Research Journal*, *31*(3), 645–673. https://doi.org/10.3102/00028312031003645

Calabro, F. J., Murty, V. P., Jalbrzikowski, M., Tervo-Clemmens, B., & Luna, B. (2020). Development of hippocampal–prefrontal cortex interactions through adolescence. *Cerebral Cortex*, *30*(3), 1548–1558. https://doi.org/10.1093/cercor/bhz186

Cerasoli, C. P., Nicklin, J. M., & Nassrelgrgawi, A. S. (2016). Performance, incentives, and needs for autonomy, competence, and relatedness: A meta-analysis. *Motivation and Emotion*, *40*, 781–813.

Chang, M.-L. (2013). Toward a theoretical model to understand teacher emotions and teacher burnout in the context of student misbehavior: Appraisal, regulation and coping. *Motivation and Emotion*, *37*(4), 799–817.

Claro, S., Paunesku, D., & Dweck, C. S. (2016). Growth mindset tempers the effects of poverty on academic achievement. *Proceedings of the National Academy of Sciences*, *113*(31), 8664–8668.

Cornelius-White, J. (2007). Learner-centered teacher-student relationships are effective: A meta-analysis. *Review of Educational Research*, *77*(1), 113–143.

Culyba, A. J., Ginsburg, K. R., Fein, J. A., Branas, C. C., Richmond, T. S., & Wiebe, D. J. (2016). Protective effects of adolescent-adult connection on male youth in urban environments. *Journal of Adolescent Health*, *58*(2), 237–240.

Davidson, A. (2015). *Social determinants of health: A comparative approach*. Oxford University Press.

De Bruyckere, P., & Kirschner, P. A. (2016). Authentic teachers: Student criteria perceiving authenticity of teachers. *Cogent Education*, *3*(1), Article 1247609.

Deci, E. L., & Ryan, R. M. (1985). Conceptualizations of intrinsic motivation and self-determination. In E. L. Deci & R. M. Ryan (Eds.) *Intrinsic motivation and self-determination in human behavior* (pp. 11–40). Springer.

Dixson, D. D., Worrell, F. C., & Mello, Z. (2017). Profiles of hope: How clusters of hope relate to school variables. *Learning and Individual Differences*, *59*, 55–64. https://doi.org/10.1016/j.lindif.2017.08.011

Dumontheil, I. (2016). Adolescent brain development. *Current Opinion in Behavioral Sciences, 10*, 39–44

Dweck, C. S., & Leggett, E. L. (1988). A social-cognitive approach to motivation and personality. *Psychological Review, 95*(2), 256–273.

Eddy, C. L., Huang, F. L., Cohen, D. R., Baker, K. M., Edwards, K. D., Herman, K. C., et al. (2020). Does teacher emotional exhaustion and efficacy predict student discipline sanctions? *School Psychology Review, 49*(3), 239–255. https://doi.org/10.1080/2372966X.2020.1733340

Elmore, G. (2024, September 18). *The power of belonging in children's lives* [Conference keynote presentation]. Colorado Department of Education 2024 Landscape Conference, Colorado Springs, CO.

Erskine, R. G. (2018). *Life scripts: A transactional analysis of unconscious relational patterns.* Routledge.

Education Resource Strategies. (2024). *Examining school-level teacher turnover trends from 2021–2023: A new angle on a pervasive issue.* Education Resource Strategies. Accessed at www.erstrategies.org/tap/teacher-turnover-trends-analysis on June 2, 2025.

Fisher, D., & Frey, N. (2021). New thinking about student engagement. *Educational Leadership, 79*(4).

Frei, F. X., & Morriss, A. (2020). Begin with trust. *Harvard Business Review, 98*(3), 112–121.

GBH News. (1990). *Raw video: Nelson Mandela visits Madison Park HS in Roxbury in 1990* [Video file]. Accessed at www.youtube.com/watch?v=b66c6OkMZGw on September 30, 2024.

Ginwright, S. A. (2022). *The four pivots: Reimagining justice, reimagining ourselves.* North Atlantic Books.

Gregory, G., & Kaufeldt, M. (2015). *The motivated brain: Improving student attention, engagement, and perseverance.* ASCD.

Gujral, H. K., & Kaur, J. (2018). Life script: Determinants and outcomes. *International Journal of Research in Economics and Social Sciences (IJRESS), 8*(3), 738–747.

Hambrick, E. P., Brawner, T. W., Perry, B. D., Brandt, K., Hofmeister, C., & Collins, J. O. (2019). Beyond the ACE score: Examining relationships between timing of developmental adversity, relational health and developmental outcomes in children. *Archives of Psychiatric Nursing, 33*(3), 238–247. https://doi.org/10.1016/j.apnu.2018.11.001

Harmsen, R., Helms-Lorenz, M., Maulana, R., & van Veen, K. (2018). The relationship between beginning teachers' stress causes, stress responses, teaching behaviour and attrition. *Teachers and Teaching, 24*(6), 626–643.

Hasel, M. C., & Grover, S. L. (2017). An integrative model of trust and leadership. *Leadership & Organization Development Journal, 38*(6).

Hashimoto, T., Takeuchi, H., Taki, Y., Sekiguchi, A., Nouchi, R., Kotozaki, Y., et al. (2015). Neuroanatomical correlates of the sense of control: Gray and white matter volumes associated with an internal locus of control. *NeuroImage, 119*, 146–151. https://doi.org/10.1016/j.neuroimage.2015.06.061

Herzog, J. I., & Schmahl, C. (2018). Adverse childhood experiences and the consequences on neurobiological, psychosocial, and somatic conditions across the lifespan. *Frontiers in Psychiatry, 9*(420).

Hodges, T. (2018, October 25). *School engagement is more than just talk*. Accessed at www.gallup.com/education/244022/school-engagement-talk.aspx on September 30, 2024.

Houchens, G. W., Zhang, J., Davis, K., Niu, C., Chon, K. H., & Miller, S. (2017). The impact of positive behavior interventions and supports on teachers' perceptions of teaching conditions and student achievement. *Journal of Positive Behavior Interventions, 19*(3), 168–179. https://doi.org/10.1177/1098300717696938

Howard, J. L., Bureau, J. S., Guay, F., Chong, J. X. Y., & Ryan, R. M. (2021). Student motivation and associated outcomes: A meta-analysis from self-determination theory. *Perspectives on Psychological Science, 16*(6), 1300–1323. https://doi.org/10.1177/1745691620966789

Hu, Y., Shmygelska, A., Tran, D., Eriksson, N., Tung, J. Y., & Hinds, D. A. (2016). GWAS of 89,283 individuals identifies genetic variants associated with self-reporting of being a morning person. *Nature Communications, 7*, Article 10448. https://doi.org/10.1038/ncomms10448

Hutchison, E. D. (2019). *Dimensions of human behavior: The changing life course* (6th ed.). SAGE.

Ingersoll, R. M., Merrill, E., Stuckey, D., & Collins, G. (2018). *Seven trends: The transformation of the teaching force.* Updated October 2018. CPRE Research Report# RR 2018-2. Consortium for Policy Research in Education.

Jones, C. (@CJ1two). (2012, October 5). *Why should we have to go to class if we came here to play FOOTBALL, we ain't come to play SCHOOL, classes are POINTLESS.* [Tweet]. Twitter. Accessed at https://www.al.com/sports/2017/05/cardale_jones_references_aint.html on April 21, 2025.

Junker, R., Donker, M. H., & Mainhard, T. (2021). Potential classroom stressors of teachers: An audiovisual and physiological approach. *Learning and Instruction, 75*, Article 101495.

Kelley, M. S., & Lee, M. J. (2018). When natural mentors matter: Unraveling the relationship with delinquency. *Children and Youth Services Review, 91*, 319–328. https://doi.org/10.1016/j.childyouth.2018.06.002

Kim, G. J.-S., & Hill, G. (2018). *Healing our broken humanity: Practices for revitalizing the church and renewing the world*. InterVarsity Press.

Klassen, R. M., Perry, N. E., & Frenzel, A. C. (2012). Teachers' relatedness with students: An underemphasized component of teachers' basic psychological needs. *Journal of Educational Psychology, 104*(1), 150–165. https://doi.org/10.1037/a0026253

Knighton, R. (2022). *Positive deviant teachers: How beliefs, relational dynamics with students, and administrator leadership style impact their success with disengaged students* [Doctoral dissertation, University of Lethbridge, Canada]. Opus University of Lethbridge. https://hdl.handle.net/10133/6335

Koplan, C., & Chard, A. (2015). Adverse early experiences. In M. Compton & R. Shim (Eds.), *The social determinants of mental health*. American Psychiatric Publishing.

Larson, K. E., Nguyen, A. J., Orozco Solis, M. G., Humphreys, A., Bradshaw, C. P., & Lindstrom Johnson, S. (2020). A systematic literature review of school climate in low and middle income countries. *International Journal of Educational Research, 102*, Article 101606. https://doi.org/10.1016/j.ijer.2020.101606

LeMahieu, P. G., Nordstrum, L. E., & Gale, D. (2017). Positive deviance: Learning from positive anomalies. *Quality Assurance in Education: An International Perspective, 25*(1), 109–124.

Lemov, D. (2021). *Teach like a champion 3.0: 63 techniques that put students on the path to college.* Jossey-Bass.

Levy, T. (2021, December 20). *Understand your life script.* Accessed at https://evergreenpsychotherapycenter.com/understand-your-life-script on April 21, 2024.

Liang, C. T. H., Rocchino, G. H., Gutekunst, M. H. C., Paulvin, C., Melo Li, K., & Elam-Snowden, T. (2020). Perspectives of respect, teacher–student relationships, and school climate among boys of color: A multifocus group study. *Psychology of Men and Masculinities, 21*(3), 345–356.

Marques, S. C., Lopez, S. J., Fontaine, A. M., Coimbra, S., & Mitchell, J. (2015). How much hope is enough? Levels of hope and students' psychological and school functioning. *Psychology in the Schools, 52*(4), 325–334. http://dx.doi.org/10.1002/pits.21833

Maslow, A. H. (1999). *Toward a psychology of being* (3rd ed.). Simon & Schuster.

Mason, B. A., Hajovsky, D. B., McCune, L. A., & Turek, J. J. (2017). Conflict, closeness, and academic skills: A longitudinal examination of the teacher–student relationship. *School Psychology Review, 46*(2), 177–189.

McGrath, K. F., & Van Bergen, P. (2015). Who, when, why and to what end? Students at risk of negative student–teacher relationships and their outcomes. *Educational Research Review, 14*, 1–17.

McLeod, S. (2018, May 21). *Maslow's hierarchy of needs.* Accessed at www.simplypsychology.org/maslow.html on September 30, 2024.

Meltzer, A., Muir, K., & Craig, L. (2016). Being trusted: The perspectives of trusted adults about engaging with young people. *Children and Youth Services Review, 63*, 58–66. https://doi.org/10.1016/j.childyouth.2016.02.010

Miller, E. (2013, January 25). *Teamwork With a Cause.* [Video]. YouTube. www.youtube.com/watch?v=itf8lJIeiXU.

Miller, D. (2009). *The book whisperer: Awakening the inner reader in every child.* Jossey-Bass.

Mitchell, R. M., Kensler, L., & Tschannen-Moran, M. (2018). Student trust in teachers and student perceptions of safety: Positive predictors of student identification with school. *International Journal of Leadership in Education, 21*(2), 135–154. https://doi.org/10.1080/13603124.2016.1157211

Moreno, A. (2022). *Purpose-driven learning: Unlocking and empowering our students' innate passion for learning.* Routledge.

Nate Wylie Studios. (2014, May 23). *Speech to change your life today! Admiral McRaven "make your bed" motivational words of wisdom* [Video file]. Accessed at www.youtube.com/watch?v=sBAqF00gBGk on February 27, 2025.

Noble-Carr, D., Barker, J., McArthur, M., & Woodman, E. (2014). Improving practice: The importance of connections in establishing positive identity and meaning in the lives of vulnerable young people. *Children and Youth Services Review, 47*, 389–396. https://doi.org/10.1016/j.childyouth.2014.10.017

Oberle, E., Gist, A., Cooray, M. S., & Pinto, J. B. R. (2020). Do students notice stress in teachers? Associations between classroom teacher burnout and students' perceptions of teacher social–emotional competence. *Psychology in the Schools, 57*(11), 1741–1756.

O'Hara, M. (1989). Person-centered approach as conscientização: The works of Carl Rogers and Paulo Freire. *Journal of Humanistic Psychology, 29*(1), 11–35.

Organisation for Economic Co-operation and Development. (n.d.). *Secondary graduation rate.* Accessed at https://data.oecd.org/students/secondary-graduation-rate.htm on April 25, 2024.

Ouweneel, E., Schaufeli, W. B., & Le Blanc, P. M. (2013). Believe, and you will achieve: Changes over time in self-efficacy, engagement, and performance. *Applied Psychology: Health and Well-Being, 5*(2), 225–247.

Pascale, R., Sternin, J., & Sternin, M. (2010). *The power of positive deviance: How unlikely innovators solve the world's toughest problems.* Harvard Business Press.

Phan, H. P. (2013). Examination of self-efficacy and hope: A developmental approach using latent growth modeling. *The Journal of Educational Research, 106*(2), 93–104. https://doi.org/10.1080/00220671.2012.667008

Pianta, R. C., & Allen, J. P. (2008). Building capacity for positive youth development in secondary school classrooms: Changing teachers' interactions with students. In M. Shinn & H. Yoshikawa (Eds.), *Toward positive youth development: Transforming schools and community programs* (pp. 21–39). Oxford University Press.

Pink, D. H. (2018). *Drive: The surprising truth about what motivates us.* Canongate Books.

Quin, D. (2017). Longitudinal and contextual associations between teacher–student relationships and student engagement: A systematic review. *Review of Educational Research, 87*(2), 345–387.

Roazzi, A., Attili, G., Di Pentima, L., & Toni, A. (2016). Locus of control in maltreated children: The impact of attachment and cumulative trauma. *Psicologia: Reflexão e Crítica, 29*(8). https://doi.org/10.1186/s41155-016-0025-9

Roberts, D. (2023). *Lessons learned and cherished: The teacher who changed my life.* Andscape Books.

Romero, L. S. (2015). Trust, behavior, and high school outcomes. *Journal of Educational Administration, 53*(2), 215–236.

Roorda, D. L., Jak, S., Zee, M., Oort, F. J., & Koomen, H. M. Y. (2017). Affective teacher–student relationships and students' engagement and achievement: A meta-analytic update and test of the mediating role of engagement. *School Psychology Review, 46*(3), 239–261.

Rubens, S. L., Feldman, D. B., Soliemannjad, R. R., Sung, A., & Gudiño, O. G. (2020). Hope, daytime sleepiness, and academic outcomes in low-income, Latinx youth. *Child and Youth Care Forum, 49*(5), 743–757.

Ruiz, M. (1997). *The four agreements: A practical guide to personal freedom.* Amber-Allen Pub.

Shernoff, D. J., Csikszentmihalyi, M., Schneider, B., & Shernoff, E. S. (2014). Student engagement in high school classrooms from the perspective of flow theory. In M. Csikszentmihalyi (Ed.), *Applications of flow in human development and education* (pp. 475–494). Springer.

Shin, D. D., & Kim, S.-I. (2019). Homo curious: Curious or interested? *Educational Psychology Review, 31*(4), 853–874.

Siegel, D. J. (2013). *Brainstorm: The power and purpose of the teenage brain.* Penguin.

Sinek, S. (2009, September). *How great leaders inspire action* [Video file]. TED Conferences. Accessed at www.ted.com/talks/simon_sinek_how_great_leaders_inspire_action on August 2, 2024.

Snyder, C. R. (2002). Hope theory: Rainbows in the mind. *Psychological Inquiry, 13*(4), 249–275.

Spilt, J. L., & Koomen, H. M. Y. (2009). Widening the view on teacher–child relationships: Teachers' narratives concerning disruptive versus nondisruptive children. *School Psychology Review, 38*(1), 86–101.

Sujadi, E., & Aulianisya, L. (2020). Locus of control and student achievement. *Indonesian Journal of Counseling and Development, 2*(1), 52–58.

Tschannen-Moran, M. (2017). Trust in schools. In G. Noblit (Ed.), *Oxford Encyclopedia of Research in Education*. Oxford University Press.

Tschannen-Moran, M., & Hoy, W. K. (2000). A multidisciplinary analysis of the nature, meaning, and measurement of trust. *Review of Educational Research, 70*(4), 547–593. https://doi.org/10.3102/00346543070004547

U.S. Department of Education. (2012). *Facts about teaching.* Accessed at www.ed.gov/teaching/national-conversation on February 14, 2025.

Wadsworth, M., & Butterworth, S. (2011). Early life. In M. Marmot & R. Wilkinson (Eds.), *Social determinants of health.* Oxford University Press.

Watson, J. C. (2017). Examining the relationship between self-esteem, mattering, school connectedness, and wellness among middle school students. *Professional School Counseling, 21*(1), 108–118.

Wood, K. (2020). *Learning leadership: A dialogic phenomenon of high school principal practice* [Doctoral dissertation, University of Lethbridge, Canada]. ProQuest. www.proquest.com/openview/48d408f25237023113ec38debdec08b1/1?pq-origsite=gscholar&cbl=44156

Yeager, D. S., Dahl, R. E., & Dweck, C. S. (2018). Why interventions to influence adolescent behavior often fail but could succeed. *Perspectives on Psychological Science, 13*(1), 101–122.

Index